Foreword

Many a reader has been tempted to interpret parts of Milton's *Samson Agonistes* as autobiographical, particularly those sections in which Samson denigrates himself — "Now blind, disheart'n'd, sham'd, dishonor'd, quell'd" — but a revealing passage from a personal letter should prove a sufficient deterrent.

> Surely I have ground to congratulate myself, for many have made a figure by their published writings whose living voice and daily conversation have presented next to nothing that was not low and common: if, then, I can attain the distinction of seeming myself equal in mind and manners to any writings of mine that have been tolerably to the purpose, there will be the double effect that I shall so have added weight personally to my writings, and shall receive back by way of reflection from them credit, how small soever it may be, yet greater in proportion. For, in that case, whatever is right and laudable in them, that same shall I seem not more to have derived from authors of high excellence than to have fetched forth pure and sincere from the inmost feelings of my own mind and soul. I am glad, therefore, to know that you are assured of my tranquillity of spirit in this great affliction of loss of sight, and also of the pleasure I have in being civil and attentive to the reception of visitors from abroad. Why, in truth, should I not bear gently the deprivation of sight, when I may hope that it is not so much lost as revoked and retracted inwards, for the sharpening rather than the blunting of my mental edge. Whence it is that I neither think of books with anger nor quite intermit the study of them, greviously though they have mulcted me, — were it only that I am instructed against such moroseness by the example of King Telephus of the Mysians, who refused not to be cured in the end by the weapon that had wounded him.

Thus wrote John Milton to Emeric Bigot, a young French correspondent on 24 March 1656 of his unabated love for books. What the great man says here is quite typical and reflects his lifelong passion for books and the ideals they reflect.

It is unnecessary to rehearse here a long biographical account stressing Milton's every known utterance relating to books, for every graduate student in English knows the story of young John Milton's inbred love of learning and how his parents had to ration his study time, so great was his thirst for knowledge and so delicate his health. Although no one knows the extent of his scrivener father's library, Professor Donald L. Clark has done pioneer work in investigating the training young Milton later received at St. Paul's School and the books in the library there.

As often happens with high-spirited youths, the traditional values of his university precipitated a violent reaction, and Milton was expelled for insubordination. After a cooling-off period, however, he returned to acquit himself with honor. More to the point, the polished rhetoric of his Cambridge-produced *Prolusions* reflects a strong reading background in the Graeco-Roman and Judaeo-Christian traditions and in the literary traditions of his native tongue. In spite of his good showing at Cambridge, Milton was dissatisfied with his education and retired to the family country house at Horton to read his way through the literary masterpieces overlooked by his tutors. In order to do this, he obviously had to have a plentiful supply of books which the rapidly expanding printing industry obligingly provided. Fortunately he also had an indulgent, rich father who could supply the where-withal for the leisure and the library. We may plausibly conjecture, in addition, that many books passed back and forth between him and sympathetic friends and neighbors and that he made occasional trips to nearby Oxford to acquire new reading materials. Like many a serious youth, Milton kept a commonplace book, and other than allusions picked up from his early poetry, prolusions, and academic exercises, it is the only evidence at this point in his life we have of his reading, of which two fine studies have been made: the late James Holly Hanford's "The Chronology of Milton's Private Studies," *PMLA*, XXXVI, 251-341, and Miss Ruth Mohl's edition of his Commonplace Book in the first volume of the Yale Prose.

After his sojourn in the buccolic retreat at Horton, Milton undertook a Continental *wanderjahr* surpassed in brilliance only by Boswell's and perhaps Byron's. In France and Italy he impressed nearly everyone with his charm, good looks, and sensible conversation laced with wit, his depth and breadth of learning, and his remarkable familiarity with the life style and literature of his hosts. Following dazzling social triumphs in Florence and Rome, he captivated the aging Manso in Naples who presented him with gifts of books, probably autographed copies or his own works, possibly rare editions of their mutual idol, Tasso. Nor did he neglect the opportunities to flesh out his library with book bargains readily available in Italy. In Venice, where the selections were especially plentiful because of the prolific local printing industry, he packed up his purchases and shipped them home by sea while he took the high road to Lac Leman, the arduous passage over the Alps to Geneva, bastion of Protestantism.

At home in London once more, Milton took up school-teaching, got married, and moved to a large house in Aldersgate Street which would, happily, accommodate his books. Edward Phillips tells us that he moved twice more before his Secretaryship in the Cromwell government, to a great house in the Barbican and to a somewhat smaller one in High Holborn that looked backward onto Lincoln's Fields Inn, each time a possible adjustment to his burgeoning collection of books.

It seems reasonable to assume that while Milton could read for himself he continued to buy books as the spirit moved him. After his blindness, however, more than likely he cut down on such expenses, although we are told by various biographers that he kept up with the world of books by having someone read to him regularly. Indeed, it was this onerous duty which grated most harshly on his daughters and allegedly caused their disaffection. Part of their unhappiness seems to have been rooted in money matters, for Elizabeth Fisher testified during the probate of Milton's will that the girls stole books from their blind father and sold them to the women of Dunghill. Apparently they thought their father too stingy with their pocket money and sold books surreptitiously to second hand book dealers to augment their allowances, or perhaps they thought their father had unwisely invested in books money that should have rightfully gone into their dowries. Milton doubtlessly reminded them dryly that they had the same dowry their mother Mary Powell had, that, in point of fact, their money was tied up in their Grandfather Powell's estate, from which he had never collected a penny of that which was lawfully his. At any rate, Milton's enslavement to the bibliophile's passion, surely one of the least infirmities of a noble mind, continued in spite of his blindness. So deeply ingrained was the habit of acquisition, he even toyed with the idea of buying an atlas, certainly the last book a blind man needed or could profit by and the one which would most afflict and inflame his tender sensibilities.

His unfortunate financial straits doubtlessly prevented Milton's giving his library *en bloc* to an institution — even if such an idea ever crossed his mind. Perhaps he gave some of his books as momentoes to old friends and admirers — such as the young Frenchman, Emeric Bigot — who came to pay their respects to him; perhaps he cautioned his widow to be chary of dealers and charlatans who would deprecate his beloved books' true value; indubitably he kept by his side well-thumbed old favorites to distract his mind when the miseries of the gout became too acute or the tedium of eternal darkness grew oppressive. Had he possessed fewer books he might have parcelled them out individually to friends in his will, as did Ben Jonson and John Donne; or, had his sight continued unimpaired he might have left us shelf lists of his collection; needless to say, he did neither. Obviously, however, books were an extremely important element in Milton's life, and I hope this conjectural catalogue of his library and ancillary reading — the furniture of his mind, as it were — which is only a partial record of his immense range of knowledge, will shed new light on his bibliographic milieu.

* * * * *

Although this project has taken much time and considerable labor, it is a preliminary work, and I look forward to the day when Miltonic scholarship has turned up enough new evidence to justify a revised edition. Some books from Milton's library have been positively identified — they have his authenticated signature and/or holograph notations — and others can be reasonably assigned to his possession (for a time at least; there is always the possibility that he borrowed a given book), for he quotes from them accurately, proving that he had the book at his fingertips or that he made extensive notes in his commonplace book. Other titles can be likewise added to the list, for Milton alludes to some works in such a manner as to make positive identification possible; others are somewhat doubtful to my mind, but I have included them because reputable scholars far more knowledgeable than I in such arcane matters have made a case for inclusion. Still other pedants seem to believe that every book published in Milton's lifetime, indeed anything that was ever published (and occasionally things that were moldering away in manuscript) on a subject peripherally touching on Miltonic themes, had a profound influence on his thinking. Giving as many people the benefit of as many doubts as I could, I have included many titles that strike me as patently absurd; they are here simply as part of the record. Others were simply too silly for inclusion; for example, nearly every volume crossing a bookseller's counter with a name vaguely resembling John Milton's (including initials and all foreign variations) on the flyleaf has been assigned to his library at one time or another. Those that could be satisfactorily eliminated have been given the heave.

My system is simplicity itself. Authors are alphabetically arranged; following an author's name is any other name by which he might also be known in square brackets. On the following line is the title of the book nominated for inclusion in Milton's library. Short titles are the general rule; occasionally full titles are given if they tend to throw light on the character and contents of the book. Following the title comes the date and place of publication of those works which survive from Milton's library and from those books he noted in his Commonplace Book which are identifiable as the precise edition he used. All other titles have been checked to ascertain that they were in print and available for Milton's purchase or perusal. On the same line is a symbol indicating my classification of the work: [V] means the work was in Milton's library or that there is sufficient internal evidence in his works to indicate that he read it; [*] indicates a possibility that Milton owned the work or that his references or allusions to it lead one to believe the possibility of his having owned it; [?] is, obviously, a questionable inclusion, an association copy, or a fatuous attribution. Underneath comes a veritable treasure trove of information: an abbreviation of the title of Milton's work in which the book is mentioned and a reference to a standard edition of Milton's works (either the Columbia Milton or the Yale Prose) in which the citation can be checked out. The indexers of the Columbia Milton helpfully included references to works generally thought to have been alluded to by Milton; these are included under the designation NDX and a small Roman numeral for the volume of the *Index*, e.g., NDX CM, ii, 1083.

It may appear that I have been inconsistent on occasion in citing some titles; for example, in a string of Latin titles by a given author, one may crop up in English. I chose to follow the lead of the majority of students of Milton who have previously cited the work rather than following the dictates of conformity. Although it may be momentarily distracting, the citation is in no case confusing.

I have tried to carry out a duty to students of Milton and of intellectual history and to those interested in libraries. I hope this work will be improved with the assistance of Miltonists and book lovers everywhere who will offer corrections and gentle reproof in an attempt to enlarge our insight into the intellectual development of John Milton.

I gratefully acknowledge a long series of personal debts for help with this volume. The Folger Shakespeare Library staff in Washington, D.C., hospitably provided much assistance and innumerable courtesies. The friendship and encouragement of Roy Flannagan, John Shawcross, Philip Highfill, Milton Crane, Robert Walker, John Lievsay, Charles Mish, Daniel Atwood, Jeanne Roberts, and Richard DeMolen, *et alii ad infinitum,* pushed and pulled me through many a dark hour. I wish also to give special thanks to Professor Theressa Wilson Brown, quondam Chairman of the Division of English and Speech at The District of Columbia Teachers College, for helpfully arranging my teaching schedule so as to allow me as much free time as possible to devote to research, and a grave bow to my colleagues there for concurring without demur.

And finally, I dedicate this work to my severest critics and brightest inspiration: Ann, the boys, and Cleo.

Arlington, Virginia   J. C. B.
September 1974

Abbreviations to Milton's Works

A	Animadversions upon the Remonstrants Defense
AP	Apology against a Pamphlet
AR	Areopagitica
BN	Brief Notes upon a late Sermon
C	Colasterion
CPB	Commonplace Book
CD	Christian Doctrine
CG	Reason of Church-government urg'd against Prelaty
COR	Correspondence
CP	A Treatise of Civil Power
DDD	Doctrine and Discipline of Divorce
1D	First Defense
2D	Second Defense
E	Of Education
G	Accidence Commenc't Grammar
H	Considerations...to remove Hirelings out of the Church
HB	History of Britain
HM	History of Moscovia
K	Eikonoklastes
LO	Art of Logic
MB	The Judgment of Martin Bucer
MAR	Marginalia
O	Observations on the Articles of Peace
P	Of Prelatical Episcopacy
POS	A Postscript

PROL	Prolusions
R	Of Reformation
RJP	Response of John Phillips
SD	Pro se Defensio
T	Tetrachordon
TH	Theme on Early Rising
TKM	Tenure of Kings and Magistrates
TR	Of True Religion, Heresy, Schism, Toleration
W	The Ready and Easy Way to Establish a Free Commonwealth

Other Abbreviations

CM	The Works of John Milton. Frank Allen Patterson, gen. ed. New York City: Columbia University Press, 1931-38.
YP	Complete Prose Works of John Milton. Don M. Wolfe, gen. ed. New Haven, Conn.: Yale University Press, 1953- .
NDX	Index to the Columbia Edition of the Works of John Milton. New York City: Columbia University Press, 1940.
V	A volume known to have been in Milton's library or to have been read by him.
*	A possible or likely candidate for inclusion.
?	A doubtful work.

Following is a list of books frequently referred to in the text. Books that are referred to only once or twice in the text have appropriate bibliographical information given there.

Cawley, Robert R. _Milton and the Literature of Travel_. Princeton, N. J.: Princeton University Press, 1951.

Clark, Donald L. _John Milton at St. Paul's School, a Study of Ancient Rhetoric in English Renaissance Education_. New York City: Columbia University Press, 1948.

Conklin, George N. _Biblical Criticism and Heresy in Milton_. New York City: King's Crown Press, 1949.

Corcoran, Sister Mary Irma. _Milton's Paradise with Reference to the Hexameral Background_. Washington: Catholic University of America Press, 1945.

Edmundson, George. _Milton and Vondel_. London: Trübner, 1885.

Evans, J. M. _Paradise Lost and the Genesis Tradition_. Oxford: The Clarendon Press, 1968.

Fletcher, Harris F. _Milton's Rabbinical Readings_. Urbana: University of Illinois Press, 1930.

French, John M. _The Life Records of John Milton_. New Brunswick, N. J.: Rutgers University Press, 1949-58. 5 vols.

Hughes, Merritt Y. _John Milton: Complete Poems and Major Prose_. New York City: Odyssey Press, 1957.

_____. _Paradise Regained, The Minor Poems and Samson Agonistes. Complete and Arranged Chronologically_. New York City: Odyssey Press, 1937.

McColley, Grant. _Paradise Lost: An Account of Its Growth and Major Origins, with a Discussion of Milton's Use of Sources and Literary Patterns_. Chicago: Packard, 1940.

Parker, William R. _Milton: A Biography_. Oxford: The Clarendon Press, 1968.

_____. _Milton's Contemporary Reputation_. Columbus: Ohio State University Press, 1940.

_____. _Milton's Debt to Greek Tragedy in Samson Agonistes_. Baltimore: Johns Hopkins University Press; London: Milford, 1937.

Prince, F. T. _The Italian Element in Milton's Verse_. Oxford: The Clarendon Press, 1954.

Samuel, Irene. _Plato and Milton_. Ithaca, N. Y.: Cornell
     University Press, 1947.

Saurat, Denis. _La Pensée de Milton_. Paris: Alcan, 1920.

Smart, John S., ed. _The Sonnets of Milton_. Glasgow:
     Maclehose, Jackson, 1921.

Svendsen, Kester. _Milton and Science_. Cambridge, Mass.:
     Harvard University Press, 1956.

West, Robert H. _Milton and the Angels_. Athens: University
     of Georgia Press, 1955.

Whiting, George W. _Milton's Literary Milieu_. Chapel Hill:
     University of North Carolina Press; London: Oxford
     University Press, 1939.

Symbols for journals cited follow the standard forms given
at the beginning of recent _PMLA_ bibliographies.

1. Abelard, Peter.

> EXPOSITIO IN GENESIM. (?)

>> See Sr. M. I. Corcoran, MILTON'S PARADISE.

2. ABINGTONS AND ALISBURIES PRESENT MISERIES. BOTH WHICH
TOWNES BEING LATELY LAMENTABLY PLUNDERED BY PRINCE ROB-
ERT AND HIS CAVILIERS. (?)

>> See G. W. Whiting, MILTON'S LITERARY MILIEU.

3. Acevedo, Alonso.

> CREACION DEL MUNDO. (?)

>> See Grant McColley, PARADISE LOST.

Adams, Clement.

> HM   CM, X, 382.
> A reference Milton probably picked up from
> Purchas or Hakluyt, qq.v.

4. Adams, Thomas.

> MEDITATIONS ON THE CREED. (?)

>> See J. M. Evans, PARADISE LOST AND THE GENESIS
>> TRADITION.

5. Adamus, Melchoir.

> VITAE GERMANORUM THEOLOGORUM. (*)

> MB   YP, II, 428.

6. Adrichomius.

> THEATRUM TERRAE SANCTAE. (?)

>> See Robert R. Cawley, MILTON AND THE LITERATURE
>> OF TRAVEL; G. W. Whiting, MILTON'S LITERARY MI-
>> LIEU.

1

7. Adrichomius.

    URBIS HIEROSOLIMAE DESCRIPTIO. (?)

        See no. 6.

8. Aelianus.

    DE INSTRUENDIS ACIEBUS. (V)

        E   YP, II, 412.
        See J. H. Hanford, "Milton and the Art of War,"
        SP, XVIII (1921), 232-66; W. R. Parker, MILTON,
        p. 853.

9. Aelianus, Claudius.

    VARIA HISTORIA. (?)

        NDX   CM, i, 25.

10. Aelred.

    DE GENEALOGIA REGUM ANGLORUM, in HISTORIAE ANGLICANAE
    SCRIPTORES X, ed. Sir Roger Twysden, q.v. (V)

        See Constance Nicholas, INTRODUCTION AND NOTES
        TO MILTON'S HISTORY OF BRITAIN, p. 155.

11. Aelred.

    DE VITA SANCTI EDWARDI REGIS ET CONFESSORIS, in Twys-
    den, q.v. (V)

        See no. 10.

12. Aeschylus.

    TRAGOEDIAE VII. (V)

        NDX   CM, i, 26.
        Milton pays high homage to Aeschylus in the
        foreword to SAMSON AGONISTES and clearly al-
        ludes to EUMENIDES in EIKONOKLASTES (YP, III,
        589) and other places (the Columbia Milton
        INDEX lists thirty-odd allusions). For a full
        discussion of Milton's intimate knowledge of
        Aeschylus, see W. R. Parker, MILTON'S DEBT TO
        GREEK TRAGEDY IN SAMSON AGONISTES.

Aeschylus.

    SUPPLICES, in TRAGOEDIAE VII.

        1D   YP, IV, 439-40.
        See no. 12.

13. Aesop.

    FABULAE. (*)
        CG   YP, I, 834.
        LO   CM, XI, 203.

14. Agrippa von Nettesheim, Heinrich Cornelius.

    OCCULTA PHILOSOPHIA. (?)

        See Robert H. West, MILTON AND THE ANGELS.

15. Ainsworth, Henry.

    ANNOTATIONS UPON THE FIVE BOOKES OF MOSES. (?)

        See Sr. M. I. Corcoran, MILTON'S PARADISE.

16. Alberti, Leandro.

    DESCRITTIONE DI TUTTA L'ITALIA. (?)

        See J. S. Smart, THE SONNETS OF MILTON,
        pp. 122-23.

17. Alcaeus.

    CARMENA. (?)

        1D   YP, IV, 441.
        NDX   CM, i, 37.

18. Alciatus, Andraeus.

    ΠΑΡΕΡΓΩΝ JURIS. (V)

        T   YP, II, 714.

19. Alcman.

    CARMINA. (?)

3

MAR   CM, XVIII, 294.

20. ALCORAN OF MOHAMET. (?)

        See W. R. Parker, MILTON, p. 369.

Alcuin.

        HB   CM, X, 186, 189, 196.
        DDD   YP, II, 231-32.
        Milton cites the authority of Alcuin in CPB,
        DDD, and HB, but did not know him firsthand;
        he knew him, says H. Glicksman, "Sources of
        Milton's History of Britain," WISCONSIN STUDIES
        IN LANGUAGE AND LITERATURE, XI (1920), p. 140,
        through William of Malmsbury, q.v.

21. Alexander of Hales.

        SUMMA THEOLOGICA. (?)

        See Sr. M. I. Corcoran, MILTON'S PARADISE.

22. Alexander, Sir William.

        DOOMES-DAY. (?)

        See Stella Revard, "Milton's Eve and the Evah
        of Sir William Alexander's Doomes-day," PELL,
        III,ii (Spring 1967), 181-86.

23. Alfraganius.

        EX ALFRAG. DE ORTU ET OCCASU PLANETARUM, ET DE OC-
        CULTATIONIBUS EORUM SUB RADIIS SOLIS, in DE SPHAERA
        of Sacrobosco, q.v. (?)

        See Allan H. Gilbert, "Milton's Textbook of
        Astronomy," PMLA, XXXVIII (1923), 297-307.

Alfred.

        HB   CM, X, 221.
        Translator of Boethius's CONSOLATION OF PHILO-
        SOPHY, q.v.

        Translator of Bede's HISTORIA ECCLESIASTICA
        GENTIS ANGLORUM, q.v.

24. Allen, William ⌈ pseud. Edward Sexby and Silius, or Silas,
                      Titus⌉.

    KILLING NO MURDER. (?)

        See W. R. Parker, MILTON, pp. 541, 1071.

    Almoni, Peloni.

        Pseud. used by unknown author of A COMPENDIUS
        DISCOURSE, q.v.

25. Ambrose.

    COMMENTARIUM IN EPISTOLAM I AD CORINTHIOS. (V)

        T   YP, II, 698.
        MB   YP, II, 460.

26. Ambrose.

    COMMENTARIUM IN EPISTOLAM I AD TIM. (V)

        CD   CM, XIV, 265.

27. Ambrose.

    COMMENTARY ON MATTHEW. (V)

        CD   CM, XIV, 267.
        MAR   CM, XVIII, 275.

28. Ambrose.

    DE DIGNITATE CONDITIONIS HUMANAE. (?)

        See Sr. M. I. Corcoran, MILTON'S PARADISE.

29. Ambrose.

    DE PARADISO. (?)

        See Sr. M. I. Corcoran, MILTON'S PARADISE.

30. Ambrose.

    ENARRATIONES IN XII PSALMOS DAVIDICOS. (?)

                            5

See Sr. M. I. Corcoran, MILTON'S PARADISE.

31. Ambrose.

EPISTOLAE. (?)

lD   YP, IV, 393, 413.

32. Ambrose.

EXPOSITIONIS IN LUCAM. (V)

T   YP, II, 697.
See W. R. Parker, MILTON, pp. 148, 285, 806.

33. Ambrose.

HEXAEMERON LIBRI SEX. (?)

See Sr. M. I. Corcoran, MILTON'S PARADISE.

34. Ambrose.

ORATIO IN AUXENTIUM DE TRADENDIS BASILICIS. (?)

lD   YP, IV, 413.

35. Ambrose, Isaac.

WAR WITH DEVILS, in COMPLEAT WORKS. (?)

See Robert H. West, MILTON AND THE ANGELS.

36. Ames, William.

CONSCIENTIA. Amsterdam, 1635. (V)

See J. M. French, LIFE RECORDS, I, 291-92.
Milton's copy is in the Princeton University
Library.

37. Ames, William.

MEDULLA THEOLOGIAE (THE MARROW OF SACRED DIVINITY).
(V)

DDD   YP, II, 232, 275.

6

```
T           YP, III, 610.
CD          CM, XVII, 173.  Milton's quotation
            is in Latin.
```

38. Ammianus Marcellinus.

RERUM GESTARUM. Ed. Henricus Valensius ₍Henri de
Valois₎. (V)

```
HB          CM, X, 93, 94, 95, 96, 97.
```
See Constance Nicholas, INTRODUCTION AND NOTES
TO MILTON'S HISTORY OF BRITAIN, p. 62.

39. Ammianus Marcellinus.

HISTORIAE. Trans. Philemon Holland. (?)

See H. Glicksman, "Sources of Milton's History
of Britain," WISCONSIN STUDIES IN LANGUAGE AND
LITERATURE, XI (1920), 113.

40. Anacreon.

TEII CARMINA. (*)

```
MAR         CM, XVIII, 283, 287, 301
NDX         CM, i, 53.
```

41. Anastasius Bibliothecarius.

HISTORIA ECCLESIASTICA. (V)

See W. R. Parker, MILTON, p. 502.

42. Andreini, Giovanni Battista.

L'ADAMO. (?)

```
NDX         CM, i, 58.
```

43. Andrewes, Lancelot.

A SUMMARIE VIEW OF THE GOVERNMENT BOTH OF THE OLD
AND NEW TESTAMENT, in CERTAIN BRIEFE TREATISES, q.v.
(*)

```
CG          YP, I, 194.
```

7

44. Andrewes, Lancelot.

      OF EPISCOPACY. (*)

           P   YP, I, 625.

45. Andrewes, Lancelot.

      OPUSCULA QUAEDAM POSTHUMA. (?)

           A   YP, I, 734.

ANGLO-SAXON CHRONICLE. Ed. and trans. Abraham Whelock, q.v. Also see Bede.

46. AN ANSWER TO A BOOK, INTITULED, THE DOCTRINE AND DISCIP-
LINE OF DIVORCE, OR, A PLEA FOR LADIES AND GENTLEWOMEN,
AND ALL OTHER MARIED WOMEN AGAINST DIVORCE. (V)

           C   YP, II, 719.

47. AN ANSWER TO THE PETITION SENT FROM THE UNIVERSITIE OF
OXFORD. (*)

           R   YP, I, 611, 615.

48. AN ANTI-REMONSTRANCE TO THE LATE HUMBLE REMONSTRANCE.
(*)

      Intro.   YP, I, 77-78.

49. AN APOLOGY FOR BISHOPS OR, A PLEA FOR LEARNING. (*)

         AP   YP, I, 873.

50. Aphthonius.

      PROGYMNASMATA. (V)

        TH   YP, I, 1035, 1038.

51. Apicius, Coelius.

      DE ARTE COQUINARIA. (?)

        PROL   YP, I, 280.

52. APOCALYPSE OF ABRAHAM. (?)

See Edward C. Baldwin, "Some Extra-Biblical
Semitic Influences upon Milton's Story of the
Fall of Man," JEGP, XXVIII (1929), 366-401;
and "Paradise Lost and the Apocalypse of Moses,"
JEGP, XXIV (1925), 383-86.

53. APOCALYPSE OF MOSES. (?)

See no. 52.

54. Apollodorus of Athens.

BIBLIOTHECES. (V)

PROL   YP, I, 225, 232, 238, 243, 245,
            249, 250, 269, 278, 279, 283, 301.
2D   YP, IV, 564.
See Donald L. Clark, JOHN MILTON AT ST. PAUL'S
SCHOOL.

55. Apollonius Pergaeus.

CONICA. (*)

TKM   YP, III, 253.

56. Apollonius Rhodius.

ARGONAUTICA. (V)

2D   YP, IV, 584-85.
COR   YP, IV, 869.
MAR   CM, XVIII, 304, 305, 310, 321.
NDX   CM, i, 74.

57. APOLOGIA PRO CONFESSIONE. (?)

MAR   CM, XVIII, 577-78.

58. Apuleius, Lucius.

METAMORPHOSES. Trans. William Adlington as
THE XI BOOKES OF THE GOLDEN ASSE. (*)

AP   YP, I, 934.
AR   YP, II, 514.

9

```
C          YP, II, 757.
2D         YP, IV, 656.
```

59. Aquinas, St. Thomas.

SUMMA S. THOMAE AQUINATIS...CUM COMMENTARIIS...R. F.
CHRYSOSTOMI IAVELLI. (*)

```
PROL       YP, I, 259-60.
AR         YP, II, 516.
```

60. Aquinas, St. Thomas.

DE REGIMINE PRINCIPUM. (?)

```
TKM        YP, III, 190, 213.
```

61. Aratus.

PHAENOMENA & DIOSEMEIA. Guillaume Morel edition.
Paris, 1559. (V)

```
E          YP, II, 394-95.
```
Milton's autographed copy is now in the British
Museum. Milton also knew other texts of Aratus,
e.g., that of Jean de Gabiano printed at Lyons
in 1608 and Henri Estienne's folio POETAE
GRAECI PRINCIPES, q.v.; there is also evidence
that he read the scholia and consulted an un-
determined number of other editions. See
Maurice Kelley and Samuel D. Atkins, "Milton's
Annotations of Aratus," PMLA, LXX (1955), 1090-
1106. See also Donald L. Clark, JOHN MILTON AT
ST. PAUL'S SCHOOL.

ARCHAIONOMIA. Ed. and sometimes trans. William Lambarde;
in Abraham Whelock's edition of Bede, q.v.

62. Archer, John.

THE PERSONALL REIGNE OF CHRIST UPON EARTH. (?)

```
Intro.     YP, I, 149-50.
```
See Michael Fixler, MILTON AND THE KINGDOMS OF
GOD.

Aretino, Pietro. See Pietro.

63. Aretius, Benedictus.

> PROBLEMA THEOLOGICA. (V)
>
> | T | YP, II, 714. |
> |-----|-------------------|
> | LO | CM, XI, 511. |
> | MAR | CM, XVIII, 292. |

64. Ariosto, Lodovico.

> ORLANDO FURIOSO. (V)
>
> | CPB | YP, I, 418. |
> |-----|-------------------|
> | R | YP, I, 560. |
> | CG | YP, I, 811. |
> | MAR | CM, XVIII, 569-70. |
> | NDX | CM, i, 88. |
>
> A copy of the John Harington translation (London, 1591) has sometimes been thought to have belonged to Milton; the notes in it, however, are almost certainly not in Milton's hand. See W. R. Parker, MILTON, p. 884.

65. Aristides of Miletus.

> MILESIAN TALES. (?)
>
> | 2D | YP, IV, 564. |
> |----|--------------|

66. Aristophanes.

> COMOEDIAE. (*)
>
> | AR | YP, II, 495. |
> |-----|--------------------|
> | MAR | CM, XVIII, 276-77. |
>
> The marginalia in Pindar, thought by some to be Milton's, makes a clear reference to "Scholia on Aristophanes" by Spondanus; however, no such work is listed in the catalogues of the BM, BN, Bodleian, or FSL.

67. Aristophanes.

> THE BIRDS. (*)
>
> | SD | YP, IV, 783-84. |
> |----|-----------------|

68. Aristophanes.

      THE CLOUDS. (*)

          SD   YP, IV, 630.

69. Aristophanes.

      THE FROGS. (*)

          1D   YP, IV, 385.
          2D   YP, IV, 594.

70. Aristotle.

      OPERA. (V)

          CPB   YP, I, 443.
          R   YP, I, 571.
          NDX   CM, i, 89-92.

71. Aristotle.

      CATEGORIES. (*)

          PROL   YP, I, 285.
          LO   CM, XI, 123, 133, 145.

72. Aristotle.

      DE ANIMA. (*)

          PROL   YP, I, 259, 264.
          LO   CM, XI, 69.

73. Aristotle.

      DE CAELO. (*)

          PROL   YP, I, 236.

74. Aristotle.

      DE GENERATIONE ANIMALIUM. (?)

          A   YP, I, 720.
          PROL   YP, I, 263.
          E   YP, II, 390.

75. Aristotle.

    DE INTERPRETATIONE. (V)

        LO   CM, XI, 307, 325.

76. Aristotle.

    DE PARTIBUS ANIMALIUM. (V)

        PROL   YP, I, 263.
        E   YP, II, 390.
        LO   CM, XI, 67, 245.

77. Aristotle.

    ETHICS. (V)

        R   YP, I, 571, 572, 584.
        DDD   YP, II, 283, 292, 314, 346.
        E   YP, II, 379, 396.
        AR   YP, II, 521, 527.
        T   YP, II, 646.
        C   YP, II, 745.
        TKM   YP, III, 202.
        1D   YP, IV, 521.
        COR   YP, IV, 839.
        LO   CM, XI, 47, 65.
        MAR   CM, XVIII, 278.

78. Aristotle.

    HISTORIA ANIMALIUM. (*)

        E   YP, II, 390.

79. Aristotle.

    HISTORIA NATURALIUM. (V)

        PROL   YP, I, 304.

80. Aristotle.

    MAGNA MORALIA. (V)

        LO   CM, XI, 69.

81. Aristotle.

    METAPHYSICS. (V)

        PROL   YP, I, 252, 263, 264.
        LO   CM, XI, 11, 63, 67, 87, 119, 125,
                         135, 155, 193, 233, 239, 243, 267,
                         301, 313, 475.

82. Aristotle.

    METEROLOGICA. (*)

        PROL   YP, I, 238.
        E   YP, II, 392.

83. Aristotle.

    ORGANON. (*)

        T   YP, II, 608.

84. Aristotle.

    PHYSICS. (*)

        PROL   YP, I, 237, 263, 285.
        RJP   YP, IV, 923.
        LO   CM, XI, 33, 45, 49, 63, 65, 67,
                         75, 145, 243.

85. Aristotle.

    POETICS. (*)

        CG   YP, I, 813.
        E   YP, II, 404.
        AR   YP, II, 511.
        SA   CM, I, 330.

86. Aristotle.

    POLITICS. (V)

        R   YP, I, 572.
        E   YP, II, 377, 379, 411.
        AR   YP, IT, 496.
        K   YP, III, 361; see also pp. 109-
                         21 _passim_.

```
            TKM           YP, III, 199, 203.
            1D            YP, IV, 343, 348, 356, 381, 383,
                          438, 455, 477, 504.
            2D            YP, IV, 605.
            SD            YP, IV, 813.
            RJP           YP, IV, 950.
            W             CM, VI, 136.
            N             CM, VI, 162.
            LO            CM, XI, 37.
            ACM           CM, XVIII, 499.
```

87. Aristotle.

    POSTERIOR ANALYTICS. (V)

```
            LO            CM, XI, 73, 77, 137, 245, 313, 317,
                          319, 431.
```

88. Aristotle.

    PRIOR ANALYTICS. (V)

```
            PROL          YP, I, 275.
            LO            CM, XI, 317, 333, 339, 371, 387,
                          389, 395, 405.
```

89. Aristotle.

    RHETORIC. (V)

```
            AP            YP, I, 899.
            E             YP, II, 401, 403.
            LO            CM, XI, 27, 43, 103, 175, 187, 465.
            MAR           CM, XVIII, 300.
            Intro.        YP, III, 108, 109.
```

90. Aristotle.

    TOPICS. (V)

```
            LO            CM, XI, 23, 75, 101, 119, 137, 201,
                          215, 217, 235, 273, 315, 339.
```

91. Armin, Philip.

    A TREATISE OF THE RICKETS. (?)

        A trans. of Francis Glisson's DE RACHITIDE,
        q.v. See W. R. Parker, MILTON, p. 979.

15

92. Arminius, Jacobus.

OPERA THEOLOGICA. (?)

DDD   YP, II, 293.
AR   YP, II, 519-20.

93. Armstrong, Archibald.

A BANQUET OF JESTS NEW AND OLD. (?)

See W. R. Parker, MILTON, p. 499.

94. Arnisaeus, Henningus.

DE JURE CONUBIORUM. (V)

T   YP, II, 701, 712.

95. Arnobius.

ADVERSUS GENTES. (?)

AP   YP, I, 934.
SD   YP, IV, 744.

96. Arrian ₜFlavius Arrianus₎.

DE ASCENSU ALEXANDRI. (V)

ACM   CM, XVIII, 496.

97. ARTICLES OF PEACE BETWEEN ENGLAND AND UNITED PROVINCES.
(V)

See Kester Svendsen's note no. 19, YP, IV,
706 ff.

Ascham, Antony. See Eutactus Philodemus.

98. Ascham, Roger.

TOXOPHILUS, THE SCHOOLE OF SHOOTINGE. (V)

CPB   YP, I, 502.
See W. R. Parker, MILTON, p. 842.

16

99. Ascham, Roger.

    THE SCHOLEMASTER. (*)

        E   YP, II, 358, 373.

100. Ashmole, Elias.

    THE WAY TO BLISS. (?)

        See Grant McColley, PARADISE LOST.

101. Asser ₍Asserius Menevensis, Asser of St. David's₎.

    DE REBUS GESTIS AELFREDI. (V)

        See Constance Nicholas, INTRODUCTION AND NOTES
        TO MILTON'S HISTORY OF BRITAIN, pp. 111-12;
        H. Glicksman, "Sources of Milton's History of
        Britain," WISCONSIN STUDIES IN LANGUAGE AND
        LITERATURE, XI (1920), 105-44.

102. Aston, Sir Thomas.

    REMONSTRANCE AGAINST PRESBITERY. (V)

        R   YP, I, 573, 604, 605, 606, 610.
        A   YP, I, 686.
        CG   YP, I, 854.
        AR   YP, II, 540.
        TKM   YP, III, 249.
        See Sonia Miller, "Two References in Milton's
        TENURE OF KINGS," JEGP, L (1951), 320-25.

103. Athanasius.

    AGAINST THE GENTILES. (V)

        R   YP, I, 555, 564, 566.

104. Athanasius.

    EPISTLES. (V)

        R   YP, I, 564.

105. Athanasius.

SYNOPSIS. (V)

R   YP, I, 564.

106. Athanasius.

SERMO DE CRUCE ET PASSIONE DOMMINI. (?)

1D   YP, IV, 393.

107. Athenaeus.

DEIPNOSOPHISTAE. (*)

PROL   YP, I, 220.
AP   YP, I, 880.
See Irene Samuel, PLATO AND MILTON.

108. Augustine, Saint, of Hippo.

OPERA. (?)

R   YP, I, 534, 562, 611.
HB   CM, X, 98.
CD   CM, XV, 43, 49, 195.
See Sr. M. I. Corcoran, MILTON'S PARADISE.

109. Augustine, Saint, of Hippo.

DE CIVITATE DEI. (V)

CPB   YP, I, 474.
1D   YP, IV, 375, 419.
NDX   CM, i, 115.

110. Augustine, Saint, of Hippo.

DE GENESI CONTRA MANICHAEOS. (*)

See Sr. M. I. Corcoran, MILTON'S PARADISE.

111. Augustine, Saint, of Hippo.

DE GENESI AD LITTERAM IMPERFECTUS LIBER. (*)

See no. 110.

112. Augustine, Saint, of Hippo.

    DE GENESI AD LITTERAM. (*)

        See no. 110.

113. Augustine, Saint, of Hippo.

    QUAESTIONUM IN PENTATEUCHUM LIBRI VII. (*)

        See no. 110.

114. Augustine, Saint, of Hippo.

    QUAESTIONES VETERIS ET NOVI TESTAMENTI. (?)

        See no. 110.

115. Aulus Gellius.

    NOCTES ATTICAE. (V)

PROL	YP, I, 274.
SD	YP, IV, 754.
T	YP, II, 593.
G	CM, VI, 346.
LO	CM, XI, 119, 299, 345, 465.
MC	CM, XII, 309.

116. Aurelius, Antonius Marcus.

    MEDITATIONS. (V)

AP	YP, I, 883.
1D	YP, IV, 360.

117. Aurelius Victor, Sextus.

    DE CAESARIBUS. (V)

1D	YP, IV, 465.
HB	CM, X, 89.

118. Ausonius, Decimus Magnus.

      EPIGRAMS. (V)

          MAR   CM, XVIII, 285.

119. Ausonius, Decimus Magnus.

      ECLOGUES. (V)

          MAR   CM, XVIII, 499.

120. Ausonius, Decimus Magnus.

      IDYLS. (?)

          NDX   CM, i, 116.

121. Ausonius, Decimus Magnus.

      MOSELLA. (?)

          NDX   CM, i, 116.

122. Avitus, Alcimus Ecdicius.

      DE ORIGINALI PECCATO. (?)

          NDX   CM, i, 125.

123. Avitus, Alcimus Ecdicius.

      DE ORIGE MUNDI. (?)

          NDX   CM, i, 125.

124. Avitus, Alcimus Ecdicius.

      LIBELLI DE SPIRITALIS HISTORIAE GESTIS: DE MUNDI INITIO. (?)

        See Grant McColley, PARADISE LOST; Sr. M. I. Corcoran, MILTON'S PARADISE.

125. Avitus.

      DE MOSAICAE HISTORIAE GESTIS. (?)

See J. M. Evans, PARADISE LOST AND THE GENESIS
TRADITION.

126. Babington, Gervase.

CERTAINE PLAINE, BRIEFE, AND COMFORTABLE NOTES, UPON
EUERIE CHAPTER OF GENESIS. (?)

See J. M. Evans, PARADISE LOST AND THE GENESIS
TRADITION.

127. Babington, Gervase.

WORKES. (?)

See Grant McColley, PARADISE LOST.

128. Bacon, Sir Francis.

ADVANCEMENT OF LEARNING. Oxford, 1640. (V)

PROL   YP, I, 263, 287.
E   YP, II, 370, 374.
AR   YP, II, 492.
K   YP, III, 337.
See also YP, II, 205 and CM, XVIII, 494. Marginalia in Milton's alleged copy of Malvezzi's
DISCOURSES UPON CORNELIUS TACITUS, q.v., indicate that he read Gilbert Wats's translation
of Bacon's ADVANCEMENT OF LEARNING. Of ten
possible editions, the Oxford, 1640, one is
the only one which matches Milton's page references.

129. Bacon, Sir Francis.

DE AUGMENTIS SCIENTIARUM. (V)

E   YP, II, 367.
LO   CM, XI, 25.

130. Bacon, Sir Francis.

ESSAYS. (*)

NDX   CM, i, 128.
See M. Y. Hughes' JOHN MILTON: COMPLETE POEMS
AND MAJOR PROSE, pp. 71, 233, 248, 468, 578,
631, 675.

21

131. Bacon, Sir Francis.

    NEW ATLANTIS. (V)

        AP   YP, I, 881.
        AR   YP, II, 526.

132. Bacon, Sir Francis.

    A WISE AND MODERATE DISCOURSE, CONCERNING CHURCH-AFFAIRES. (V)

        CPB   YP, I, 450-51.
        A   YP, I, 668.
        AP   YP, I, 882.
        AR   YP, II, 534, 542.
    First published in 1641, this pamphlet, written in 1589, was originally called AN ADVERTISEMENT TOUCHING THE CONTROVERSIES OF THE CHURCH OF ENGLAND. It was reprinted by Bacon's chaplain, William Rawley, in RESUSCITATIO (London, 1657), a volume of Bacon's collected papers.

133. Bacon, Roger.

    HISTORIE. (?)

        MAR   CM, XVIII, 334.
    On page 87 of his alleged copy of Ariosto, Milton makes a marginal reference: "Historie, Baken the great English necromancer." This is probably a reference to the late 16th century chap book on which Robert Greene may have based his play, THE HONORABLE HISTORY OF FRIER BACON AND FRIER BUNGAY.

Bagnols, Leon de. See Levi Ben Gerson.

134. Baillie, Robert.

    A DISSUASIVE FROM THE ERRORS OF THE TIMES. (*)

        FC   CM, I, 71.

135. Baillie, Robert.

    SATAN THE LEADER IN CHIEF TO ALL WHO RESIST THE REPARATION OF SION. (?)

See G. W. Whiting, MILTON'S LITERARY MILIEU.

136. Baillie, Robert.

LADENSIUM...THE CANTERBURIANS SELF-CONVICTION. (*)

Intro.   YP, I, 49-51, 105, 155.
R   YP, I, 585.

137. Baillie, Robert.

A LARGE SUPPLEMENT OF THE CANTERBURIAN SELF-
CONVICTION. (*)

      Intro.   YP, I, 51.

138. Baillie, Robert.

A PARALLEL...OF THE LITURGIE WITH THE MASSE-BOOK.
(?)

      Intro.   YP, I, 51.

139. Baillie, Robert.

THE UNLAWFULNESSE AND DANGER OF LIMITED EPISCOPACIE.
(?)

      Intro.   YP, I, 82.

Baker, Sir Richard. Translator of Malvezzi's DISCOURSES
UPON CORNELIUS TACITUS, q.v.

Balsamon. Editor and annotator of Photius, q.v.; Milton
twice respectfully cites him as an authority:
      T   YP, II, 685, 702.

140. THE BARBAROUS & INHUMANE PROCEEDINGS AGAINST THE PROFES-
SORS OF THE REFORMED RELIGION WITHIN THE DOMINION OF THE
DUKE OF SAVOY. (?)

            See John T. Shawcross, "A Note on the Piedmont
            Massacre," MiltonQ, VI (1972), 36.

141. Bar Cephas, Moses.

      COMMENTARIUS DE PARADISO. (?)

          See Sr. M. I. Corcoran, MILTON'S PARADISE.

142. Barclay, John.

      THE MIRROUR OF MINDES, OR, BARCLAY'S ICON ANIMORUM.
      (V)

      CG   YP, I, 796.
      The ICON is the fourth of four parts of the
      SATYRICON, a satire against Catholicism.

143. Barclay, John.

      SATYRICON. (?)

      CG   YP, I, 796.

144. Barclay, William.

      DE REGNO ET REGALI POTESTATE ADVERSUS BUCHANANUM,
      BRUTUM, BOUCHERIUM ET RELIQUOS MONARCHOMACHOS. (?)

      TKM   YP, III, 207.

145. Bar Hebraeus, Gregorius   [Abu al-Faraj].

      SCHOLIA ON THE OLD TESTAMENT. (?)

          See Sr. M. I. Corcoran, MILTON'S PARADISE.

146. Barlow, William.

      A BRIEFE DISCOVERIE OF THE IDLE ANIMADVERSIONS OF
      MARKE RIDLEY. (?)

          See Grant McColley, PARADISE LOST.

Bar Nachman. Aramaic var. of Ben Nachman, q.v.

Bar Nachmoni. Latin var. of Ben Nachman, q.v.

147. Baron, Robert.

CYPRIAN ACADEMY. (?)

See W. R. Parker, MILTON, pp. 411, 1008.

148. Baron, Robert.

POCULA CASTALIA. (?)

See W. R. Parker, MILTON, pp. 411, 1008.

149. Baronius, Cesare.

ANNALES ECCLESIASTICI. (*)

A   YP, I, 731.
See Grant McColley, PARADISE LOST.

150. Basil the Great.

OPERA. (V)

CPB   YP, I, 453.
AP   YP, I, 939.
T   YP, II, 697.
See W. R. Parker, MILTON, pp. 148, 806, 830, 841, 921.

151. Basil the Great.

HOMILIAE IX IN HEXAEMERON. (V)

CPB   YP, I, 381.

152. Basil the Great.

HOMILIA IN PSALMUM I. (V)

CPB   YP, I, 382.

153. Basil the Great.

DE FIDE. (V)

R   YP, I, 565.
AR   YP, II, 508, 510.
TKM   YP, III, 212.

154. Basil the Great.

MORALIA. (V)

K   YP, III, 518-19.

155. Basil the Great.

CONTRA EUNOMIUS. (?)

See Sr. M. I. Corcoran, MILTON'S PARADISE.

156. Basil the Great.

DE SPIRITU SANCTU. (?)

See Sr. M. I. Corcoran, MILTON'S PARADISE.

157. Bastwick, John.

LETANY OF JOHN BASTWICK. (?)

Intro.   YP, I, 42, 43, 45.

158. Bate, George.

ELENCHUS MOTUUM NUPERORUM IN ANGLIA; SIMUL AC JURIS
REGII ET PARLAMENTARII BREVIS ENARRATIO. (?)

2D   YP, IV, 598, 631.
See W. R. Parker, MILTON, pp. 582, 1093.

159. Batman, Stephen.

BATMAN UPPON BARTHOLOME, HIS BOOKE DE PROPRIETATIBUS
RERUM. (?)

DDD   YP, II, 279.
C   YP, II, 740.

160. Bayly, Robert.

A PARALLEL OR BRIEFE COMPARISON OF THE LITURGIE WITH
THE MASSE-BOOK, AND OTHER ROMISH RITUALLS. (?)

K   YP, III, 360.

161. Bayly, Thomas.

THE ROYAL CHARTER GRANTED UNTO KINGS, BY GOD HIMSELF.
(?)

TKM   YP, III, 215.
K   YP, III, 465, 569, 586.

162. Beaumont, Joseph.

PSYCHE. (?)

See J. M. Evans, PARADISE LOST AND THE GENESIS
TRADITION; Arnold Williams, "Commentaries on
Genesis as a Basis for Hexaemeral Material in
the Literature of the Late Renaissance," SP,
XXXIV (1937), 191-208.

163. Bede.

HISTORIA ECCLESIASTICA GENTIS ANGLORUM.   Ed. Abraham
Whelock. Cambridge, 1644. (V)

CPB   YP, I, 381-82, 431.
C   YP, II, 735.
2D   YP, IV, 490.
HB   CM, X, 82-194 passim.
This volume also includes Alfred's Old English
version in parallel columns, the ANGLO-SAXON
CHRONICLE, and ARCHAIONOMIA, a collection of
early English laws, edited and sometimes trans-
lated by William Lambarde. Milton also read
Bede in Jerome Commelin's RERUM BRITANNICARUM,
q.v. See also H. Glicksman, "Sources of Mil-
ton's History of Britain,' WISCONSIN STUDIES
IN LANGUAGE AND LITERATURE, XI (1920), 105-44;
Constance Nicholas, INTRODUCTION AND NOTES TO
MILTON'S HISTORY OF BRITAIN.

164. Bede.

COMMENTARIUM IN PENTATEUCHUM. (?)

See Sr. M. I. Corcoran, MILTON'S PARADISE.

165. Bellarmine, St. Robert Francis Romulus.

DISPUTATIONES...DE CONTROVERSIIS CHRISTIANAE FIDEI
ADVERSUS HUJUS TEMPORIS HAERETICOS. (?)

A   YP, I, 731.
See Sr. M. I. Corcoran, MILTON'S PARADISE.

166. Belvedere, Theodore.

LUCERNA DELLA CHRISTIANA VERITA, PER CONOSCER LA
VERA CHIESA, & LA FALSA PRETESA RIFORMATA. (?)

K   YP, III, 514.

167. Belvedere, Theodore.

TURRIS CONTRA DAMASCUM. (?)

K   YP, III, 514.

168. Bembo, Pietro.

RIMA DI M. PIETRO BEMBO. (?)

CG   YP, I, 811.
See J. S. Smart, THE SONNETS OF MILTON, pp. 34,
44, 110, 134, 136.

Ben Asher, Jacob ₍Baal ha-Turim₎. Commentator on the
        Pentateuch; found in Buxtorf's BIBLE, q.v.

169. Benbrigge, John.

GODS FURY, ENGLANDS FIRE. OR A PLAINE DISCOVERY OF
THOSE SPIRITUALL INCENDIARIES, WHICH HAVE SET CHURCH
AND STATE ON FIRE. (?)

See G. W. Whiting, MILTON'S LITERARY MILIEU.

Benedictus, Johannes.
        In Milton's alleged copy of Pindar, there is
        a note that Lucian was edited by Johannes
        Benedictus.

Ben Elijah, Isaiah. See Isaiah Aharon.

Ben Gerson, Levi ₍also Gersonides₎.
        Harris Fletcher states that Milton probably knew
        Ben Gerson through his commentaries in the rab-
        binical Bible edited by Johann Buxtorf (see

MILTON'S SEMITIC STUDIES); George N. Conklin, on the other hand, is not nearly so positive and points out that Milton's rabbinical information was readily available in other sources (see BIBLICAL CRITICISM AND HERESY IN MILTON).

Ben Gorion, Joseph. See Josippus.

Ben Halafta, Rabbi Jose.
    Perhaps the Rabbi Judas mentioned in 1D (YP, IV, 353). See Harris F. Fletcher, MILTON'S RABBINICAL READINGS and George N. Conklin, BIBLICAL CIRTICISM AND HERESY IN MILTON.

Ben Ilai, Rabbi Judah. See Ben Halafta.

170. Ben Israel, Rabbi Manasseh.

    SPES ISRAELIS. (?)

        See Michael Fixler, MILTON AND THE KINGDOMS OF GOD.

171. Benlowes, Edward.

    THEOPHILA. (?)

        See W. R. Parker, MILTON, pp. 411, 1008.

172. Bergomas, Jacobus ₍Jacopo Filippo Foresti of Bergamo₎.

    SUPPLEMENTUM CHRONICARUM. (*)

        HB   CM, X, 16.

173. Bernard, John.

    THE ANATOMIE OF THE SERVICE BOOK. (?)

        R   YP, I, 527.

174. Bernard, Richard.

    A SHORT VIEW OF THE PRAELATICALL CHURCH OF ENGLAND. (?)

```
          Intro.      YP, I, 68.
          R           YP, I, 590, 591, 592, 596, 610.
```

175. Bernardus, Justinianus ₍Bernardo Giustiniani₎.

DE ORIGINE URBIS VENETIARUM REBUSQUE AB IPSA GESTIS
HISTORIA. (V)

```
          COR         YP, I, 328.
          See J. M. French, LIFE RECORDS, I, 349-50;
          W. R. Parker, MILTON, pp. 150, 808.
```

176. Berni, Francesco.

ORLANDO INNAMORATO NUOVAMENTE COMPOSTO. (V)

```
          CPB         YP, I, 385-86, 439, 463.
          Milton quotes exactly from the Venice, 1541,
          edition; however, the text of the Milan, 1542,
          edition is identical.  Since Milton gives no
          page numbers in his notes from this book, it
          is impossible to tell which edition he used.
```

177. Berosus ₍Pseudo₎.

DE ANTIQUITATIBUS. (V)

```
          HB          CM, X, 4.
          Constance Nicholas cites the ANTIQUITATUM VARI-
          ARUM AUTORES, Lyons, 1560, edition of the false
          Berosus.  He was often printed with Solinus and
          Mela, both of whom Milton cites.  See INTRO-
          DUCTION AND NOTES TO MILTON'S HISTORY OF BRITAIN,
          p. 21.
```

178. Best, Paul.

MYSTERIES DISCOVERED. (?)

```
          MAR         CM, XVIII, 572.
          See Maurice Kelley, Library, 5th Ser., V (1950),
          49-51.
```

179. Beza, Theodore ₍Thédore de Bèze₎.

ANNOTATIONES MAJORES IN NOVUM TESTAMENTUM. (V)

```
          DDD         YP, II, 266.
```

180. Beza, Theodore.

ICONES, ID EST VERAE IMAGINES VIRORUM DOCTRINA
SUMUL ET PETATE ILLUSTRIUM. (V)

MAR   CM, XVIII, 581.
MB   YP, II, 424, 428.
"A book of portraits of reformers," now lost,
was said (in 1879) to have contained Milton's
signature. See W. R. Parker, MILTON, p. 1122.

181. Beza, Theodore.

JOB EXPOUNDED. (?)

See John M. Steadman, "Urania, Wisdom and
Scriptural Exegesis," Neophilologus, XLVII
(1963), 61-73.

182. Beza, Theodore.

TRACTATIO DE REPUDIIS ET DIVORTIIS. (V)

DDD   YP, II, 266.
T   YP, II, 656.

183. Beza, Theodore.

VINDICIAE CONTRA TYRANNOS. (*)

2D   YP, IV, 659.
The VINDICATION AGAINST TYRANTS, though frequently attributed to Beza, was published under
the pseudonymn of Stephanus Junius Brutus.
Robert W. Ayres suggests that it was probably
written by either Hubert Languet or Duplessis-
Mornay. John Phillips also cites the work in
his RESPONSE, in which Milton's hand is evident.

184. BIBLE. "Geneva Bible, 1560." (?)

See Wayne Baxter, N&Q, XI.iii (1911), 109-10,
and J. M. French, LIFE RECORDS, IV, 387; V, 125.

N.B. To reproduce every reference and allusion
to the Bible in Milton's works would be folly,
for students may easily consult the indexes
of the Columbia Milton, Yale Prose, and Parker's
MILTON. See also Harris F. Fletcher, THE USE
OF THE BIBLE IN MILTON'S PROSE and James H. Sims,

THE BIBLE IN MILTON'S EPICS.

185. BIBLE. 1581 edn. (?)

A copy with the signature "Jhon Melton" was
reported by William Jaggard in 1916. See
W. R. Parker, MILTON, p. 1122.

186. BIBLE. "Breeches Bible, 1588." (?)

See French's LIFE RECORDS, IV, 387; E. M.
Clark, N&Q, V.xii (1958), 518-19.

187. BIBLE. 1599 edn. (?)

Supposedly Milton's mother's Bible. See
French's LIFE RECORDS, I, 322.

188. BIBLE. Authorized or King James Version. London, 1611.
(V)

Milton's copy, with autograph marginalia, is
now in the British Museum. See French's LIFE
RECORDS, II, 65; V, 359, 396.

189. BIBLE. 1614 edn. (?)

An autographed copy owned by George Offor in
1856 was thought to have been destroyed in a
fire at Sotheby's in 1865. See French's LIFE
RECORDS, V, 125-26.

190. BIBLE. 1629 edn. (?)

See French's LIFE RECORDS, IV, 387; V, 126.

191. BIBLE. 1637 edn. (?)

See W. R. Parker, MILTON, p. 835.

192. Bidenbachius, Felix.

DE CAUSIS MATRIMONIALIBUS TRACTUS. (V)

T   YP, II, 712.

193. Bilson, Thomas.

      THE PERPETUALL GOVERNMENT OF CHRISTES CHURCH. (*)

          CG   YP, I, 825.

194. Bilson, Thomas.

      THE TRUE DIFFERENCE BETWEEN CHRISTIAN SUBJECTION
      AND UNCHRISTIAN REBELLION. (*)

          CG   YP, I, 825.

195. Bion.

      IDYLS. (V)

          E   YP, II, 394-95.
          See J. H. Hanford, "The Pastoral Elegy and
          Milton's Lycidas," PMLA, XXV (1910), 403-47.

196. Blaeu, Jean and Gillaume.

      LE THÉATRE DU MONDE. (?)

          See Sr. M. I. Corcoran, MILTON'S PARADISE.

197. Blondel, David.

      PSEUDO-ISIDORE AND TORRES DRUBBED. (?)

          P   YP, I, 628.
          The reference to David Blondell in NDX (CM, i,
          170) is misleading; Milton's marginal note is
          to Flavius Blondus da Forli, q.v.

198. Blondus, Flavius [Flavio Biondo da Forli].

      HISTORIARUM AB INCLINATIONE IMPERII ROMANORUM. (V)

          HB   CM, X, 106.
          See Constance Nicholas, INTRODUCTION AND NOTES
          TO MILTON'S HISTORY OF BRITAIN, p. 70.

199. Blundeville, Thomas.

      EXERCISES, CONTAINING SIXE TREATISES. (?)

          E   YP, II, 392.

200. Boccaccio, Giovanni.

          DECAMERON. (?)

                  C   YP, II, 757.
                  NDX   CM, i, 173.

201. Boccaccio, Giovanni.

          FILOCOLO. (?)

                  See Olin H. Moore, "The Infernal Council," MP,
                  XVI (1918), 186-93.

202. Boccaccio, Giovanni.

          GENEALOGIA DE GLI DEI. (*)

                  See Merritt Y. Hughes, JOHN MILTON: COMPLETE
                  POEMS AND MAJOR PROSE, pp. 52, 57, 180, 255,
                  574, 597, 599.

203. Boccaccio, Giovanni.

          VITA DI DANTE POETA FIORENTINO. Rome, 1544. (V)

                  CPB   YP, I, 438.

204. Boccaccio, Giovanni.

          VITA DI DANTE POETA FIORENTINO. Florence, 1576.
          (V)

                  Milton knew two editions of Boccaccio's LIFE
                  OF DANTE; see Ruth Mohl's discussion, YP, I,
                  438.

205. Boccalini, Trajano.

          DE' RAGGUAGLI DI PARNASSO. Venice, 1630. (V)

                  CPB   YP, I, 467-68.
                  Although ADVICE FROM PARNASSUS first appeared
                  in Venice, 1612-13 and frequently thereafter,
                  because of a peculiar printer's error in the
                  Venice, 1630, edition, Ruth Mohl chooses it as
                  Milton's.

                          34

206. Bochart, Samuel.

GEOGRAPHIA SACRA. (?)

See Robert R. Cawley, MILTON AND THE LITERATURE
OF TRAVEL.

207. Bochart, Samuel.

HIEROZOICON, SIVE BIPERTITUM OPUS DE ANIMALIBUS
SACRAE SCRIPTURAE. (?)

See Harris F. Fletcher, MILTON'S RABBINICAL
READINGS, pp. 290 ff.

208. Bodin, Jean.

COLLOQUIUM HEPTAPLOMERES. ₍MS₎ (V)

See Louis I. Bredvold, "Milton and Bodin's
HEPTAPLOMERES," SP, XXI (1924), 399-402.

209. Bodin, Jean.

DE LA DEMONOMANIE DE SORCIERS. (?)

See Robert H. West, MILTON AND THE ANGELS.

210. Bodin, Jean.

DE REPUBLICA. (V)

CPB   YP, I, 409.
CG   YP, I, 834.
TKM   YP, III, 201, 203.

211. Bodin, Jean.

LE FLEAU DES DEMONS ET SORCIERS. (?)

See M. Y. Hughes, JOHN MILTON: COMPLETE POEMS AND
MAJOR PROSE, p. 420.

212. Boehme ₍Böhme, Behmen₎, Jakob.

ANSWERS TO FORTY QUESTIONS CONCERNING THE SOUL...
AND THE CLAVIS, OR KEY. (?)

See Margaret Lewis Bailey, MILTON AND JAKOB
BOEHME: A STUDY OF GERMAN MYSTICISM IN SEVEN-
TEENTH-CENTURY ENGLAND (New York: Oxford
University Press, 1914).

213. Boehme, Jakob.

AURORA. THAT IS, THE DAY-SPRING. (?)

See no. 212.

214. Boehme, Jakob.

CONCERNING THE THREE PRINCIPLES OF THE DIVINE
ESSENCE. (?)

See no. 212; M. Y. Hughes, JOHN MILTON: COMPLETE
POEMS AND MAJOR PROSE, p. 418.

215. Boehme, Jakob.

ELECTION OF GRACE. (?)

See no. 212.

216. Boehme, Jakob.

EPISTLES OF J. BEHME. (?)

See no. 212.

217. Boehme, Jakob.

THE INCARNATION OF JESUS CHRIST. (?)

See no. 212.

218. Boehme, Jakob.

MYSTERIUM MAGNUM: OR AN EXPOSITION OF THE FIRST BOOK
OF MOSES, CALLED GENESIS. (?)

See no. 212; M. Y. Hughes, JOHN MILTON: COMPLETE
POEMS AND MAJOR PROSE, p. 422.

219. Boehme, Jakob.

177 THEOSOPHICK QUESTIONS WITH ANSWERS TO 13 OF
THEM ⌜DE SIGNATURA RERUM⌝. (?)

    See no. 212.

220. Boehme, Jakob.

    THREEFOLD LIFE OF MAN. (?)

        See no. 212; M. Y. Hughes, JOHN MILTON: COMPLETE
        POEMS AND MAJOR PROSE, pp. 217-18.

221. Boethius.

    OPERA. (?)

222. Boethius.

    CONSOLATION OF PHILOSOPHY. (*)

        Although there are editions and translations
        without number, Milton's copy is unknown. He
        probably knew Queen Elizabeth's translation
        and King Alfred's and doubtlessly read it in
        Latin as well. See John S. Coolidge, "Boethius
        and 'That Last Infirmity of Noble Mind'," PQ,
        42 (1963), 176-82.

223. Boethius.

    ON CICERO'S DE INVENTIONE. (V)

        LO   CM, XI, 113.

224. Boethius.

    ON CICERO'S "TOPICS". (V)

        LO   CM, XI, 23, 139, 193, 213, 219,
                    263, 437.

225. Boethius ⌜Boece⌝, Hector.

    SCOTORUM HISTORIAE. (V)

        HB   CM, X, 106.

226. Boiardo, Matteo Maria.

ORLANDO INNAMORATO. (V)

CPB YP, I, 391, 418, 439, 463.
MAR CM, XVIII, 577.
See Harris F. Fletcher, COLLECTION OF FIRST
EDITIONS OF MILTON'S WORKS (Urbana: University
of Illinois Press, 1953), p. 24.

227. St. Bonaventure.

BREVILOQUIUM. (?)

See Sr. M. I. Corcoran, MILTON'S PARADISE.

228. St. Bonaventure.

EXPOSITIO IN QUATUOR LIBROS SENTENTIARUM MAGISTRI
PETRI LOMBARDI. (?)

See no. 227.

Bonmatthei. See Buonmattei.

229. BOOK OF BARUCH (Slavonic). (?)

See Edward C. Baldwin, "Some Extra-Biblical
Semitic Influences upon Milton's Story of the
Fall of Man," JEGP, XXVIII (1929), 366-401.

230. BOOK OF COMMON PRAYER. (V)

A YP, I, 724, 725.
CG YP, I, 854, 856.
K YP, III, 360, 503, 504, 508.
2D YP, IV, 548, 587, 620.
RJP YP, IV, 931.

231. BOOK OF LLAN DAV (MS). (*)

K YP, III, 588.
1D YP, IV, 490.
HB CM, X, 140.
Milton may have known this unpublished MS
through Selden who purchased it and placed
it in the Bodleian in 1659.

232. BOOK OF THE CHRONICLES OF RABBI ELIEZER, THE SON OF
     HYRQANUS. (?)

        See Edward C. Baldwin, "Some Extra-Biblical
        Semitic Influences Upon Milton's Story of the
        Fall of Man," JEGP, XXVIII (1929), 366-401.

233. Boorde, Andrew.

    A DYETARY OF HELTH. (?)

        See Sr. M. I. Corcoran, MILTON'S PARADISE.

234. Bowes, Sir Jerom.

    HM   CM, X, 382.
    Milton's reference to Bowes' "Journal" was
    probably picked up from Hakluyt, q.v.

235. Bowles, Edward.

    THE MYSTERIE OF INIQUITY YET WORKING IN THE KINGDOMES
    OF ENGLAND, SCOTLAND, & IRELAND, FOR THE DESTRUCTION
    OF RELIGION TRULY PROTESTANT. (V)

    K   YP, III, 474, 475, 476.

236. Bracton, Henry de.

    DE LEGIBUS ET CONSUETUDINIBUS ANGLIAE LIBRI QUINQUE.
    (V)

    K   YP, III, 591.
    1D   YP, IV, 492 ff.

237. Bramwell, John.

    THE SERPENT SALVE. (?)

    TKM   YP, III, 201.
    K   YP, III, 429, 591.

238. Brandt, Sebastian.

    NARRENSCHIFF. Trans. by Alexander Barclay as THE
    SHIP OF FOOLS. (V)

    PROL   YP, I, 266.

239. Brent, Nathaniel.

    THE HISTORIE OF THE COUNCEL OF TRENT. (?)

        CPB   YP, I, 396.

240. Brerewood, Edward.

    THE PATRIARCHICALL GOVERNMENT OF THE ANCIENT CHURCH, in CERTAIN BRIEFE TREATISES. (V)

        CG   YP, I, 194.

241. Breydenbach.

    PREREGRINATIO IN TERRAM SANCTAM. (?)

        See Robert R. Cawley, MILTON AND THE LITERATURE OF TRAVEL.

242. Brinsley, John.

    CONSOLATION FOR OUR GRAMMAR SCHOOLES. (?)

        E   YP, II, 378.

243. Brinsley, John.

    LUDUS LITERARIUS. (?)

        E   YP, II, 381.

244. BRITISH LIGHTNING OR SUDDAINE TUMMULTS, IN ENGLAND, SCOTLAND AND IRELAND. (?)

    See G. W. Whiting, MILTON'S LITERARY MILIEU.

245. Brodaeus ⌈Turonensis⌉, Joannes, ed.

    EURIPIDIS TRAGOEDIAE. (V)

        MAR   CM, XVIII, 310, 311, 312, 315, 316, 317, 318.

246. Brompton, John.

    CHRONICON, in HISTORIAE ANGLICANAE SCRIPTORES X, ed. Sir Roger Twysden, q.v. (V)

HB   CM, X, 207, 281, 288, 295.

247. Brooke, Sir Robert.

      LA GRAUNDE ABRIDGEMENT. (?)

            C   YP, II, 756.

248. Brooke, Sir Robert.

      ASCUNS NOVEL CASES. (*)

            C   YP, II, 756.
      This work is familiarly known as "Petty Brooke."

249. Brooke, Robert Greville, Lord.

      A DISCOURSE OPENING THE NATURE OF THAT EPISCOPACIE,
      WHICH IS EXERCISED IN ENGLAND. (V)

            Intro.   YP, I, 145-48.
            AR   YP, I, 600.
            See G. W. Whiting, "Milton and Lord Brooke on
            the Church," MLN, LI (1936), 161-66, and MILTON'S
            LITERARY MILIEU.

250. Brooke, Robert Greville, Lord.

      ON THE NATURE OF TRUTH. (*)

            See M. Y. Hughes, JOHN MILTON: COMPLETE POETRY
            AND MAJOR PROSE, p. 746.

251. Browne, Sir Thomas.

      PSEUDODOXIA EPIDEMICA. (?)

            See Sr. M. I. Corcoran, MILTON'S PARADISE.

252. Browne, William.

      BRITANNIA'S PASTORALS. (V)

            MAR   CM, XVIII, 570 ff.

41

253. Bucer, Martin.

DE REGNO CHRISTI JESU SERVATORIS NOSTRI. (V)

POS   YP, I, 974.
MB   YP, I, 417, 432, 479.
2D   YP, IV, 609.

254. Bucer, Martin.

IN SACRA QUATUOR EVANGELICA, ENARRATIONES. (V)

MB   YP, II, 432, 444.
TKM   YP, III, 247.

255. Bucer, Martin.

THE ORIGINALL OF BISHOPS AND METROPOLITANS: THE
JUDGEMENT OF M. BUCER, in CERTAIN BRIEFE TREATISES.
(V)

Intro.   YP, I, 194.

256. Bucer, Martin.

SCRIPTA ANGLICANA. (V)

MB   YP, II, 418, 422.
T   YP, II, 710.

257. Buchanan, David.

A SHORT AND TRUE RELATION OF SOME MAIN PASSAGES OF
THINGS (WHEREIN THE SCOTS ARE PARTICULARLY CONCERN-
ED) FROM THE VERY FIRST BEGINNING OF THESE UNHAPPY
TROUBLES TO THIS DAY. (V)

K   YP, III, 385, 439.
Milton also cites this work as TRUTHS MANIFEST.

258. Buchanan, David.

SOME PAPERS OF THE COMMISSIONERS OF SCOTLAND. (?)

K   YP, III, 439.

259. Buchanan, George.

DE JURE REGNI APUD SCOTOS. (?)

42

```
          CPB          YP, I, 478.
          K            YP, III, 588, 590.
```

260. Buchanan, George.

　　　POEMATA QUAE EXTANT. (*)

```
          2D           YP, IV, 592.
```
Although Milton refers to Buchanan as a poet,
he is best known as a historian. See René
Galland, "Milton and Buchanan," Révue Anglo-
Américaine, XIII (1936), 326-33.

261. Buchanan, George.

　　　RERUM SCOTICARUM HISTORIA. (V)

```
          CPB          YP, I, 460, 478.
          TKM          YP, III, 223-26, 239.
          1D           YP, IV, 371, 481.
          HB           CM, X, 98, 106, 131, 147, 193,
                       203, 204, 229, 230.
          NDX          CM, i, 203.
```
See W. R. Parker, MILTON, p. 842; H. Glicksman,
"Sources of Milton's History of Britain," Wis-
consin Studies in Language and Literature, XI
(1920), 105-44; Constance Nicholas, INTRODUCTION
AND NOTES TO MILTON'S HISTORY OF BRITAIN, p. 23.

262. Bullinger, Henry.

　　　THE CHRISTEN STATE OF MATRIMONY. Trans. Miles
　　　Coverdale. (?)

　　　See William Haller, "Hail Wedded Love," ELH,
　　　XIII (1946), 79-97.

263. Bullinger, Henry.

　　　"Sermon on the Good Spirits," in SERMONUM DECADES.
　　　(?)

　　　See Robert H. West, MILTON AND THE ANGELS.

264. Buonmattei, Benedetto.

　　　DELLA LINGUA TOSCANA, LIBRI DUE. (*)

```
          COR          YP, I, 328.
          2D           YP, IV, 616.
```

265. THE BURDEN OF ENGLAND, SCOTLAND, & IRELAND: OR, THE
WATCHMANS ALARUM. (?)

    See G. W. Whiting, MILTON'S LITERARY MILIEU.

266. Burgidolensis, Herveus.

    COMMENTARY. (?)

        CG   YP, I, 777.
        See M. Y. Hughes, JOHN MILTON: PROSE SELECTIONS
        (New York, 1947), p. 78.

267. Burton, Robert.

    ANATOMY OF MELANCHOLY. (*)

        See Robert H. West, MILTON AND THE ANGELS;
        G. W. Whiting, MILTON'S LITERARY MILIEU.

268. Butler, Samuel [?].

    THE CHARACTER OF THE RUMP. (?)

        See W. R. Parker, MILTON, pp. 548-49, 1073;
        Paul B. Anderson, SP, XLIV (1947), 504-18
        (for question of authorship). THE TRANSPROSER
        REHEARSED, q.v., was also attributed to Butler,
        though Andrew Marvell throught it the work of
        Samuel Parker.

269. Buxtorf, Johann.

    HEBREW OLD TESTAMENT WITH RABBINICAL COMMENTARY.
    (?)

        See Harris F. Fletcher, MILTON'S RABBINICAL
        READINGS. Although Professor Fletcher makes
        the grand assumption that Milton was intimately
        familiar with Buxtorf's Bible and actively
        leads the student to think so also, he occas-
        ionally makes an ambiguous statement that causes
        one to sit up with a jolt; for instance, "The
        Buxtorf edition fits Milton's references to
        rabbinical apparatus, and there is no particular
        reason why this Bible, perhaps the best known
        among Christians throughout Europe of all the
        six editions up to Milton's time, should not
        have been used by him." Some of Professor
        Fletcher's arguments are more persuasive;

however, the tyro (to use one of his favorite
words) is left with niggling doubts. See
Samuel S. Stollman, "Milton's Rabbinical Readings and Fletcher," _Milton Studies_, IV (1972),
195-215.

270. Buxtorf, Johannis.

LEXICON CHALDAICUM. (*)

See H. F. Fletcher, MILTON'S RABBINICAL READ-
INGS, pp. 236-39.

271. Buxtorf, Johann, Filius.

DISSERTATIONES PHILOLOGICAE-THEOLOGICAE. (?)

See Sr. M. I. Corcoran, MILTON'S PARADISE.

272. BYZANTINAE HISTORIAE SCRIPTORES. (V)

CPB   YP, I, 436-37.

273. Caesar, Julius.

C. IULII CAESARIS QUAE EXTANT. (V)

CPB   YP, I, 400.
1D   YP, IV, 448-49.
HB   CM, X, 31-51.

274. Caesar, Julius.

COMMENTARIES. (V)

1D   CM, VII, 333.
HB   CM, X, 31-51.
LO   CM, XI, 63, 175, 207, 259, 365.

275. Caesar, Julius.

CIVIL WARS. (V)

MAR   CM, XVIII, 498.
LO   CM, XI, 53.

45

276. Cajetan ⌜Gaetano⌟, Thommaso di Vio.

      COMMENTARII...IN QUINQUE MOSAICOS LIBROS. (?)

          See Sr. M. I. Corcoran, MILTON'S PARADISE.

Calaber, Quintus. See Quintus Smyrnaeus.

277. Calepine, Ambrose.

      AMBROSII CALEPINI BERGOMATIS LEXICON. (?)

          See John M. Steadman, "Urania, Wisdom, and
          Scriptural Exegesis," Neophilologus, XLVII
          (1963), 61-73.

278. Callimachus.

      OPERA. Ed. Bonaventura Vulcanius. Leyden, 1584.
      (V)

          CG   YP, I, 815, 816.
          2D   YP, IV, 584.
          COR   YP, I, 335.
          MAR   CM, XVIII, 278, 294, 295, 297.
          NDX   CM, i, 211.
          IDYLS of Moschus and Bion are appended to
          this edition which Milton used. See Nathan
          Dane, "Milton's Callimachus," MLN, LVI (1941),
          278-79.

279. Calvin, Jean.

      A COMMENTARIE UPON THE FIRST BOOKE OF MOSES CALLED
      GENESIS. (*)

          DDD   YP, II, 246.
          See Sr. M. I. Corcoran, MILTON'S PARADISE.

280. Calvin, Jean.

      IN EPISTOLAM PRIOREM AD CORINTHIOS. (?)

          DDD   YP, II, 251.

281. Calvin, Jean.

      INSTITUTIO CHRISTIANAE RELIGIONIS. (V)

```
          DDD        YP, II, 293.
          K          YP, III, 515.
```

282. Calvin, Jean.

   MOSIS RELIQUI LIBRI QUATUOR. (*)

```
          DDD        YP, II, 296, 313.
```

283. Calvin, Jean.

   PRAELECTIONES IN DUODECIM PROPHETAS. (*)

```
          DDD        YP, II, 257, 291.
          T          YP, II, 615.
```

284. Calvin, Jean.

   PRAELECTIONES IN LIBRUM PROPHETIARUM DANIELIS. (V)

```
          TKM        YP, III, 246.
```

285. Calvisius ₍Kallwitz₎, Sethus.

   OPUS CHRONOLOGICUM. (V)

```
          HB         CM, X, 71, 101, 197, 257.
```

286. Camden, William.

   ANNALES RERUM ANGLICARUM ET HIBERNICARUM, REGNANTE
   ELIZABETHA AD ANNUM SALUTIS 1589. London, 1615-27.
   (V)

```
          CPB        YP, I, 365, 389, 421, 435, 459, 464,
                     465, 479, 481, 483, 484, 492, 502,
                     503.
          R          YP, I, 527, 528, 529, 539, 540, 542,
                     586, 615.
          CG         YP, I, 798.
```
   According to Ruth Mohl, Milton's "page references
   to Camden throughout the CPB fit this edition. A
   second part of the ANNALES appeared in Leyden in
   1625 and in London in 1627, and the fact that
   seven of Milton's fifteen entries from Camden
   have 'Vol. 2' in them shows that he must have
   used the edition in which the 'Tomus Alter' or
   Second Part was added. The 1615 edition...has

47

that Second Part, dated 1627, bound with the
First Part, dated 1615" (YP, I, 365 ff.). See
also W. R. Parker, MILTON, p. 842.

287. Camden, William.

BRITANNIA. London, 1586. (V)

R   YP, I, 539, 542.
CG   YP, I, 798.
W   CM, VI, 142.
1D   YP, IV, 505.
HB   See H. Glicksman, "Sources of Milton's History of Britain," Wisconsin Studies
in Language and Literature, XI (1920), 105-44.

288. Camden, William.

BRITANNIA. Trans. Philemon Holland. (V)

Constance Nicholas points out, "Milton's citation of certain points...indicates that he
used Philemon Holland's translation, either
the 1610 edition or its 1637 reprint, as well
the Latin BRITANNIA" (INTRODUCTION AND NOTES
TO MILTON'S HISTORY OF BRITAIN, p. 17).

289. Camden, William.

INSTITUTIO GRACAE GRAMMATICES COMPENDIARIA. (*)

See Donald L. Clark, JOHN MILTON AT ST. PAUL'S
SCHOOL.

290. Camerarius, P.

OPERAE HORARUM SUBCISIUARUM. Trans. I. Molle as
THE LIVING LIBRARIE. (?)

See Kester Svendsen, MILTON AND SCIENCE.

291. Cameron, John.

MYROTHECIUM EVANGELICUM. (V)

T   YP, II, 647.

48

292. Camoẽs, Vaz de.

OS LUSIADS. (?)

See James H. Sims, "Camoens' LUSIADS and Milton's
PARADISE LOST: Satan's Voyage to Eden," PAPERS
ON MILTON, University of Tulsa Monograph Series,
VIII (1969), 36-46.

293. Campion, Edmund.

HISTORY OF IRELAND, COLLECTED BY THREE LEARNED
AUTHORS, VIZ. MEREDITH HANMER...EDMUND CAMPION AND
EDMUND SPENSER. Dublin, 1633. (V)

CPB   YP, I, 389 ff.
See W. R. Parker, MILTON, p. 842.

294. Canne, John.

THE GOLDEN RULE, OR, JUSTICE ADVANCED. (?)

George W. Whiting in MILTON'S LITERARY MILIEU
does not say that Milton read Canne's pamphlet; rather he makes a strong case that
Canne read Milton. It seems a reasonable
assumption, however, that (human nature
being what it is) Milton would have read a
work by a friendly competitor and co-worker
in the Cromwellian vineyards that came out
immediately following his own TKM and that
advocated the same cause.

295. Cantacuzene, John.

HISTORIARUM LIBRI IV. Trans. Jacobus Pontanus.
Ingolstadt, 1603. (V)

CPB   YP, I, 488-89.

Canterus, Guilielmus. See Canter.

296. Canter, Willem.

NOVARUM LECTIONUM LIBRI SEPTEM. (V)

MAR   CM, XVIII, 288, 300, 313, 315,
                     316, 317, 318, 320, 322, 323,
                     324, 325.

Capellus, Ludovicus. See Louis Cappel.

297. Capitolinus.

"Vita M. Antonini," and "Maximini Duo," in
SCRIPTORES HISTORIAE AUGUSTAE, q.v.

1D   CM, VII, 333.
HB   CM, X, 81, 84.

298. Cappel, Louis.

CRITICA SACRA. (?)

See George N. Conklin, BIBLICAL CRITICISM AND
HERESY IN MILTON, p. 15.

299. Cappel, Louis.

SPICILEGEUM, SEU NOTAE IN NOVUM TESTAMENTUM. (V)

1D   YP, IV, 390.
CD   CM, XVII, 93.

300. Cardan, Jerome.

DE SUBTILITATE. (?)

See Robert H. West, MILTON AND THE ANGELS, p.
103.

301. Cardan, Jerome.

OPERA. (?)

A   YP, I, 671.

302. Carew, Thomas.

COELUM BRITANICUM. (?)

See Willa McClung Evans, HENRY LAWES (New York,
1941), p. 96.

Carion, John. See Melancthon.

50

303. Carr, Nicholas.

> "Epistola de morte Buceri ad Johannem Checum," in
> Bucer's SCRIPTA ANGLICANA, q.v. (V)
>
> MB   YP, II, 426, 430.

304. Cartwright, Cristopher.

> ELECTA THARGUMICO-RABBINICA, SIVE ANNOTATIONES IN
> GENESIN. (?)
>
> > See George N. Conklin, BIBLICAL CRITICISM AND
> > HERESY IN MILTON, pp. 114-15.

305. Cartwright, Thomas.

> ADMONITION TO PARLIAMENT. (V)
>
> TKM   YP, III, 248.

306. Cartwright, William.

> COMEDIES, TRAGI-COMEDIES WITH OTHER POEMS. (*)
>
> > In his sonnet to Henry Lawes, Milton praises
> > Cartwright's poem, "Ariadne Deserted by
> > Theseus," which had been set to music by
> > their mutual friend. It seems reasonable
> > that Milton would have read more than one of
> > Cartwright's poems if he found them so sing-
> > ularly praiseworthy. W. R. Parker suggests
> > some influence on Milton's prosody; see
> > MILTON, pp. 302, 907, 929.

> Casas, Bartolomé de las. See John Phillips' trans.
> THE TEARS OF THE INDIANS.

307. Casaubon, Meric.

> THE ORIGINAL AND CAUSE OF TEMPORAL EVILS. (?)
>
> > See Robert H. West, MILTON AND THE ANGELS.

308. Cassidorus Senator [his name, not a title], Flavius
     Magnus Aurelius.

> CHRONICON. (V)

HB   CM, X, 86.
See Constance Nicholas, INTRODUCTION AND NOTES
TO MILTON'S HISTORY OF BRITAIN, pp. 56-57.

309. Castalion, ₍Châteillon₎, Sébastian.

        DIALOGUES ON SACRED HISTORY. (?)

        CPB   YP, I, 412.

310. Castell, Edmund.

        LEXICON HEPTAGLOTTON, HEBRAICUM, CHALDAICUM, SYRIA-
        CUM, SAMARITANUM, AETHIOPICUM, ARABICUM, CONJUNCTIM
        ET PERSICUM SEPARATIM. (?)

        See George N. Conklin, BIBLICAL CRITICISM AND
        HERESY IN MILTON, p. 20.

311. CATECHESIS ECCLESIARUM QUAE IN REGNO POLONIAE & DUCATU
      LITHUANIAE. (V)

        See W. R. Parker, MILTON, pp. 395, 995.

312. Cato.

        DE RE RUSTICA. (V)

        E   YP, II, 388.
        See W. R. Parker, MILTON, p. 852.

313. Cato.

        DISTICHA MORALIA. (*)

        E   YP, II, 383, 384.
        See Donald L. Clark, JOHN MILTON AT ST. PAUL'S
        SCHOOL.

314. Cats, Jacob.

        'S WERELTS BEGIN, MIDDEN, EYNDE, BESLOTEN IN DEN
        TROU-RINGH, MET DEN PROEF-STEEN VAN DEN SELVEN. (?)

        See Geoffrey Bullough, "Milton and Cats,"
        ESSAYS IN ENGLISH LITERATURE FROM THE RENAIS-
        SANCE TO THE VICTORIAN AGE PRESENTED TO A. S. P.
        WOODHOUSE, ed. Millar Maclure and F. W. Watt

                            52

(Toronto: University of Toronto Press, 1964),
pp. 103-24.

315. Cats, Jacob.

FACES AUGUSTAE, SIVE POEMATIA, QUIBUS ILLUSTRIORES
NUPTIAE, A NOBILI & ILLUSTRI VIRO...JAM A CASPARE
BARLAEO & CORNELIO BOYO LATINO CARMINE CELEBRANTUR.
(?)

See no. 314.

316. Catullus.

CARMINA. (V)

COR	YP, II, 768, 769, 771.
1D	YP, IV, 364.
2D	YP, IV, 648.
AR	CM, IV, 301.
G	CM, VI, 331.
LO	CM, XI, 159, 209, 235, 253, 427.

317. Caxton, William.

THE GOLDEN LEGEND, translation of Jacobus de
Voragine's LEGENDA AUREA SANCTORUM. (?)

CG   YP, I, 857.

318. Caxton, William.

MIRROUR OF THE WORLD. (?)

See Sr. M. I. Corcoran, MILTON'S PARADISE.

319. Cebes.

πιΝΑΞ , OR TABLE. (V)

E   YP, II, 384.

320. Cedrenus, Georges.

COMPENDIUM HISTORIARUM A MUNDO CONDITIO USQUE AD
ISAACIUM COMNENUM IMPERATOREM. (V)

```
                CPB        YP, I, 394.
                R          YP, I, 546, 577-78.
                P          YP, I, 636, 649.
```

321. Celsus, Aulus Cornelius.

    DE RE MEDICA. (V)

                E   YP, II, 391, 393.
                G   CM, VT, 329.

322. Cerda, Joannes Ludovicus de la.

        P. VERGILII MARONIS AENEIDOS...ARGUMENTIS EXPLICAT-
        IONIBUS, NOTIS ILLUSTRATI. (V)

                COR   YP, II, 771.
                MAR   CM, XVIII, 279.

323. CERTAIN BRIEFE TREATISES, WRITTEN BY DIVERSE LEARNED
      MEN, CONCERNING THE ANCIENT AND MODERNE GOVERNMENT
      OF THE CHURCH. (V)

                Nine short tracts, three of which appear under
                one title; each is also listed under the
                individual author. See YP, I, 193-94, 738,
                768.

324. Chamberlayne, Edward.

        THE PRESENT WARRE PARALLEL'D. OR, A BRIEFE RELATION
        OF THE FIVE YEARES CIVIL WARRES OF HENRY THE THIRD,
        WITH THE EVENT AND ISSUE OF THAT UNNATURALL WARR.
        (?)

                TKM   YP, III, 344.

325. Chamierus [Chamier], Danielus.

        PANSTRATIAE CATHOLICAE. (V)

                T   YP, II, 697.

326. Chancelor, Richard.

        "Discourse."

                HM   CM, X, 382.
```
```

Milton's reference probably comes from Purchas
or Hakluyt, qq.v.

327. Charitopolus, Manuel, Patriarch of Constantinople.

DECRETUM DE JURE PATRONATUS, in Leunclavius's
IURIS GRAECO-ROMANI, q.v. (?)

CPB   YP, I, 407.

328. Charitopolus, Manuel.

DECRETUM DE TRANSLATIONE EPISCOPORUM, in Leunclavius's
IURIS GRAECO-ROMANI, q.v. (?)

CPB   YP, I, 407.

329. Charitopolus, Manuel.

SOLUTIONES QUARUNDUM QUAESTIONUM, in Leunclavius's
IURIS GRAECO-ROMANI, q.v. (V)

CPB   YP, I, 417.

Charles I, King of England.
Proclamations, speeches, public correspondence,
etc. not included. EIKON-BASILIKE, q.v., an
attribution; also attributed to John Gauden.

Charondas.
In "Of Education" Milton recommends the "extol-
l'd remains" of several Greek law-givers, including Charondas. Twenty paragraphs attributed
to him are included in Johannes Stobaeus's
SENTENTIAE, q.v.; there is a slight possibility
that Milton knew Charondas through that source,
though it is more likely that he knew him only
by reputation, probably through Aristotle and
Diodorus Siculus. See YP, II, 398-99.

Châteillon. See Sébastian Castalion.

330. Chaucer, Geoffrey.

THE WORKS OF OUR ANCIENT AND LEARNED ENGLISH POET,
GEFFREY CHAUCER, NEWLY PRINTED. London, 1602. (V)

```
CPB          YP, I, 402, 406, 416, 472-73.
PROL         YP, I, 272.
R            YP, I, 570, 579, 580, 595.
A            YP, I, 667.
NDX          CM, i, 248.
```

Cheke, Sir John. See Thomas Cranmer et al., REFORMATIO LEGUM ECCLESIASTICARUM.

```
MB           YP, II, 423.
T            YP, II, 716, 717.
S            CM, I, 62.
```

331. CHESTER PLAYS, I AND II. (?)

See Allan H. Gilbert, "Milton and the Mysteries," SP, XVII (1920), 147-69.

332. Chiabera, Gabriel.

CANZONETTA. (?)

COR   YP, II, 768, 771-72.

333. CHILDREN OF BELIALL, OR, THE REBELLS. (?)

See G. W. Whiting, MILTON'S LITERARY MILIEU.

334. Chillingsworth, William.

THE RELIGION OF PROTESTANTS. (?)

See George N. Conklin, BIBLICAL CRITICISM AND HERESY IN MILTON.

335. Chimentelli, Valerio.

MARMOR PISANUM DE HONORE BISELLI. (?)

```
2D           YP, IV, 617.
COR          CM, XII, 315.
```

336. CHRONICLES OF JERAHMEEL. (?)

See Edward C. Baldwin, "Some Extra-Biblical Semetic Influences upon Milton's Story of the Fall of Man," JEGP, XXVIII (1929), 366-401.

337. Chrysostom, St. John.

    OPERA GRAECÉ. (?)

        W. R. Parker (MILTON, p. 805, n. 21) questions
whether Milton owned the Chrysostom edited by
Sir Henry Savile with the assistance of John
Hales (London, 1610-13). If the annotations
in a copy of Pindar alleged to be Milton's
were genuine, then he certainly would have been
quite familiar with it. In it someone comment-
ing on Antistrophe III quotes in Greek from
Chrysostom and gives an exact reference:
"Chrysost. T.4: in Proaemio ad Philip. p.3.1.8."
See CM, XVIII, 281. At the same place there is
a reference to Dounaeus' emendation of Chrysostom. Andrew Downes's contribution to Sir
Henry's edition was "Notae in homilias S. Jo.
Chrysostomi in epistt. Pauli et in Acta apostolorum" in Vol. VIII, beginning p. 230. Of all
the editions of Chrysostom available to Milton,
that of Sir Henry Savile is the only one to
match this reference. See note at Pindar.

338. Chrysostom, St. John.

    HOMILIAE XXI DE STATUIS AD POPULUM ANTIOCHENUM
HABITAE. (?)

    See Sr. M. I. Corcoran, MILTON'S PARADISE.

339. Chrysostom, St. John.

    HOMILIAE LXVII IN CAPUT GENESEOS. (V)

    CPB   YP, I, 364, 416-17.
For reasons well known, Miss Ruth Mohl prefers
the Venice, 1549, edition to Sir Henry Savile's.
See also W. R. Parker, MILTON, p. 805; Sr. M. I.
Corcoran, MILTON'S PARADISE.

340. Chrysostom, St. John.

    HOMILY LXXXV ON MATTHEW'S GOSPEL. (?)

    K   YP, III, 518.
See W. R. Parker, MILTON, p. 805.

341. Chrysostom, St. John.

HOMILY XXIII UPON THE EPISTLE TO THE ROMANS. (?)

TKM   YP, III, 211.
1D   YP, IV, 382 ff., 489.
See W. R. Parker, MILTON, p. 805.

342. Chrysostom, St. John.

ORATIONES LXXX. Paris, 1604. (V)

Milton's copy is in the library of Ely Cathedral.
See J. M. French, THE LIFE RECORDS OF JOHN MIL-
TON, I, 296, 304; V, 382.

343. Cicero.

OPERA OMNIA QUAE EXTANT. (V)

Constance Nicholas narrows down the dozens of
editions available to Milton to Venice, 1582-
83, and EPISTOLARUM AD ATTICUM (Venice, 1563
or 1570), both published by Aldus, as sources
for HB. See INTRODUCTION AND NOTES TO MILTON'S
HISTORY OF BRITAIN, p. 37, and Donald L. Clark,
JOHN MILTON AT ST. PAUL'S SCHOOL.

344. Cicero.

ACADEMIC QUESTIONS. (V)

G   CM, VI, 333.
LO   CM, XI, 49, 53.

345. Cicero.

AD FRATREM. (V)

LO   CM, XI, 199, 207.

346. Cicero.

AD LENTULUM. (V)

LO   CM, XI, 183.

347. Cicero.

AD QUINTUM FRATREM. (V)

LO　　　　　CM, XI, 287.

348. Cicero.

AUCTOR AD HERENNIUM. (V)

MAR　　　　　CM, XVIII, 307.

349. Cicero.

BRUTUS. (*)

PROL　　　　YP, I, 219.
COR　　　　　YP, I, 311, 331.
K　　　　　　YP, III, 461.
2D　　　　　YP, IV, 585.

350. Cicero.

DE AMICITIA. (*)

E　　　　　　YP, II, 396.
TKM　　　　　YP, III, 214.
1D　　　　　YP, IV, 317.
RJP　　　　　YP, IV, 952.

351. Cicero.

DE DIVINATIONE. (V)

LO　　　　　CM, XI, 441.
NDX　　　　　CM, i, 299.

352. Cicero.

DE DOMO SUA. (?)

NDX　　　　　CM, i, 299.

353. Cicero.

DE FATO. (V)

59

```
          LO          CM, XI, 31, 33, 349, 363.
          MAR         CM, XVIII, 307.


354.  Cicero.

          DE FINIBUS BONORUM ET MALORUM.  (V)

              CG          YP, I, 770.
              E           YP, II, 396, 402.
              AR          YP, II, 499.
              TKI.        YP, III, 214.
              G           CM, VI, 334.
              LO          CM, XI, 105, 445.
              NDX         CM, i, 299.


355.  Cicero.

          DE HARUSPICUM RESPONSIS.  (V)

              DDD         YP, II, 295.


356.  Cicero.

          DE INVENTIONE RHETORICA.  (V)

              T           YP, II, 588.
              LO          CM, XI, 113, 167, 239.


357.  Cicero.

          DE LEGE AGRARIA.  (V)

              G           CM, VI, 349, 350.
              1D          YP, IV, 485-86.
              LO          CM, XI, 85, 187, 207, 425.


358.  Cicero.

          DE LEGIBUS.  (V)

              DDD         YP, II, 310.
              TKM         YP, III, 214.
              1D          YP, IV, 383, 459.
              LO          CM, XI, 201.
              NDX         CM, i, 299.


359.  Cicero.
```

DE NATURA DEORUM. (V)

PROL	YP, I, 225, 245, 280, 291, 303, 304.
AR	YP, II, 494, 499.
TKM	YP, III, 214.
RJP	YP, IV, 935.
LO	CM, XI, 31, 37, 47, 207, 217, 281, 495.

360. Cicero.

DE OFFICIIS. (V)

DDD	YP, II, 323.
E	YP, II, 377, 396.
TKM	YP, III, 214.
K	YP, III, 361.
1D	YP, IV, 351.
SD	YP, IV, 745.
G	CM, VI, 330.
LO	CM, XI, 165, 187, 247, 421, 443.
MAR	CM, XVIII, 307.

361. Cicero.

DE ORATORE. (V)

PROL	YP, I, 217, 219, 240, 246, 268, 274, 311.
E	YP, II, 402, 403.
SD	YP, IV, 771, 773.
RJP	YP, IV, 911.
LO	CM, XI, 23, 129, 207.

362. Cicero.

DE PARTITIONE ORATORIA. (V)

LO	CM, XI, 35, 279.

363. Cicero.

DE PROVINCIIS. (*)

1D	YP, IV, 343.

364. Cicero.

DE RE PUBLICA. (?)

AR	YP, II, 497.
1D	YP, IV, 536.
NDX	CM, i, 299.

365. Cicero.

DE SENECTUTE. (V)

PROL	YP, I, 295, 305.
AR	YP, II, 498.
2D	YP, IV, 585, 586.
NDX	CM, i, 299.
LO	CM, XI, 253.

366. Cicero.

DE UNIVERSO. (?)

NDX	CM, i, 299.

367. Cicero.

DIVINATIO IN VERREM[sic]: IN CAECILIUM DIVINATIO.
(V)

LO	CM, XI, 195-96.

368. Cicero.

EPISTOLAE AD FAMILIARES. (V)

PROL	YP, I, 273.
1D	YP, IV, 536.
SD	YP, IV, 744.
G	CM, VI, 344.
NDX	CM, i, 299.

369. Cicero.

EPISTOLARUM AD ATTICUM. (V)

T	YP, II, 655.
RJP	YP, IV, 952.
G	CM, VI, 339, 350.
HB	CM, X, 36.
LO	CM, XI, 251.

```
              MAR          CM, XVIII, 305.
              See no. 343.


370.  Cicero.

         IN CATILINAM.  (V)

              K            YP, III, 441.
              2D           YP, IV, 581.
              LO           CM, XI, 147, 159, 173, 183, 185,
                           187, 443.
              NDX          CM, i, 299.


371.  Cicero.

         IN PISONEM.  (V)

              DDD          YP, II, 295.
              AR           YP, II, 498.
              1D           YP, IV, 442, 536.
              RJP          YP, IV, 899.
              LO           CM, XI, 195, 217.


372.  Cicero.

         IN TOGA CANDIDA.  (?)

              2D           YP, IV, 581, 648.


273.  Cicero.

         IN VATINIUM.  (?)

              SD           YP, IV, 739, 743.


374.  Cicero.

         IN VERREM.  (V)

              G            CM, VI, 331, 335, 336, 346, 350.
              LO           CM, XI, 173, 191, 221, 291, 483.
              SD           YP, IV, 756.
              AR           YP, II, 539.


375.  Cicero.

         ORATOR.  (V)
```

```
          LO          CM, XI, 129.

376.  Cicero.

          PARADOX.  (V)

          LO          CM, XI, 133.

377.  Cicero.

          PHILIPPICAE.  (V)
              1D          YP, IV, 332, 352, 383, 402, 444,
                            469, 501, 504.
              LO          CM, XI, 159, 161, 183, 191, 195,
                            199, 209, 217, 289, 451.

378.  Cicero.

          PRO A. LINCINIO ARCHIA POETA.  (V)
              PROL        YP, I, 288.
              LO          CM, XI, 189, 249.
              NDX         CM, i, 300.

379.  Cicero.

          PRO L. CORN. BALBO.  (?)
```

          The brilliant scholarship and erudition of the
          indexors of The Columbia Milton notwithstanding,
          I cannot find anything resembling a reference
          to this entry in OF REFORMATION (CM, III, 34).
          Nor is it indexed in The Yale Prose.

```
380.  Cicero.

          PRO CLUENTIO.  (V)
              G           CM, VI, 349.
              LO          CM, XI, 451.

381.  Cicero.

          PRO FLACCO.  (V)
              1D          YP, IV, 388, 449.
```

382. Cicero.

    PRO FONTEIO. (V)

        LO   CM, XI, 183.

383. Cicero.

    PRO LEGE MANILIA. (V)

        G   CM, VI, 344.
        LO   CM, XI, 197.

384. Cicero.

    PRO LIGARIO. (V)

        LO   CM, XI, 47, 51, 109.

385. Cicero.

    PRO MARCELLO. (V)

        LO   CM, XI, 35, 127, 133, 173, 185,
                    189, 491.

386. Cicero.

    PRO MILONE. (V)

        1D   YP, IV, 439.
        LO   CM, XI, 147, 187, 273, 285, 355.

387. Cicero.

    PRO MURENA. (V)

        AP   YP, I, 945.
        2D   YP, IV, 662.
        LO   CM, XI, 107, 139, 159, 171, 177,
                    187, 233, 255, 411.

388. Cicero.

    PRO PLANCIO. (V)

        1D   YP, IV, 388.
        2D   YP, IV, 643.

```
          G          CM, VI, 336.
          LO         CM, XI, 207.


389. Cicero.

        PRO POMPEIO. (V)

          LO         CM, XI, 107.


390. Cicero.

        PRO QUINTO. (V)

          G          CM, VI, 349.
          LO         CM, XI, 443.


391. Cicero.

        PRO C. RABIRIO PERDUELLIONIS REO. (V)

          1D         YP, IV, 350.
          2D         YP, IV, 659.
          LO         CM, XI, 455.


392. Cicero.

        PRO ROSCIO AMERINO. (V)

          SD         YP, IV, 752.
          G          CM, VI, 349.
          LO         CM, XI, 349.


393. Cicero.

        PRO ROSCIO COMOEDO. (V)

          LO         CM, XI, 89.


394. Cicero.

        PRO SESTIO. (V)

          1D         YP, IV, 464, 466.
          RJP        YP, IV, 950.
          G          CM, VI, 331, 345.
          LO         CM, XI, 197.
```

395. Cicero.

> PRO SULLA. (V)
>
>> LO   CM, XI, 161.

396. Cicero.

> SOMNIUM SCIPIONIS. (?)
>
>> PROL   YP, I, 235.

397. Cicero.

> TOPICA. (V)
>
>> LO   CM, XI, 23, 33, 45, 95, 111, 117,
>>   131, 133, 169, 177, 187, 205, 211,
>>   215, 219, 279, 285, 451, 459.

398. Cicero.

> TUSCULANAE DISPUTATIONES. (V)
>
>> PROL   YP, I, 241.
>> AR   YP, II, 499.
>> NDX   CM, i, 300.
>> LO   CM, XI, 107, 141, 161, 257, 357,
>>   407.
>> R   CM, III, 34.

399. Cinnamus ₍Sinnamus₎, Johannes.

> HISTORIA. (*)
>
>> See W. R. Parker, MILTON, pp. 502, 1061.

400. Clanvowe, Sir Thomas.

> THE CUCKOO AND THE NIGHTINGALE, in Speght's edn. of
> Chaucer, q.v. (V)
>
>> See J. S. Smart, THE SONNETS OF MILTON (Oxford:
>> The Clarendon Press, 1966), pp. 41, 43; M. Y.
>> Hughes, JOHN MILTON: COMPLETE POEMS AND MAJOR
>> PROSE, p. 53.

401. Clapmarius, Arnoldus [not Clapmorius as in CM].

    DE ARCANIS RERUMPUBLICARUM. (V)

        MAR   CM, XVIII, 493-500 passim.
        See J. M. French, THE LIFE RECORDS OF JOHN
        MILTON, II, 305.

402. Claudianus, Claudian.

    OPERA. (V)

        COR   CM, XII, 9.
        1D   YP, IV, 460.

403. Claudianus, Claudian.

    DE BELLO GILDONICO. (V)

        SD   YP, IV, 795.
        HB   CM, X, 97.

404. Claudianus, Claudian.

    DE LAUDIBUS STILICHONIS. (V)

        HB   CM, X, 97.
        NDX   CM, i, 311.

405. Claudianus, Claudian.

    DE NUPTIIS HONORII AUGUSTI EPITHALAMIUM. (*)

        HB   CM, X, 97.
        NDX   CM, i, 311.

406. Claudianus, Claudian.

    DE IV CONSULATU HONORII. (*)

        NDX   CM, i, 311.

407. Claudianus, Claudian.

    DE VI CONSULATU HONORII. (V)

        1D   YP, IV, 389.

408. Claudianus, Claudian.

> DE RAPTU PROSERPINAE. (V)

>> COR   YP, I, 316-17.
>> NDX   CM, i, 311.

409. Claudianus, Claudian.

> IN RUFINUM. (*)

>> NDX   CM, i, 311.

Cleaver, Richard. Co-author (with John Dod, q.v.) of GODLY FORM OF HOUSEHOLD GOVERNMENT.

410. Cleland, James.

> INSTITUTION OF A YOUNG NOBLE MAN. (?)

>> E   YP, II, 370, 415.

Clemens, Titus Flavius. See Clement of Alexandria.

411. Clement of Alexandria.

> HORTATORY ADDRESS TO THE GREEKS. (V)

>> AR   YP, II, 517.

412. Clement of Alexandria.

> OPERA. (V)

>> R   YP, I, 551.
>> 1D   YP, IV, 350.
>> SD   YP, IV, 744.
>> P   YP, I, 647.

413. Clement of Alexandria.

> PAEDAGOGOS. (V)

>> CPB   YP, I, 392.

414. Clement of Alexandria.

> STROMATA. (V)
>
> | CPB | YP, I, 385, 394-95. |
> | P | YP, I, 632, 647-48. |

415. Clement Romanus, St.

> TWO EPISTLES. (V)
>
> | CG | YP, I, 780, 792. |

416. Clenardus, Nicolaus.

> INSTITUTIONES IN LINGUAM GRAECAM. (?)
>
> See Donald L. Clark, JOHN MILTON AT ST. PAUL'S SCHOOL.

417. Cochlaeus [Dobeneck], Johannes.

> MISCELLANEORUM LIBRI PRIMI TRACTATUS QUARTUS. CON-
> SILIUM JO. COCHLAEI SUPER NEGOCIO LUTHERANO AD...
> CARD. & ARCHIEPISCOPUM MOGUNTINUM. (V)
>
> | TKM | YP, III, 244. |
> | AP | YP, I, 901. |

418. Codinus, Georgius.

> DE OFFICIIS MAGNAE ECCLESIAE ET AULAE CONSTANTIN-
> OPOLITANAE, in BYZANTINAE HISTORIAE SCRIPTORES, q.v.
> (V)
>
> | CPB | YP, I, 437. |

419. Codinus, Georgius.

> EXCERPTA DE ANTIQUITATIBUS CONSTANTINOPOLITANTIS.
> (V)
>
> See W. R. Parker, MILTON, p. 502.

420. Coke, Sir Edward.

> COMMENTARY UPON LITTLETON, THE FIRST PART OF THE
> INSTITUTES OF THE LAWS OF ENGLAND. (V)

```
        C          YP, II, 729, 735.
        H          CM, VT, 74.
        1D         YP, IV, 505.
```

421. Cole, Peter.

      A TREATISE OF THE RICKETS. (?)

          Intro.   YP, IV, 143-44.

422. Colet, John.

      GRAMMATICES RUDIMENTIS. (?)

          E   YP, II, 370.

423. Colet, John.

      STATUTES OF DEAN COLET. (MS) (?)

          E   YP, II, 373.

Collier, Jeremy. See Comenius.

424. Collinne, William.

      THE SPIRIT OF THE PHANATIQUES DISSECTED. (?)

          See W. R. Parker, MILTON, pp. 549, 1073.

425. Columella, L. Junius Moderatus.

      DE RE RUSTICA. (V)

          E   YP, II, 388.
          See W. R. Parker, MILTON, p. 852.

426. Comenius, Joannes Amosus.

      CONATUUM COMENIANORUM PRAELUDIA. (?)

          E   YP, II, 364, 365.

427. Comenius, Joannes Amosus.

      JANUA LINGUARUM RESERATA. (?)

E   YP, II, 364, 365.

428. Comenius, Joannes Amosus.

   NATURAL PHILOSOPHY REFORMED BY DIVINE LIGHT. (?)

   Intro. YP, IV, 137-41.

429. Comenius, Joannes Amosus.

   PANSOPHIAE PRODROMUS. (?)

   E   YP, II, 364, 365.

430. Comenius, Joannes Amosus.

   A PATTERN OF UNIVERSAL KNOWLEDGE. (?)

   Intro. YP, IV, 137-41.

431. Comenius, Joannes Amosus.

   PORTA SAPIENTIAE RESERATA; SIVE PANSOPHIAE CHRISTI-
   ANAE SEMINARIUM. (?)

   E   YP, II, 364, 365.

432. Comenius, Joannes Amosus.

   A REFORMATION OF SCHOOLES. (?)

   E   YP, II, 364, 365.
   A translation of no. 429.

433. Comestor, Petrus.

   HISTORIA SCHOLASTICA. (?)

   See Sr. M. I. Corcoran, MILTON'S PARADISE.

434. Commelin, Jerome.

   RERUM BRITANNICARUM, ID EST ANGLIAE, SCOTIAE,
   VICINARUMQUE INSULARUM AC REGIONUM, SCRIPTORES
   VETUSTIORES. Heidelberg, 1587. (V)

   CPB   YP, I, 369, 381, 413, 474.

This collection of histories includes Bede,
Gildas, Geoffrey of Monmouth, Guiliam of
Nevers, and John Frossard. The copy of the
Heidelberg edition in the Houghton Library
has been identified by J. M. French as Milton's own copy. See "Milton's Annotated Copy
of Gildas," HSNPL, XX (1938), 75-80.

435. Commines, Philippe de.

LES MEMOIRES. (V)

CPB   YP, I, 379, 384, 405, 457, 482.
K   YP, III, 450.
1D   YP, IV, 506.

436. Comnena, Anna.

HISTORIA CONSTANTINOPOLITANA. (?)

COR   CM, XII, 89.

437. A COMPENDIUS DISCOURSE, PROVING EPISCOPACY TO BE OF
APOSTOLICALL, AND CONSEQUENTLY OF DIVINE INSTITUTION.
Attrib. to Peloni Almoni. (V)

Intro.   YP, I, 104, 118, 119, 121, 122.
R   YP, I, 550.
P   YP, I, 619, 627, 631, 632, 639,
             644.
CG   YP, I, 778.

438. CONCILIORUM OMNIUM TAM GENERALIUM QUAM PROVINCIALIUM...
SIXTI V. PONTIFICIS MAXIME. (V)

T   YP, II, 696-99.
Milton quotes from vols. I, II, IV.

439. CONFESSION OF FAITH. (?)

CG   YP, I, 771.

440. Constantius Lugdenensis ⌜Constance of Lyon⌝.

VITA SANCTI GERMANI EPISCOPI ANTISIODORENSIS. (?)

HB   CM, X, 107, 108, 109, 112.
It appears the life was available only in MS;

Milton probably knew Constantius through Usher
or Bede. See Constance Nicholas, INTRODUCTION
AND NOTES TO MILTON'S HISTORY OF BRITAIN, p.
71.

441. CONSTITUTIONS AND CANONS. (V)

        CG   YP, I, 823.

442. Conti, Natale.

    MYTHOLOGIAE. (*)

        T   YP, II, 597.
        K   YP, III, 453, 463.
        COR   CM, XII, 309.
        See John M. Steadman, "Urania, Wisdom, and
        Scriptural Exegesis," Neophilologus, XLVII
        (1963), 61-73.

443. Cook, John.

    KING CHARLES HIS CASE. (*)

        1D   YP, IV, 363, 379.
        See S. I. Wolff, "Milton's 'Advocatum nescio
        Quem': Milton, Salmasius and John Cook," MLQ,
        II,iv (December 1941), 599.

444. Cooper, Thomas.

    THESAURUS LINGUAE ROMANAE ET BRITANNICAE. (?)

        MAR   CM, XVIII, 581.
        See John M. Steadman, "Urania, Wisdom, and
        Scriptural Exegesis," Neophilologus, XLVII
        (1963), 61-73.

445. Corbet, John.

    EPISTLE CONGRATULATORIE OF LYSIMACHUS NICANOR OF
    THE SOCIETIE OF JESU, TO THE COVENATERS IN SCOT-
    LAND. (V)

        A   YP, I, 667.
        AP   YP, I, 905.

446. Cornelius Nepos.

    VITA ATTICI. (*)

        G   CM, VI, 343.
        AR   YP, II, 498.
        NDX   CM, ii, 1358.

    CORPUS IURIS CIVILIS. See Justinian I.

447. Coryate, Thomas.

    CORYAT'S CRUDITIES. (*)

        K   YP, III, 566.

448. Costanzo, Angelo di.

    HISTORIA DEL REGNO DI NAPOLI. (V)

        CPB   YP, I, 364-65, 506-07.

    Coventry, Francis. See Grotius' DE VERITATE RELIGIONIS
    CHRISTIANAE.

    Coverdale, Miles. Translator of Bullinger's THE CHRIST-
    EN STATE OF MATRIMONY, q.v.

449. Cowley, Abraham.

    DAVIDËIS, in POEMS. (?)

        See Grant McColley, PARADISE LOST.

450. Cranmer, Thomas.

    REFORMATIO LEGUM ECCLESIASTICARUM. (V)

        R   YP, I, 535.
        T   YP, II, 717.

451. Crantz, George.

    LECTORI, in Vlacq's edn. of Alexander More's FIDES
    PUBLICA, q.v. (V)

SD   YP, IV, 723.

Crashaw, Richard.   Translator of Marini's STRAGE DEGLI
INNOCENTI, q.v.

452. Creccelius, John.

COLLECTANEA EX HISTORIJS. Frankfurt, 1614. (V)

An annotated copy in the Huntington Library is
thought by some to be Milton's. See J. M.
French, LIFE RECORDS OF JOHN MILTON, I, 280;
W. R. Parker, MILTON, pp. 124, 787. Professor
Maurice Kelley says the annotations are not
in Milton's hand.

453. Cromwell, Oliver.

ORDERS OF THE LORD PROTECTOR FOR PUTTING INTO
EXECUTION THE LAWS MADE AGAINST PRINTING UNLICENSED
BOOKS. (*)

A   YP, II, 163.
Propinquity notwithstanding, Cromwell's proclamations, speeches, public correspondence, etc.
are not included.

454. Ctesias.

DE REBUS PERSICIS ET INDICIS, in Herodotus's HISTORY,
q.v. (*)

1D   YP, IV, 436.

455. Culman, Leonhard.

SENTENTIAE PUERILES. (?)

E   YP, II, 386.

456. CURSOR MUNDI. (?)

See Sr. M. I. Corcoran, MILTON'S PARADISE.

457. Curtius Rufus, Quintus.

DE REBUS GESTIS ALEXANDRI MAGNI. (*)

```
            MAR          CM, XVIII, 496.
            NDX          CM, i, 416.
            CG           YP, I, 792.
```

458. Cuspinianus ₍Spiess-Hammer₎, Johannes.

HISTORIA CAESARUM ET IMPERATORUM ROMANORUM. Frankfurt, 1601. (V)

```
            CPB          YP, I, 417, 435, 436, 460, 470, 474.
            2D           YP, IV, 683.
```
See W. R. Parker, MILTON, p. 882.

459. Cyprian, Caecilius.

OPERA. Ed. Pamelius; commentary by Golartius.
Paris, 1593. (V)

```
            CPB          YP, I, 392-93, 395, 403-04, 490.
            R            YP, I, 534, 544, 546, 561, 562,
                         563, 564.
            CG           YP, I, 840.
            A            YP, I, 675, 676.
            MB           YP, II, 450.
            H            CM, VI, 86.
            CD           CM, XIV, 261.
```
Professor Ruth Mohl says, "Sister Dorothy Mer-
cedes of St. Joseph's College, Brooklyn, has
identified the 1593 edition as the Golartius
edition which Milton refers to in CHURCH-GOVERN-
MENT and which was probably also the source of
his entry ₍in the CPB₎." Milton probably consulted other editions, for his numbering of
Cyprian's EPISTLES differs in OF REFORMATION
from that in this edition.

460. Cyril, Saint, of Alexandria.

DE ADORATIONE IN SPIRITU ET VERITATE. (?)

See Sr. M. I. Corcoran, MILTON'S PARADISE.

461. Cyril, Saint, of Alexandria.

GLAPHYRORUM IN GENESIM. (?)

See Sr. M. I. Corcoran, MILTON'S PARADISE.

462. Cyril, Saint, of Alexandria.

HOMILIAE IN GENESIM. (?)

```
```

See Sr. M. I. Corcoran, MILTON'S PARADISE.

463. Cyril, Saint, of Jerusalem.

CATECHESES. (?)

See Sr. M. I. Corcoran, MILTON'S PARADISE.

464. Damascene, St. John.

DE FIDE ORTHODOX. (?)

See Sr. M. I. Corcoran, MILTON'S PARADISE.

465. Daneau, Lambert.

THE WONDERFUL WOORKMANSHIP OF THE WORLD. (?)

See Sr. M. I. Corcoran, MILTON'S PARADISE.

466. Dante Alighieri.

DANTE CON L'ESPOSITIONE DI M. BERNARDINO DANIELLO.
Venice, 1568. (V)

CPB	YP, I, 366, 371, 384, 405-06, 418-19, 472, 476.
R	YP, I, 558-59.
CG	YP, I, 752, 842.
NDX	CM, i, 426-27.

See Irene Samuel, DANTE AND MILTON: THE COMEDIA
AND PARADISE LOST (Ithaca, N. Y.: Cornell University Press, 1966); Irene Samuel, "The Valley
of Serpents," PMLA, LXXVIII (1963), 449-51;
E. E. Kellett, "Milton and Dante," RECONSIDER-
ATIONS (Cambridge: Cambridge University Press,
1928); Oscar Kuhns, "Dante's Influence on Milton," MLN, XIII (January 1898), 1-11.

467. Dante Alighieri.

LA COMEDIA. Ed. and commentary by Cristoforo Landino. (?)

See Irene Samuel, DANTE AND MILTON, p. vi.

468. Dante Alighieri.

LA COMEDIA. Ed. and commentary by Alesandro Vellutello. (?)

See Irene Samuel, DANTE AND MILTON, p. vi.

469. Dante Alighieri.

L'AMOROSO CONVIVIO. Venice, 1529. (V)

Milton's copy is in the New York Public
Library. See Maurice Kelley, "Milton's
Dante-Della Casa-Varchi Volume," BNYPL,
LXVI (1962), 499-504.

470. Dati, Carlo.

ESEQUIE DELLA MAESTA CHRISTIANISS: DI LUIGI XIII.
IL GIUSTO, RE DI FRANCIA E DI NAVARRA, CELEBRATE
DI FIRENZE DALL. ALTEZZA SERENISSIMA DI FERDINANDO
GRANDUCA DI TOSC., E DISCRITTE DA CARLO DATI. (V)

COR	YP, II, 765.
ED	CM, I, 137.
2D	CM, VIII, 123.

471. Davanzati Bostichi, Bernardo.

SCISMA D'INGHILTERRA CON ALTRE OPERETTE. (V)

AR   YP, IT, 504, 518.
See Harris Fletcher, "Milton's 'Vicar of Hell',"
JEGP, XLVII (1948), 387-89; "Milton's Private
Library--An Additional Title," PQ, XXVIII (1949),
72-76.

472. Davenport, Christopher ₍also known as Franciscus Sancta
Clara, Francis Hunt, and Francis Coventry₎.

APOLOGIA EPISCOPORUM SEU SACRI MAGISTRATUS. (*)

R   YP, I, 527.

473. Davenport, Christopher.

PARAPHRASTICA EXPOSITIO ARTICULORUM CONFESSIONIS
ANGLICANAE. (?)

R   YP, I, 528.

474. Davies, Sir John.

ORCHESTRA: OR A POEME OF DAUNCING. (*)

NDX   CM, i, 431.
See M. Y. Hughes, JOHN MILTON: COMPLETE POEMS
AND MAJOR PROSE, p. 317.

475. Davies, John, of Hereford.

WITTES PILGRIMAGE. (?)

NDX   CM, i, 431.

476. Davies, John, of Hereford.

MIRUM IN MODUM. (?)

See M. Y. Hughes, JOHN MILTON: COMPLETE POEMS
AND MAJOR PROSE, pp. 65, 194.

477. Davison, Francis.

A POETICAL RHAPSODY. (?)

NDX   CM, i, 431.

478. Davity ﹐d'Avity﹐, Pierre.

LES ESTATS, EMPIRES, ET PRINCIPAUTEZ DU MONDE. (V)

E   YP, II, 389.
See Allan H. Gilbert, "Pierre Davity: His 'Geo-
graphy' and Its Use by Milton," The Geographical
Review, VII, 322-38.

DeDieu, Louis. See Dieu.

479. LES DELICES DE LA SUISSE. (?)

MAR   CM, XVIII, 575.
A ghost-book, neither seen nor heard of since
a Mr. Herber outbid Thomas DeQuincey for it
in 1809; it was said to have had Milton's own
notes in the margins. See Horace A. Eaton,
THOMAS DEQUINCEY (N.P., 1936), p. 181.

480. Della Casa, Giovanni.

> RIME ET PROSE. Venice, 1563. (V)
>
>> Milton's copy with title page inscribed in his
>> own hand is in the New York Public Library.
>> See Maurice Kelley, BNYPL, LXVI (1962), 449-
>> 504; Harris Fletcher, INTLELLECTUAL DEVELOPMENT
>> OF JOHN MILTON, II, 301; Smart's edition of the
>> Sonnets (Glasgow, 1921), pp. 30-34; and CM,
>> XVIII, 345.

481. Delrio, Martin.

> LES CONTROVERSES ET RECHERCHES MAGIQUES. (?)
>
>> See Robert H. West, MILTON AND THE ANGELS.

482. Delrio, Martin.

> SYNTAGMA TRAGOEDIAE LATINAE, SEU FRAGMENTA VETERUM
> TRAGICORUM ET L. ANN. SENECAE TRAGOEDIAE, CUM COM-
> MENTARIIS. (?)
>
>> COR   YP, II, 771.

483. Demetrius.

> DE ELOCUTIONE. (V)
>
>> DDD   YP, II, 338.
>> E   YP, II, 402-03.
>> Although Milton makes reference to the Athenian
>> orator Demetrius Phalereus, ON STYLE was act-
>> ually written by another, later Demetrius.

484. Demosthenes.

> DE CORONA. (*)
>
>> AP   YP, I, 887-88.
>> See Donald L. Clark, JOHN MILTON AT ST. PAUL'S
>> SCHOOL.

485. De Sales, St. Francis.

> TRAITÉ DE L'AMOUR DE DIEU. (?)

See Sr. M. I. Corcoran, MILTON'S PARADISE.

Diaconus. See Paulus Diaconus.

486. Didymus Calcenterus.

"Scholia in Hom." (?)

MAR CM, XVIII, 302, 303.
Didymus, a contemporary of Cicero and Augustus,
was said to have written over 3,500 books, but
now he's known through fragments preserved in
the Venetian Scholia. The reference in the mar-
gin of the alleged Milton Pindar is quite clear,
but how Milton would have known Didymus is a
pretty puzzle.

487. Dieu, Louis de.

ANIMADVERSIONES. COMMENT. IN QUATUOR EVANGELIA,
IN QUO COLLATIS SYRI IMPRIMIO ARABII EVANGELII
HEBRAEI, VULGATI, D. ERASMI ET BEZAE VERSIONIBUS,
DIFFICILIA LOCA ILLUSTRANTUR ET VARIAE LECTIONES
CONFERUNTUS. (?)

See George N. Conklin, BIBLICAL CRITICISM AND
HERESY IN MILTON.

488. Digby, Lord George.

THE THIRD SPEECH OF THE LORD GEORGE DIGBY, TO THE
HOUSE OF COMMONS, CONCERNING BISHOPS, AND THE
CITIE PETITION. (*)

CG YP, I, 787, 803, 854.
See G. W. Whiting, MILTON'S LITERARY MILIEU.

489. Dio ｢Cocceianus, Dion, Dion Cassius, Dio Cassius｣, Cassius.

ROMAN HISTORY. (V)

CG YP, I, 770.
PROL YP, I, 258, 298.
1D YP, IV, 360, 399, 443, 447, 465.
TKM YP, III, 206.
HB CM, X, 42, 49, 50, 51, 53, 56, 65,
67, 68, 69, 74, 76, 80, 81, 83, 84,
85, 86.

82

MAR   CM, XVIII, 328.
See H. Glicksman, "Sources of Milton's History
of Britain," Wisconsin Studies in Language and
Literature, XI (1920), 105-44.

490. Diodati, Jean.

ANSWER SENT TO THE ECCLESIASTICAL ASSEMBLY AT LON-
DON. (?)

RJP   YP, IV, 906, 914.

491. Diodati, John.

PIOUS ANNOTATIONS UPON THE HOLY BIBLE.   (V)

T   YP, II, 615.
SD   YP, IV, 748, 787, 799, 817.

492. Diodorus Siculus.

BIBLIOTHECA HISTORIA.   (V)

E   YP, II, 376.
1D   YP, IV, 433-36.
HB   CM, X, 3, 50.
COR   CM, XII, 103.
See Sr. M. I. Corcoran, MILTON'S PARADISE;
G. W. Whiting, MILTON'S LITERARY MILIEU.

493. Diogenes Laertius.

LIVES AND OPINIONS OF EMINENT PHILOSOPHERS.   (V)

AP   YP, I, 879.
AR   YP, II, 495, 498, 523.
E   YP, II, 397.
RJP   YP, IV, 904.
See M. Y. Hughes, JOHN MILTON: COMPLETE POEMS
AND MAJOR PROSE, p. 1025.

494. Dionysius the Areopagite (Pseudo).

DE CAELESTI HIERARCHIA.   (?)

See Robert H. West, MILTON AND THE ANGELS.

495. Dionysius of Halicarnassus.

    THE ROMAN ANTIQUITIES. (V)

        T   YP, II, 593.
        1D   YP, IV, 498.
        RJP   YP, IV, 920.

496. Dionysius Periegetes.

    PERIEGESIS. (V)

        E   YP, II, 391, 395.
        See Donald L. Clark, JOHN MILTON AT ST. PAUL'S
        SCHOOL.

497. Diotogenes the Pythagorean.

    LIBRUM DE REGNO. [A fragment preserved in Stobaeus,
    q.v.] (V)

        1D   YP, IV, 438.

498. A DIRECTORY FOR PUBLIQUE WORSHIP OF GOD THROUGHOUT THE
THREE KINGDOMS OF ENGLAND, SCOTLAND, AND IRELAND. (V)

        K   YP, III, 366, 503, 508.
        RJP   YP, IV, 931.

Dobeneck, Johann. See Cochlaeus.

499. Dod, John, and Richard Cleaver.

    GODLY FORM OF HOUSEHOLD GOVERNMENT. (?)

        See William Haller, "Hail Wedded Love," ELH,
        XIII (1946), 79-97.

500. Donne, John.

    DEVOTIONS UPON EMERGENT OCCASIONS. (?)

        See Grant McColley, PARADISE LOST.

501. Dorotheus.

   VITAE APOSTOLORUM AC PROPHETARUM, in ECCLESIASTICAE
   HISTORIAE AUTORES, q.v. (*)

      CPB   YP, I, 376-77.
      See W. R. Parker, MILTON, p. 803.

502. Douglas, Lady Eleanor.

   SAMSON'S FALL. (?)

      See W. R. Parker, MILTON, pp. 368-69.

Dounaeus ⌈Andrew Downes⌉. See Chrysostom's OPERA.

503. Downame, George.

   DIALECTIKS, in P. RAMI VEROMANDUI REGII PROFESSORIS
   DIALECTICAE LIBRI...CUM COMMENTARIUS GEORGII DOWNAMI
   ANNEXIS. (V)

      A   YP, I, 672, 694.
      LO   CM, XI, 487.
      See W. S. Howell's LOGIC AND RHETORIC IN ENGLAND,
      1500-1700 (Princeton, 1956), pp. 208-09; he
      traces Milton's debt to Downham ⌈sic⌉. Cf. P. A.
      Duhamel, "Milton's Alleged Ramism," PMLA, LXVII
      (1952), 1035-53; Fr. Walter J. Ong, HLB, VIII
      (1954), 151-62; J. M. French, "Milton, Ramus,
      and Edward Phillips," MP, XLVII (1949), 82-87;
      W. J. Ong, RAMUS: METHOD, AND THE DECAY OF DIA-
      LOGUE (Cambridge, Mass.: Harvard University
      Press, 1958).

504. Downame, John.

   THE CHRISTIAN WARFARE AGAINST THE DEVILL WORLD AND
   FLESH. (?)

      See John M. Steadman, "'Like Turbulencies': The
      Tempest as Adversity Symbol" in MILTON'S EPIC
      CHARACTERS: IMAGE AND IDOL (Chapel Hill: Univer-
      sity of North Carolina Press, 1962).

505. Drayton, Michael.

   POLY-OLBION. (?)

A   YP, II, 529, 551.
See Jack B. Oruch, "Imitation and Invention in
the Sabrina Myths of Drayton and Milton,"
Anglia, XC (1972), 60-70.

506. Drummond, William, of Hawthornden.

POEMS. Ed. and preface by Edward Phillips. (*)

See W. R. Parker, MILTON, p. 989.

507. Drusius, Johannes.

ANNOTATIONES and PARALLEL SACRA, in CRITICI SACRI,
ed. John Pearson, Bp. of Chester, et al. (?)

See George N. Conklin, BIBLICAL CRITICISM AND
HERESY IN MILTON.

508. Dryden, John.

HEROIC STANZAS CONSECRATED TO THE MEMORY OF HIS
HIGHNESS OLIVER, LATE LORD PROTECTOR. (?)

Milton remarked that Dryden was a "good rimist,
but no poet." Milton's widow, however, miti-
gated the harshness of the remark. See W. R.
Parker, MILTON, pp. 584, 1096.

509. Dryden, John.

ASTRAEA REDUX. A POEM. (?)

See no. 508.

510. Dryden, John [?].

S'TOO HIM BAYES. (?)

See Hugh Macdonald, JOHN DRYDEN: A BIBLIOGRAPHY
(Oxford, 1939), pp. 196, 209, for attributed
authorship. Also see W. R. Parker, MILTON, pp.
630, 1145-46.

511. Dryden, John.

"The Fall of Angels and Man in Innocence," MS of

THE STATE OF INNOCENCE. (?)

> Dryden registered his MS for publication on
> 17 April 1674. Parker makes interesting con-
> jectures as to why it was delayed in appearing
> (MILTON, p. 635). That Dryden sent a copy for
> Milton's perusal is not altogether unlikely.

512. Du Bartas, Guillaume de Saluste, seigneur du Bartas.

LA SEPMAINE OU CREATION. Trans. Joshua Sylvester,
DU BARTAS HIS DIVINE WEEKES AND WORKS. (V)

> See George Coffin Taylor, MILTON'S USE OF DU
> BARTAS (Cambridge, Mass.: Harvard University
> Press, 1934).

513. Du Chesne, André.

HISTOIRE D'ANGLETERRE, D'ECOSSE, ET D'IRLANDE. (V)

> CPB   YP, I, 399, 483.
> See W. R. Parker, MILTON, p. 842. Milton's
> page references fit the Paris, 1634 and 1641,
> editions.

Du Jon. See Junius.

514. Du Moulin, Louis [?].

IRENAEI PHILADELPHI EPISTOLA AD RENATUM VERIDAEUM.
(*)

> R   YP, I, 581.

515. Du Moulin, Peter.

POEMATUM LIBELLI TRES. (?)

> See W. R. Parker, MILTON, pp. 612, 1132.

516. Du Moulin, Pierre.

DE LA VOCATION DES PASTEURS. (?)

> A   YP, I, 734.

517. Du Moulin, Pierre.

REGII SANGUINIS CLAMOR. (V)

2D   YP, IV, 252 ff. passim.
Milton did not know, of course, that Du Moulin
was the author of THE CRY OF THE ROYAL BLOOD;
he fingered Alexander More as the culprit and
addressed his reply to him rather than Du Moulin.

518. Duree, John.

THE SEVERALL FORMES OF GOVERNMENT, RECEIV'D IN THE
REFORMED CHURCHES, in CERTAIN BRIEFE TREATISES, q.v.

CG   YP, I, 194.

519. Dury, John.

A CASE OF CONSCIENCE, WHETHER IT BE LAWFUL TO ADMIT
JEWS INTO A CHRISTIAN COMMON-WEALTH. (?)

Although Dury was a friend of Milton's, there
is no evidence that Milton read his pamphlet,
and they certainly differed in their attitudes
towards the Jews.

520. Dury, John.

ΕΙΚΟΝΟΚΛΑΣΤΗΣ.   (*)

A French translation of Milton's book (London,
1652). See W. R. Parker, MILTON, pp. 424, 1019-
20.

Dury, John. See Sameul Hartlib's edn. of THE REFORMED
SCHOOL.

521. Eachard, John.

THE GROUNDS & OCCASIONS OF THE CONTEMPT OF THE
CLERGY AND RELIGION. (?)

See W. R. Parker, MILTON, pp. 631, 1147.

522. Eadmer.

HISTORIA NOVORUM IN ANGLIA. (V)

HB   CM, X, 252, 263, 264, 305, 309.
See H. Glicksman, "Sources of Milton's History
of Britain," Wisconsin Studies in Language and
Literature, XI (1920), 105-44; Constance Nicho-
las, INTRODUCTION AND NOTES TO MILTON'S HISTORY
OF BRITAIN, p. 147.

523. Eden, Sir Richard, and Richard Willes.

THE HISTORY OF TRAVAYLE IN THE WEST AND EAST INDIES.
(?)

See Robert R. Cawley, MILTON AND THE LITERATURE
OF TRAVEL.

524. ΕΙΚΩΝ ΑΛΗΘΙΝΗ, THE POURTRAICTURE OF TRUTHS MOST
SACRED MAJESTY. (*)

K   YP, III, 147.
MAR   CM, XVIII, 576.
See W. R. Parker, MILTON, p. 369; Warren H.
Lowenhaupt, "The Writing of Milton's EIKONO-
KLASTES," SP, XX (January 1923), 29-51; G. W.
Whiting, MILTON"S LITERARY MILIEU, chapt. XIII.

525. EIKON BASILIKE: THE POURTRAICTURE OF HIS SACRED MAJESTIE
IN HIS SOLITUDES AND SUFFERINGS. (V)

Intro.   YP, III, 51 ff. passim.

526. EIKON EPISTE. OR, THE FAITHFUL POURTRAICTURE OF A
LOYALL SUBJECT, IN VINDICATION OF EIKON BASILIKE. IN
ANSWER TO AN INSOLENT BOOK, INTITULED EIKON ALETHINE.
(*)

Intro. YP, III, 152.
See Warren H. Lowenhaupt, "The Writing of Milton's EIKONOKLASTES," SP, XX (January 1923),
46.

527. Elsynge, Henry.

THE ANCIENT METHOD AND MANNER OF HOLDING PARLIAMENTS
IN ENGLAND. (?)

See W. R. Parker, MILTON, p. 1061; David Masson, THE LIFE OF JOHN MILTON, V, 285.

528. Elyot, Sir Thomas.

BIBLIOTHECA ELIOTAE. (?)

See John M. Steadman, "Urania, Wisdom, and Scriptural Exegesis," Neophilologus, XLVII (1963), 61-73.

529. ENCOMIUM EMMAE REGINAE. Ed. André DuChesne, in HISTORIAE NORMANNORUM SCRIPTORES ANTIQUI. (V)

HB   CM, X, 267, 268, 276, 281, 283. See H. Glicksman, "Sources of Milton's History of Britain," Wisconsin Studies in Language and Literature, XI (1920), 105-44; Constance Nicholas, INTRODUCTION AND NOTES TO MILTON'S HISTORY OF BRITAIN, pp. 153-54.

530. ENGLANDS COMPLAINT TO JESUS CHRIST AGAINST THE BISHOPS CANONS OF THE LATE SINFUL SYNOD. (?)

TKM   YP, III, 249.

531. ENGLANDS REMEMBRANCER OF LONDONS INTEGRITY, OR NEWS FROM LONDON. (?)

See G. W. Whiting, MILTON'S LITERARY MILIEU.

532. THE ENGLISH POPE, OR A DISCOURSE WHEREIN THE LATE MYSTICAL INTELLIGENCE BETWIXT THE COURT OF ENGLAND, AND THE COURT OF ROME IS IN PART DISCOVERED. (V)

K   YP, III, 527.

533. Ephrem [or Ephraim] Syrus, St.

SCRIPTURAL EXEGESIS. (?)

See Sr. M. I. Corcoran, MILTON'S PARADISE.

534. Epictitus.

SIMPLICII COMMENTARIUS IN ENCHIRIDION EPICTETI. (?)

1D   YP, IV, 430.

535. Epiphanius.

    ADVERSUS HAERESES. (V)

        T   YP, II, 697.
        MB   YP, II, 451.
        See Sr. M. I. Corcoran, MILTON'S PARADISE.

536. Epiphanius.

    Anchoratus. (?)

        See Sr. M. I. Corcoran, MILTON'S PARADISE.

537. Epiphanius.

    PANARION. (*)

        A   YP, II, 518.

538. Episcopisu, Simon.

    OPERA THEOLOGICA. (?)

        See George N. Conklin, BIBLICAL CRITICISM AND
        HERESY IN MILTON, pp. 38, 69.

539. Erasmus, Desiderius.

    OPERA OMNIA. (*)

        SD   YP, IV, 744.
        AP   YP, I, 901.

540. Erasmus, Desiderius.

    ADAGIA. (?)

        See W. Hilton Kelliher, "Erasmus' ADAGIA and
        Milton's MANE CITUS LECTUM FUGE," MiltonQ, V
        (1971), 73-74.

541. Erasmus, Desiderius.

    ANNOTATIONES IN MATTHAEUM. (*)

                    T   YP, II, 709.

542. Erasmus, Desiderius.

        COMMENTARY ON I CORINTHIANS. (*)

                    MB   YP, II, 478.

543. Erasmus, Desiderius.

        DE RATIONE STUDII. (?)

                    E   YP, II, 390.

544. Erasmus, Desiderius.

        COLLOQUIORUM FAMILIARIUM OPUS. (*)

                    PROL   YP, I, 274.
        See Donald L. Clark, JOHN MILTON AT ST. Paul'S
        SCHOOL, pp. 37 ff., 57, 100, 213; the Antwerp,
        1564, edition was used as a textbook at St.
        Paul's.

545. Erasmus, Desiderius.

        ENCOMIUM MORIAE. (V)

                    PROL   YP, I, 274.
        See G. W. Whiting, MILTON'S LITERARY MILIEU.

546. Erasmus, Desiderius.

        RESPONSIO AD DISPUTATIONEM CUIUSDAM PHIMOSTOMI DE
        DIVORTIO. (V)

                    T   YP, II, 620.
                    SD   YP, IV, 725.

547. Estienne, Henri.

        POETAE GRAECI PRINCIPES HEROICI CARMINIS, & ALII
        NONNULLI...EXCUDEBAT HENRICUS STEPHANUS. (V)

                    MAR   CM, XVIII, 287, 318, 323, 327.
        Estienne's THESAURUS includes Homer, Hesiod,
        Orpheus, Callimachus, Aratus, Nicander,

                            92

Theocritus, Moscus, Bion, Dionysius, Kolou-
thous, Tryphiodorus, Musaeus, Theogonies,
Phokylides, Pythagorus; it also included Herodotus' exegesis on the life of Homer, Plutarch's life of Homer, Dion Chrysostum's
"Of Homer," and Porphorios' "Homeric Questions."
See Maurice Kelley and Samuel D. Atkins,
"Milton's Annotations of Aratus," PMLA, LXX
(1955), 1090-1106.

548. Ethelwerd.

CHRONICORUM LIBRI QUATUOR. Ed. Sir Henry Savile,
in RERUM ANGLICARUM SCRIPTORES POST BEDAM. (V)

HB   CM, X, 109, 114, 115, 116, 120,
            123, 164, 168, 175, 182, 185, 201,
            212, 225, 241.
See H. Glicksman, "Sources of Milton's History
of Britain," Wisconsin Studies in Language and
Literature, XI (1920), 105-44.

549. ETYMOLOGICUM MAGNUM. (V)

MAR   CM, XVIII, 303.

550. Eucherius, St., of Lyons.

COMMENTARII IN GENESIM. (?)

See Sr. M. I. Corcoran, MILTON'S PARADISE.

551. Euclid.

ELEMENTA GEOMETRICA. (V)

TKM   YP, III, 253.

552. Eumenius.

PANEGYRICI. (V)

HB   CM, X, 88, 89, 90, 91, 92.

553. Euripides.

EURIPIDIS TRAGOEDIAE. Geneva, 1602. (V)

93

NDX   CM, i, 602-03,
CG   YP, I, 814.
E   YP, II, 398.
Milton's annotated Euripides is in the Bodleian.
See W. R. Parker, MILTON'S DEBT TO GREEK TRAGEDY
IN SAMSON AGONISTES (Baltimore, 1937); D. L.
Clark, JOHN MILTON AT ST. PAUL'S SCHOOL; M. Y.
Hughes, JOHN MILTON: COMPLETE POEMS AND MAJOR
PROSE, p. 533; Maurice Kelley and Samuel D.
Atkins, "Milton's Annotations of Euripides,"
JEGP, LX (1961), 680-87.

554. Euripides.

    ALCESTIS. (V)

        MAR   CM, XVIII, 308.
        NDX   CM, i, 603.
        E   YP, II, 398.
        See no. 553.

555. Euripides.

    ANDROMACHE. (V)

        MAR   CM, XVIII, 305.
        NDX   CM, I, 603.
        See no. 553.

556. Euripides.

    BACCHAE. (V)

        CD   CM, XIV, 247.
        MAR   CM, XVIII, 314.
        NDX   CM, i, 603.
        See no. 553.

557. Euripides.

    CYCLOPS. (V)

        MAR   CM, XVIII, 314.
        NDX   CM, i, 603.
        See no. 553.

558. Euripides.

DANAË. (V)

    MAR   CM, XVIII, 320.
    NDX   CM, i, 603.
    See no. 553.

559. Euripides.

ELECTRA. (V)

    MAR   CM, XVIII, 320.
    NDX   CM, i, 603.
    See no. 553.

560. Euripides.

HECUBA. (V)

    MAR   CM, XVIII, 280, 299, 305, 308,
                     314.
    See no. 553.

561. Euripides.

HELENA. (V)

    NDX   CM, i, 603.
    See no. 553.

562. Euripides.

HERACLES. (V)

    NDX.   CM, i, 603.
    PROL   CM, XII, 121.
    MAR   CM, XVIII, 319.
    2D   YP, IV, 590-91.
    See no. 553.

563. Euripides.

HERACLIDAE. (V)

    TKM   YP, III, 205.
    1D   YP, IV, 440.
    MAR   CM, XVIII, 315.
    See no. 553.

564. Euripides.

    HIPPOLYTUS. (V)

        NDX   CM, i, 603.
        MAR   CM, XVIII, 305.
        See no. 553.

565. Euripides.

    ION. (V)

        NDX   CM, i, 603.
        MAR   CM, XVIII, 318, 324.
        See no. 553.

566. Euripides.

    IPHIGENIA IN AULIS. (V)

        CD   CM, XIV, 247.
        MAR   CM, XVIII, 310.
        NDX   CM, i, 603.
        See no. 553.

567. Euripides.

    IPHIGENIA IN TAURIS. (V)

        NDX   CM, i, 603.
        MAR   CM, XVIII, 310.
        See no. 553.

568. Euripides.

    MEDEA. (V)

        NDX   CM, i, 603.
        MAR   CM, XVIII, 307.
        T   YP, II, 577-78.
        See no. 553.

569. Euripides.

    ORESTES. (V)

        NDX   CM, i, 603.
        1D   YP, IV, 590.
        PROL   CM, XII, 121.
        MAR   CM
        See no. 553.

570. Euripides.

> PHOENISSAE. (V)
>
> > NDX   CM, i, 603.
> > MAR   CM, XVIII, 305, 306.
> > See no. 553.

571. Euripides.

> RHESUS. (V)
>
> > CD   CM, XIV, 247.
> > MAR   CM, XVIII, 311.
> > NDX   CM, i, 603.
> > See no. 553.

572. Euripides.

> SUPPLICES. (V)
>
> > 1D   YP, IV, 440, 455.
> > CD   CM, XV,. 237.
> > MAR   CM, XVIII, 309.
> > NDX   CM, i, 603.
> > See no. 553.

573. Euripides.

> TROADES. (V)
>
> > NDX   CM, i, 603.
> > MAR   CM, XVIII, 313.
> > See no. 553.

574. Eusebius of Caesarea.

> ONOMASTICON URBIUS ET LOCORUM SACRAE SCRIPTURAE. (?)
>
> > See Robert H. West, MILTON AND THE ANGELS.

575. Eusebius Pamphilius.

> DE VITA CONSTANTINI, in ECCLESIASTICAE HISTORIAE AUTORES. (V)
>
> > CPB   YP, I, 376-77, 380, 430-31, 433.

```
R          YP, I, 554.
CG         YP, I, 840.
```

576. Eusebius Pamphilius.

EVANGELICAL PREPARATION. (*)

AR   YP, II, 517.

577. Eusebius Pamphilius.

HISTORIA ECCLESIASTICA, in ECCLESIASTICAE HISTORIAE
AUTORES. (V)

```
CPB        YP, I, 376-77, 392, 393, 395, 417,
           420.
R          YP, I, 549, 550, 551, 563.
P          YP, I, 630, 634, 635, 640, 641,
           642, 644, 646, 647, 648, 649.
A          YP, I, 725, 729, 734.
DDD        YP, II, 334.
AR         YP, II, 511.
T          YP, II, 637, 693.
SD         YP, IV, 744.
```

578. Eustathius.

IN HOMERI ILIADES ET ODYSSEAE. (?)

MAR   CM, XVIII, 277-305.

579. Eustratius.

IN ARISTOTELIS MORALIA NICHOMACHIO A DOCTISSIMAE
EXPLANATIONES. (?)

MAR   CM, XVIII, 305-06.

580. Eutropius, Flavius.

BREVIARIUM AB URBE CONDITA CUM PAULI ADDITAMENTIS
ET VERSIONIBUS GRAECIS. (V)

HB   CM, X, 80, 89, 90, 92.
See H. Glicksman, "Sources of Milton's History
of Britain," Wisconsin Studies in Language and
Literature, XI (1920), 105-44.

581. Eutropius.

DE GESTIS ROMANORUM, in RERUM ROMANORUM SCRIPTORES.
(V)

  R   YP, I, 554, 557.

582. Evagrius.

HISTORIA, in ECCLESIASTICAE HISTORIA AUTORES. (V)

  CPB   YP, I, 377, 482.
  P   YP, I, 629-30.

Fabius. See Quintilian.

583. Fabricus, Johannes.

CODEX APOCRYPHUS NOVI TESTAMENTI. (?)

  See Sr. M. I. Corcoran, MILTON'S PARADISE.

584. Fagius, Paulus.

THARGUM, HOC EST, PARAPHRASIS ONKELI CHALDAICA IN
SACRA BIBLIA...ADDITIS IN SINGULA FERE CAPITA SUC-
CINCTIS ANNOTATIONIBUS, AUTORE PAULO FAGIO. (V)

  DDD   YP, II, 239, 243, 246, 344.
  MB   YP, II, 435.
  T   YP, II, 710.
  SD   YP, IV, 725.

Fairfax, Edward. See Tasso.

Falkenburg, Gerard.
  MAR   CM, XVIII, 278-79, 281, 302.
  See Bonaventura Vulcanius' edition of Cali-
  machus, to which was added Falkenburg's
  epitaph on John Fleming.

585. THE FAMOUS & RENOWNED HISTORY OF MORINDOS A KING OF
SPAIN. (?)

  See Timothy J. O'Keeffe, "An Analogue to
  Milton's 'Sin' and More on the Tradition,"
  MiltonQ, V (1971), 74-77.

586. Farnaby, Thomas.

INDEX RHETORICUS. (?)

See Donald L. Clark, JOHN MILTON AT ST. PAUL'S
SCHOOL.

587. Farnaby, Thomas.

SYSTEMA GRAMMATICUM. (V)

E   YP, II, 382.
An association copy (London, 1641) with a mar-
ginal correction of a Greek letter at p. 102
which may be in Milton's hand is in the Harvard
College Library. See Washington Moon, N&Q, II.
vi (10 July 1858), 39.

588. Featley, Daniel.

THE DIPPERS DIPT. (V)

T   YP, II, 144, 583.

589. Fenner, Dudley.

SACRA THEOLOGIA, SIVE VERITAS QUAE EST SECUNDUM
PIETATEM. AD UNICAE & VERAE METHODI LEGES DESCRIPTA,
& IN DECEM LIBROS PER DUDLEIUM FENNERUM DIGESTA. (V)

TKM   YP, III, 248-49.

590. Ferrarius, Phillipus.

LEXICON GEOGRAPHICUM. (?)

See J. S. Smart, THE SONNETS OF MILTON, p. 123.

591. Ficino, Marsilio.

ANTHOLOGY OF NEO-PLATONIC WORKS. (?)

Includes Iamblichus' DE MYSTERIIS AEGYPTIORUM,
CHALDAEORUM, ASSYRIORUM, Hermes Trismagistus'
PIMANDER, Proclus' IN PLATONICUM ALCIBIADEM DE
ANIMA, ATQUE DAEMONE, Porphyry's DE DIUINUS
ATQUE DAEMONIBUS and DE SACRIFICO ET MAGIA, and
Psellus' DE DAEMONIBUS. See Robert H. West,
MILTON AND THE ANGELS.

592. Filmer, Sir Robert.

    ANARCHY OF A LIMITED OR MIXED MONARCHY. (?)

        Intro.   YP, II, 70.

593. Filmer, Sir Robert.

    NECESSITY OF THE ABSOLUTE POWER OF ALL KINGS. (?)

        Intro.   YP, II, 69.

594. Filmer, Sir Robert.

    OBSERVATIONS CONCERNING THE ORIGINALL OF GOVERNMENT.
    (*)

        Intro.   YP, II, 70.
        See W. R. Parker, MILTON, p. 410.

595. Filmer, Sir Robert.

    PATRIARCHA. ₍MS icrculating before 1642; pub. 1680.₎
    (?)

        Intro.   YP, II, 69-70.
        TKM   YP, II, 198, 200, 202, 209, 220,
                    229.

596. Fitzherbert, Sir Anthony.

    LA VIEUX NATURA BREVIUM. (V)

        MAR   CM, XVIII, 576.
        See W. R. Parker, MILTON, p. 1122.

597. Fleta.

    COMMENTARIUS JURIS ANGLICANI SIC NUNCUPATUS, SUB
    EDWARDO REGE PRIMO SUO CIRCA ANNOS ABHINC CCCXL AB
    ANONYMO CONSCRIPTUS. (V)

        K   YP, III, 415, 591-92.
        1D   YP, IV, 486, 492, 493.

598. Fletcher, Giles the Elder.

    ADONIS and ELEGIA, in POEMATUM GVALTERI HADDONI. (*)

See Warren B. Austin, "Milton's LYCIDAS and Two
Latin Elegies by Giles Fletcher, the Elder,"
SP, XLIV (1947), 41-55. Professor Austin suggests "that the two Fletcher poems had each a
different kind of possible influence upon LY-
CIDAS" and discusses them separately; however,
he asserts "since the poems occur in the same
volume, whatever tends to show that Milton had
one in mind will increase the likelihood that
he was influenced by the other also" (p. 42).
Following that line of reasoning, it is equally
logical that Milton read Walter Haddon's LUCUB-
RATIONES and other poems in the volume.

599. Fletcher, Giles the Elder.

DE LITERIS ANTIQUAE BRITANNIAE. (*)

See Leicester Bradner, MUSAE ANGLICANAE (New
York, 1940), p. 39.

600. Fletcher, Giles the Elder.

OF THE RUSSE COM ON WEALTH. London, 1591. (V)

See D. S. Mirsky, ed., A BRIEF HISTORY OF
MOSCOVIA (london, 1921), p. 14; he states
that Milton certainly made use of Fletcher's
work.

601. Fletcher, Giles the Elder.

THE HISTORY OF RUSSIA. (?)

Another edition of no. 600, q.v.

602. Fletcher, Giles.

CHRISTS VICTORIE IN HEAVEN. (*)

NDX   CM, i, 679.
See J. M. Evans, PARADISE LOST AND THE GENESIS
TRADITION, p. 233.

603. Fletcher, John.

THE FAITHFULL SHEPHERDESSE. (?)

NDX   CM, i, 379-80.

See H. E. Cory, SPENSER, THE SCHOOL OF THE
FLETCHERS, AND MILTON (Berkeley: University
of California Press, 1912); Thomas Newton's
LIFE (1749 edn.), I, iv; and Warton (1785
edn.), p. 126.

604. Fletcher, Joseph.

THE HISTORIE OF THE PERFECT-CURSED-BLESSED MAN.
(?)

See Grant McColley, PARADISE LOST.

605. Fletcher, Phineas.

THE PURPLE ISLAND. (*)

NDX   CM, i, 380.
See E. C. Baldwin, "Milton and Phineas Fletcher,"
JEGP, XXXIII (1934), 544-46; A. B. Grosart, POEMS
OF PHINEAS FLETCHER (Blackburn, 1869), I, ccxii,
ccxci-ii, ccxcix.

606. Florence of Worcester.

CHRONICON EX CHRONICIS. (V)

HB   CM, X, 109, 114, 120, 123, 124,
            132, 139, 150, 158, 176, 178, 180,
            182, 183, 194, 212, 213, 218, 224,
            225, 233, 249, 251, 252, 254, 257,
            259, 260, 261, 270, 279, 281, 291,
            307, 315.
See H. Glicksman, "Sources of Milton's History
of Britain," Wisconsin Studies in Language and
Literature, XI (1920), 105-44.

Florus, Lucius Annaeus. See Florus, Publius Annius.

Florus, Lucius Julius. See Florus, Publius Annius.

607. Florus, Publius Annius.

RERUM ROMANORUM. (*)

A   YP, II, 555.
SD   YP, IV, 776, 963.
HB   CM, X, 25.

608. Fludd, Robert.

      ANATOMIAE AMPHITHEATRUM. (?)

         See Robert H. West, MILTON AND THE ANGELS.

609. Fludd, Robert.

      DR. FLUDD'S ANSWER UNTO M. FOSTER OR THE SQUEEZING
      OF PARSON FOSTER'S SPONGE. (?)

         See Robert H. West, MILTON AND THE ANGELS.

610. Fludd, Robert.

      INTEGRUM MORBORUM MYSTERIUM. (?)

         See Robert H. West, MILTON AND THE ANGELS.

611. Fludd, Robert.

      MEDICINA CATHOLICA. (?)

         See Robert H. West, MILTON AND THE ANGELS.

612. Fludd, Robert.

      MOSAICALL PHILOSOPHY. (?)

         See Robert H. West, MILTON AND THE ANGELS.

613. Fludd, Robert.

      PHILOSOPHIA SACRA. (?)

         See Robert H. West, MILTON AND THE ANGELS.

614. Fludd, Robert.

      RESPONSUM AD HOPLOCRISMA-SPONGUM. (?)

         See Robert H. West, MILTON AND THE ANGELS.

615. Fludd, Robert.

      UTRIUSQUE COSMI HOSTORIA. (?)

See Robert H. West, MILTON AND THE ANGELS.

Foresti, Jacopo Filippo. See Jacobus Bergomas.

616. Fortescue, Sir John.

DE LAUDIBUS LEGUM ANGLIAE. (*)

1D   YP, IV, 505.

617. Foxe, John.

ACTS AND MONUMENTS. (V)

R   YP, I, 524 ff.
A   YP, I, 678-79.
CG   YP, I, 794.
MB   YP, II, 424, 425.
AR   YP, II, 502, 548.
2D   YP, IV, 586.
W. T. Hale says Milton used the seventh edition
(London, 1631-32) of Foxe's ACTS AND MONUMENTS
in the preparation of THE JUDGEMENT OF MARTIN
BUCER. See D. Douglas Waters, "Milton and the
'Mistress-Missa' Tradition," MiltonQ, VI (1972),
6-8.

Franchini, Francesco. Pseud. of Ranutius Gherus, q.v.

618. Francklin, Richard.

ORTHOTONIA, SEU TRACTATUS DE TONIS IN LINGUIA
GRAECANIA. (?)

MAR   CM, XVIII, 297.

619. Freigius, Joannes Thomas.

P. RAMI PROFESSIO REGIA. (V)

LO   CM, XI, 497.
See W. R. Parker, MILTON, p. 325; Leo Miller,
"Milton Edits Freigius' 'Life of Ramus'," Renais-
sance and Reformation, VII, iii (1972), 112-14.

620. Frishlin, Nicodemus.

OPERUM POETICORUM. (*)

MAR CM, XVIII, 578.
See W. R. Parker, MILTON, p. 1122. A copy
of this book (Strassburg, 1595), now in the
Harvard College Library, has the initials
"J. M." on the title page and is enclosed
in an oak case made from Milton's Barbican
house.

621. Frontinus, Sextus Julius.

STRATEGEMATICON. (V)

CPB YP, I, 375.
E YP, II, 412.
Milton quite possibly may have used the
London, 1539, edition or the Antwerp, 1585,
edition which was published with Flavius
Renatus' DE RE MILITARI, q.v.

622. Fuller, Nicholas.

MISCELLANEORUM THEOLOGICORUM LIBRI III. (?)

See Grant McColley, PARADISE LOST.

623. Fuller, Thomas.

A HISTORY OF THE HOLY WARRE. (?)

See E. N. S. Thompson, "Milton's Knowledge
of Geography," SP, XVI (1919), 148-71.

624. Fuller, Thomas.

PISGAH-SIGHT OF PALESTINE. (?)

See Robert R. Cawley, MILTON AND THE LITERATURE
OF TRAVEL.

625. Gaddi, Jacopo.

ADLOCUTIONES. (?)

2D YP, IV, 616.
See W. R. Parker, MILTON, pp. 824, 829.

626. Gaddi, Jacopo.

    DE SCRIPTORIBUS NON-ECCLESIASTICIS, GRAECIS, LAT-
INIS, ITALICIS. (?)

        See W. R. Parker, MILTON, pp. 824, 829.

627. Gaddi, Jacopo.

    ELOGIA. (?)

        See W. R. Parker, MILTON, pp. 824, 829.

628. Gaddi, Jacopo.

    POEMATA. (?)

        See W. R. Parker, MILTON, pp. 824, 829.

Gaetano, Thomas. See Cajetan.

629. Gafori, Franchini.

    PRACTICA MUSICE. (?)

        See John M. Steadman, "Urania, Wisdom, and
Scriptural Exegesis," Neophilologus, XLVII
(1963), 61-73.

630. Gafori, Franchini.

    THEORICA MUSICE. (?)

        See no. 629.

631. Galen.

    DE HIPPOCRATIS ET PLATONIS DECRETIS. (V)

        LO   CM, XI, 431.
        Milton's reference is to DE PLACITIS HIPPOCRATIS
        PLATONIS, II; the work is more familiarly known,
        however, as noted above. An interesting history
        of the various editions of this and others of
        Galen's works can be found in Richard J. Durling,
        "A Chronological Census of Renaissance Editions
        and Translations of Galen," Journal of the War-
        burg and Courtauld Institutes, nos. 3-4, 1961.

632. Galen.

DE OPTIMA SECTA AD THRASYBULUM. (*)

LO   CM, XI, 133.

633. Galilei, Galileo.

DIALOGO...DUE MASSIMI SISTEMI DEL MONDO TOLEMAICO
E COPERNICANO. (?)

NDX   CM, i, 728.
A   YP, II, 538.
For two quite different opinions on Milton's
use of Galileo see Allan H. Gilbert, "Milton
and Galileo," SP, XIX (1922), 152-85, and
Grant McColley, "The Astronomy of PARADISE
LOST," SP, XXIV (1937), 209-47; see also
M. H. Nicolson's "Milton and the Telescope,"
ELH, II (1935), 1-32.

634. Gascoigne, George.

POEMS. (?)

NDX   CM, i, 732.

635. Gataker, Thomas.

DE NOVI INSTRUMENTI STYLO DISSERTATIO. (V)

MAR   CM, XVIII, 306.
See George N. Conklin, BIBLICAL CRITICISM
AND HERESY IN MILTON, p. 21.

636. Gauden, John.

THE RELIGIOUS AND LOYAL PROTESTATION, OF JOHN
GAUDEN, DR. IN DIVINITIE: AGAINST THE PRESENT
DECLARED PURPOSES AND PROCEEDINGS OF THE ARMY
AND OTHERS: ABOUT THE TRYING AND DESTROYING
OUR SOVERAIGN LORD THE KING. SENT TO A COLONELL,
TO BEE PRESENTED TO THE LORD FAIRFAX, AND HIS
COUNCELL OF WARRE. (*)

TKM   YP, III, 191, 195.

Gauden, John. See also EIKON BASILIKE.

637. Gazeus, Angelinus.

    PIA HILARIA. (?)

        NDX   CM, i, 733.
        See M. Y. Hughes, JOHN MILTON: COMPLETE POEMS
        AND MAJOR PROSE, p. 295.

Gelasius.
        MB   YP, II, 451.
        Probably the first pope of that name, but
        perhaps Cyzicenus Gelasius, Bishop of Caesa-
        rea, who wrote extensively on the Nicean
        Council.

638. Gell, Robert.

    SERMON TOUCHING GOD'S GOVERNMENT OF THE WORLD BY
    ANGELS. (*)

        NDX   CM, i, 734.

639. Gell, Robert.

    STELLA NOVA, A NEW STAR. (?)

        See W. R. Parker, MILTON, p. 368.

640. Geminus.

    PHAINOMENA. (V)

        E   YP, II, 391.

641. GENESIS B. (?)

        See J. W. Lever, "PARADISE LOST and the Anglo-
        Saxon Tradition," RES, XXIII (1947), 97-106,
        and J. M. Evans, PARADISE LOST AND THE GENESIS
        TRADITION, p. 255.

642. Geoffrey of Monmouth.

    HISTORIA REGNUM BRITANNIAE, in Commelin's RERUM
    BRITANNICARUM, q.v. (V)

        CPB   YP, I, 369.
        NDX   CM, i, 740.

HB   CM, X, 6, 23, 25, 30, 49, 56, 83,
            90, 106, 122, 125, 128, 131, 150.
See H. Glicksman, "Sources of Milton's History
of Britain," Wisconsin Studies in Language and
Literature, XI (1920), 105-44.

643. Geraldus, Giglius ₍Lilius Gregorius₎.

    DE DEIS GENTUS LIBRI SIVE SYNTAGMATA. (V)

        COR   YP, II, 771.

644. Gerard, John.

    HERBALL. (?)

        NDX   CM, i, 741.
        See M. Y. Hughes, JOHN MILTON: COMPLETE POEMS
        AND MAJOR PROSE, pp. 403, 442; Kester Svendsen,
        MILTON AND SCIENCE, pp. 31-32.

    Gerardus, Hessel.
            Milton notes at the end of his HISTORY OF MUS-
            COVIA that Hessel Gerardus was one of his
            sources of information by way of Purchas,
            part 3.1.3, q.v.

645. Gerhardus, Johannis.

    LOCORUM THEOLOGICORUM. (V)

        T   YP, II, 608, 688, 712.

    Gersonides. See Levi Ben Gerson.

646. Gherus, Ranutius ₍Francesco Franchini, pseud.₎.

    DELITIAE C. C. ITALORUM POETARUM. (?)

        See J. S. Smart, THE SONNETS OF MILTON, p. 124.

647. Gilbert, William.

    DE MAGNETE. (?)

        See Grant McColley, PARADISE LOST.

110

648. Gilbert, William.

DE MUNDO NOSTRO SUBLUNARI PHILOSOPHIA NOVA. (?)

See Grant McColley, PARADISE LOST.

649. Gilby, Anthony.

AN ADMONITION TO ENGLAND AND SCOTLAND TO CALL THEM
TO REPENTANCE. (?)

K   YP, III, 396.

650. Gilty, Anthony.

DE OBEDIENTIA. (?)

TKM   YP, III, 249.
See Sonia Miller, "Two References in Milton's
TENURE OF KINGS," JEGP, L (1951), 320-25, for
a masterful job of unraveling the complicated
way by which Milton mistakenly attributed a
quotation to Gilby.

651. Gildas.

DE EXCIDIO ET CONQUESTU BRITANNIAE, in Commelin's
RERUM BRITANNICARUM, q.v. (V)

CPB   YP, I, 413, 474.
1D   YP, IV, 489.
2D   YP, IV, 552.
TKM   YP, III, 221.
HB   CM, X, 12, 23, 30, 33, 69, 83, 88,
             92, 94, 97, 103, 104, 105, 106, 107,
             109, 110, 111, 112, 115, 117, 118,
             119, 122, 123, 127, 128, 129, 130,
             131, 133, 134, 136, 137, 141, 196,
             318, 319.

652. Gill, Alexander.

LOGONOMIA ANGLICA. (*)

See W. R. Parker, MILTON, pp. 14, 711; Arthur
Barker, "Milton's Schoolmasters," MLR, XXXII
(1937), 517-36.

653. Gill, Alexander.

THE SACRED PHILOSOPHY OF THE HOLY SCRIPTURE. (?)

See Donald L. Clark, JOHN MILTON AT ST. PAUL'S
SCHOOL, p. 77.

654. Gill, Alexander.

A TREATISE CONCERNING THE TRINITIE OF PERSONS IN
UNITIE OF THE DEITIE. (*)

Intro.   YP, II, 198.

655. Gill, Alexander, Jr.

ΠΑΡΕΡΓΑ, SIVE POETICI CONATUS ALEXANDRI AB ALEXANDRO
GIL LCNDINENSIS, AB ALIQUAMMULTIS ANTEHAEC EXPETITI,
TANDEM IN LUCEM PRODEUNT. (*)

See W. R. Parker, MILTON, p. 120.

656. Gilles, Pierre.

HISTOIRE ECCLESIASTIQUE DES EGLISES REFORMÉES...EN
QUELQUES VALÉES DE PIEDMONT...APELÉES EGLISES
VAUDOISES. Geneva, 1644. (V)

CPB   YP, I, 379.
TKM   YP, III, 227.
K   YP, III, 513-14.
H   CM, VI, 81.

657. Giraldus, Giglio [Lilius] Gregorius.

DE DEIS GENTIUM. (?)

COR   CM, XII, 309.
CPB   YP, I, 469-70.

658. Giraldi Cintio, Giovanni Battista.

DISCORSI...INTORNO AL COMPORRE DE I ROMANZI DELLE
COMEDIE, E DELLE TRAGEDIE, E DI ALTRE MANIERE DI
POESIE. (?)

CG   YP, I, 813.

112

659. Girard, Bernard de, Sieur du Haillan.

    DE L'ESTAT ET SUCCEZ DES AFFAIRES DE FRANCE. (V)

        0   YP, III, 314.

660. Girard, Bernard de, Sieur du Haillan.

    L'HISTOIRE DE FRANCE. (V)

CPB	YP, I, 378-79, 383, 398, 400, 404, 405, 407, 441, 446, 450, 455, 461, 462, 473.
TKM	YP, III, 218.
1D	YP, IV, 420, 481.
RJP	YP, IV, 947-48.

Giustiniani, Bernardo. See Justinianus Bernardus.

661. Glassius ₍Glass₎, Solomon.

    PHILOLOGIAE SACRAE. (?)

        See George N. Conklin, BIBLICAL CRITICISM AND HERESY IN MILTON, pp. 64, 93-94.

662. Glisson, Francis.

    DE RACHITIDE. (?)

        See W. R. Parker, MILTON, p. 979.

663. Glycas, Michael.

    ANNALES. (*)

        COR   CM, XII, 89.
        See W. R. Parker, MILTON, pp. 502, 1061.

664. Gomarus, Franciscus.

    DAVIDIS LYRA. (?)

        CG   YP, I, 816.
        See Israel Baroway, "The Bible as Poetry in the English Renaissance," *JEGP*, XXXII (1933), 477.

113

665. Goodman, Christopher.

HOW SUPERIOR POWERS OGHT TO BE OBEYD. (V)

TKM   YP, III, 250-51.
DDD   YP, II, 223.

666. Goodman, Godfrey.

THE FALL OF MAN. (?)

See Grant McColley, PARADISE LOST.

667. Goodwin, John.

ANAPOLOGESIATES ANTAPOLOGIAS: OR, THE INEXCUSABLE-
NESSE OF THAT GRAND ACCUSATION OF THE BRETHREN,
CALLED ANTAPOLOGIA. (?)

See G. W. Whiting, MILTON'S LITERARY MILIEU.

668. Goodwin, John.

ANTI-CAVALIERISME, OR, TRUTH PLEADING AS WELL THE
NECESSITY, AS THE LAWFULNESS OF THIS PRESENT WAR,
FOR THE SUPPRESSION OF THAT BUTCHERLY BROOD OF
CAVAILIERING INCENDIARIES, WHO ARE NOW HAMMERING
ENGLAND, TO MAKE AN IRELAND OF IT. (?)

See G. W. Whiting, MILTON'S LITERARY MILIEU.

669. Goodwin, John.

ΘΕΟΜΑΧΙΑ , OR, THE GRAND IMPRUDENCE OF MEN RUN-
NING THE HAZARD OF FIGHTING AGAINST GOD. (?)

See G. W. Whiting, MILTON'S LITERARY MILIEU.

670. Gosson, Stephen.

THE SCHOOLE OF ABUSE. (?)

PROL   YP, I, 304.
AP   YP, I, 886.

671. Gouge, William.

OF DOMESTICALL DUTIES. (?)

114

See William Haller, "Hail Wedded Love, *ELH*, XIII (1946), 79-97.

Gourdon, William, of Hull.
At the end of his HISTORY OF MUSCOVIA, Milton notes that William Gourdon of Hull was one of his sources; it seems likely that Purchas's PILGRIMES, q.v., was his immediate source.

Govéa. See Pedro Gobeo de Victoria.

672. Gower, John.

CONFESSIO AMANTIS. London, 1532. (V)

CPB YP, I, 497.
AP YP, I, 946-47.
2D YP, IV, 651.

673. Gower, John.

MIROUR DE L'OMME. (?)

See John S. P. Tatlock, "Milton's Sin and Death," *MLN*, XXI (1906), 239-40, who notes a curiously close parallel between Gower's description and Milton's. The only manuscript known, however, was published first in 1899, and there is no evidence that Milton ever knew it or owned it.

674. Grant, Edwardus.

GRAECAE LINGUAE SPICILEGIUM...IN QUATUOR HORREA COLLECTUM. (?)

See Donald L. Clark, JOHN MILTON AT ST. PAUL'S SCHOOL.

675. Gratian.

DECRETUM GRATIANI. (*)

CG YP, I, 777.
DDD YP, II, 351.

115

676. GREAT BRITAINS MISERY; WITH THE CAUSES AND CURE. (?)

    See G. W. Whiting, MILTON'S LITERARY MILIEU.

677. Gregoras, Nicephoras.

   BYZANTINAE HISTORIAE LIBRI XI. (V)

    CPB   YP, I, 434, 483, 488.

678. Gregory I [Gregorius Magnus].

   EPISTOLAE. (V)

    T   YP, II, 705.

679. Gregory of Nyssa.

   OPERA. Paris, 1638. (V)

    CPE   YP, I, 397-98.

680. Gregory of Nyssa.

   AN APOLOGETICAL EXPLANATION OF THE HEXAEMERON. (?)

    See Sr. M. I. Corcoran, MILTON'S PARADISE.

681. Gregory of Nyssa.

   DE HOMINIS OPIFICIO. (?)

    See Sr. M. I. Corcoran, MILTON'S PARADISE.

682. Gregory of Nyssa.

   DE VIRGINITATE. (V)

    CPB   YP, I, 397-98.
    AP   YP, I, 873.

683. Gregory of Nyssa.

   TREATISE ON THE SOUL. (V)

    CD   CM, XV, 43.

684. Gregory of Tours, St.

> HISTORIAE FRANCORUM. (?)
>
> > 1D   YP, IV, 395.

Greville, Robert. See Lord Brooke.

685. Griffith, Matthew.

> THE FEAR OF GOD AND THE KING. (V)
>
> > BN   CM, VI, 151.
> > See W. R. Parker, MILTON, pp. 551, 1073.

686. Grimes, Ethog.

> ENGLAND AND SCOTLAND UNITED, DISJOYNED. (?)
>
> > See G. W. Whiting, MILTON'S LITERARY MILIEU.

687. Grotius, Hugo.

> ADAMUS EXUL. (*)
>
> > NDX   CM, i, 840.
> > See W. R. Parker, MILTON, p. 824. Donald A.
> > Roberts says, "It may certainly be assumed
> > that ADAMUS EXUL had some place in Milton's
> > thoughts when he considered the subject of
> > Adam and Eve [in the Cambridge Manuscript
> > list of possible topics for tragedies]" YP,
> > IV, 615. An even stronger case for Milton's
> > knowledge of Grotius and his influence is made
> > in J. M. Evans's PARADISE LOST AND THE GENESIS
> > TRADITION, pp. 212-16.

688. Grotius, Hugo.

> AD GENESIN. (?)
>
> > See Sr. M. I. Corcoran, MILTON'S PARADISE.

689. Grotius, Hugo.

> ANNOTATIONES AD VETERUM TESTAMENTUM. (V)
>
> > See George N. Conklin, BIBLICAL CRITICISM AND

117

690. Grotius, Hugo.

    ANNOTATIONES IN LIBROS EVANGELIORUM. (V)

DDD	YP, II, 238, 329, 335, 344.
T	YP, II, 715.
MB	YP, II, 433-34.
CP	CM, VI, 17-18.

691. Grotius, Hugo.

    CHRISTUS PATIENS, in POEMATA. (?)

        The title of this play was used by Milton
in the Cambridge Manuscript list of possible
tragedy topics.

692. Grotius, Hugo.

    DE JURE BELLI ET PACIS. (?)

    2D   YP, IV, 615.

693. Grotius, Hugo.

    DE VERITATE RELIGIONIS CHRISTIANAE. Trans. (probab-
ly) Francis Coventry, q.v., as TRUE RELIGION EX-
PLAINED AND DEFENDED. (V)

    MAR   CM, XVIII, 318.

694. Grotius, Hugo.

    POEMATA COLLECTA. (?)

    2D   YP, IV, 615.

695. Gruter, Jan.

    FLORILEGIUM ETHICOPOLITICUM. (?)

    SD   YP, IV, 749.

696. Gruter, Jan.

INSCRIPTIONES ANTIQUAE TOTIUS ORBIS ROMANI. (?)

    SD   YP, IV, 749-50.

Grynaeus, Simon.
    Grynaeus is cited by Milton among those who
    gave "testimonies of the high approbation
    which learned men have given of Martin Bucer."
    MB   YP, II, 422.

697. Gualtherius [Walther], Rodolphus.

    ARCHETYPI HOMILIARUM IN QUATUOR EVANGELIA. (V)

    T   YP, II, 711.
    LOR   CM, XI, 513.

698. Guarini, Giovanni Battista.

    IL PASTOR FIDO E LE RIME DEL SIG. B. G. (*)

    NDX   CM, i, 841.
    See M. Y. Hughes, JOHN MILTON: COMPLETE POEMS
    AND MAJOR PROSE, p. 135; F. T. Prince, THE
    ITALIAN ELEMENT IN MILTON'S VERSE, pp. 146-68.

699. Guicciardini, Francesco.

    HISTORIA D'ITALIA. Florence, 1636. (V)

    CPB   YP, I, 442-43, 471.
    See W. R. Parker, MILTON, p. 883.

700. Guillim, John.

    A DISPLAY OF HERALDRIE. (V)

    CPB   YP, I, 473.
    See W. R. Parker, MILTON, p. 842.

Guntzer, Christopher. See Erhard Kieffer.

701. Haddon, Walter.

    POEMATUM GVALTERI HADDONI. (?)

    MB   YP, II, 426.

T   YP, II, 716, 717.
See no. 598.

702. Hájek, Václav Wenceslas.

THE HISTORY OF THE BOHEMIAN PERSECUTION, FROM THE
BEGINNING OF THEIR CONVERSION TO CHRISTIANITY IN
THE YEAR 894 TO THE YEAR 1632. (V)

K   YP, III, 513-14.

703. Hakewill, George.

AN APOLOGIE OF THE POWER AND PROVIDENCE OF GOD IN
THE GOVERNMENT OF THE WORLD. (?)

PROL   YP, I, 302.
See Victor Harris, ALL COHERENCE GONE (Chicago, 1949), pp. 160-63; Howard Schultz,
MILTON AND FORBIDDEN KNOWLEDGE (New York,
1955), pp. 93-95.

704. Hakewill, William, trans. and ed.

MODUS TENENDI PARLIAMENTUM: MANNER OF HOLDING
PARLIAMENTS. (?)

1D   YP, IV, 485, 491, 493.
Milton may or may not have read Hakewill's
translation; in fact, he refers to the text
as an "ancient manuscript entitled THE MAN-
NER OF HOLDING PARLIAMENT." According to
Maude V. Clarke, there are twenty five manu-
scripts extant dating from the end of the
fourteenth to the beginning of the sixteenth
centuries, of which six are translations--
two French and four English. See M. V. Clarke,
MEDIEVAL REPRESENTATION AND CONSENT (London,
1936); W. R. Parker, MILTON, p. 1061.

705. Hakluyt, Richard.

THE PRINCIPAL NAVIGATIONS OF THE ENGLISH NATION.
(*)

HM   CM, X, 331-33, 335-41, 353, 363,
            366, 370-73, 382.
At the end of HISTORY OF MUSCOVIA Milton
cites "The Papers of Mr. Hakluyt" as one of

120

his sources; presumably it was a reference to this work. See L. C. Tihany, _PQ_, XIII (1934), 305-06; Harris Fletcher, _PQ_, XX (1941), 501-11.

706. Hall, John.

THE DISCOVERER. (*)

See W. R. Parker, MILTON, p. 960.

707. Hall, John.

HORAE VACIVAE, OR ESSAYS. (?)

See W. R. Parker, MILTON, pp. 307, 931.

708. Hall, John.

POEMS. (?)

See W. R. Parker, MILTON, pp. 307, 931.

709. Hall, John.

A SERIOUS EPISTLE TO MR. WILLIAM PRYNNE. (?)

See W. R. Parker, MILTON, p. 967.

710. Hall, Joseph.

A COMMON APOLOGY OF THE CHURCH OF ENGLAND; AGAINST THE...BROWNISTS. (V)

AP   YP, I, 877.

711. Hall, Joseph.

A DEFENSE OF THE HUMBLE REMONSTRANCE. (V)

See the Preface and Notes to ANIMADVERSIONS by R. Kirk and William P. Baker, YP, I, 653-56.

712. Hall, Joseph.

EPISCOPACIE BY DIVINE RIGHT ASSERTED. (V)

Intro.   YP, I, 653-56.

713. Hall, Joseph.

AN HUMBLE REMONSTRANCE. (V)

Intro.   YP, I, 653-56.

714. Hall, Joseph.

A MODEST CONFUTATION OF A SLANDEROUS AND SCUR-
RILOUS LIBELL, ENTITULED, ANIMADVERSIONS UPON
THE REMONSTRANTS DEFENSE AGAINST SMECTYMNUUS.
(V)

Intro.   YP, I, 653-56.

715. Hall, Joseph ⌈Mercurius Britannicus⌉.

MUNDUS ALTER ET IDEM. (V)

A   YP, I, 697.
AP   YP, I, 880, 881, 914.

716. Hall, Joseph.

OCCASIONAL MEDITATIONS. (*)

A   YP, I, 696.

717. Hall, Joseph.

THE PASSION SERMON PREACHED AT PAULE'S CROSSE ON
GOOD-FRIDAY, APR. 14.1609. (V)

AP   YP, I, 877.

718. Hall, Joseph.

THE PEACE OF ROME. (?)

A   YP, I, 731.

719. Hall, Joseph.

RESOLUTIONS AND DECISIONS OF DIVERS PRACTICAL

CASES OF CONSCIENCE. (*)

    See W. R. Parker, MILTON, p. 969.

720. Hall, Joseph.

    A SHORT ANSWER TO THE TEDIOUS VINDICATION OF
    SMECTYMNUUS. (V)

        Intro.   YP, I, 653-56.

721. Hall, Joseph.

    THE TRUE PEACE-MAKER. (?)

        A   YP, I, 669.

722. Hall, Joseph ₍Virgidemiae₎.

    VIRGIDEMIARUM, SIXE BOOKES...OF TOOTH-LESSE SATYRS.
    ₍Includes TOOTHLESS SATYRS, THREE LAST BOOKS OF
    BYTING SATYRS.₎ (V)

        A   YP, I, 668, 670.
        AP   YP, I, 880, 930.

723. Hammond, Henry.

    OF RESISTING THE LAWFULL MAGISTRATE UNDER COLOUR
    OF RELIGION. (?)

        K   YP, III, 348-49.

724. Hammond, Henry.

    OF THE ZELOTS AMONG THE JEWES. (?)

        K   YP, III, 348-49.

725. Hammond, Henry.

    PARAPHRASES AND ANNOTATIONS ON THE NEW TESTAMENT.
    (?)

        See George N. Conklin, BIBLICAL CRITICISM AND
        HERESY IN MILTON, p. 43.

726. Hammond, Henry.

POWER OF THE KEYS. (?)

See Leo Miller, "Milton, Salmasius and Hammond: The History of an Insult," Renaissance
and Reformation, IX (1973), 108-15.

726a. Hammond, Henry.

TO THE RIGHT HONOURABLE, THE LORD FAIRFAX, AND HIS
COUNCELL OF WARRE, THE HUMBLE ADDRESSE OF HENRY
HAMMOND. (?)

Intro.   YP, III, 99, 105.
TKM   YP, III, 195.

727. Harding, Thomas.

A CONFUTATION OF A BOOKE INTITULED AN APOLOGY OF
THE CHURCH OF ENGLAND. (?)

DDD   YP, II, 322.
This is a most uncertain candidate for inclusion, for many Reformed writers charged
that the Pope derived revenue from Roman
brothels; Harding's book, however, deals with
the charge at length.

728. Hardyng, John.

CHRONICLE. (V)

CPB   YP, I, 495.
See W. R. Parker, MILTON, p. 842.

Harington, John. See Ariosto.

729. Harmar, Samuel.

VOX POPULI, OR GLOSTERSHERES DESIRE: WITH, THE WAY
AND MEANS TO MAKE A KINGDOME HAPPY (BY GODS HELP.)
BY SETTING UP OF SCHOOLE-MASTERS IN EVERY PARISH
THROUGHOUT THE LAND GENERALLY. (?)

E   YP, II, 381, 415.
Although Harmar anticipated Milton's plea
for public education, whether Milton knew
VOX POPULI is uncertain.

124

730. "Harrington."

> THE CENSURE OF THE ROTA UPON MR MILTONS BOOK. (?)
>
>> See W. R. Parker, MILTON, pp. 558-60, 1074;
>> Paul B. Anderson, "Anonymous Critic of Milton:
>> Richard Leigh? or Samuel Butler?" SP, XLIV (1947),
>> 504-18; W. R. Parker, MILTON'S CONTEMPORARY REP-
>> UTATION, pp. 280-83.

731 THE HARROWING OF HELL (MS). (?)

> See Sr. M. I. Corcoran, MILTON'S PARADISE.

732. Hartlib, Samuel.

> A DESCRIPTION OF THE FAMOUS KINGDOME OF MACARIA. (?)
>
> Intro.   YP, I, 157-59.

733. Hartlib, Samuel.

> THE REFORMED SCHOOL. (?)
>
> E   YP, II, 207.
> This work is a revision of J. Dury's book of
> the same name.

734. Hayward, Sir John.

> THE LIFE AND RAIGNE OF KING EDWARD THE SIXT. London,
> 1630. (V)
>
> CPB   YP, I 504.
> R   YP, I, 529, 530, 531, 533, 535-36.
> A   YP, I, 678, 692.
> See W. R. Parker, MILTON, p. 842.

735. Heath, Robert.

> PARADOXICAL ASSERTIONS AND PHILOSOPHICAL PROBLEMS.
> (?)
>
> See Grant McColley, PARADISE LOST.

736. Hegesippus.

> MEMOIRS, in Esubius, q.v. (?)

```
          P          YP, I, 645-46.
          R          YP, I, 549.
```

737. Heimbach, Peter.

ADLOCUTIO GRATULARIA. (?)

See W. R. Parker, MILTON, p. 1059.

738. Heinsius, Daniel.

ARISTARCHUS SACER, SIVE AD NONNI IN JOHANNEM META-PHRASIN CONTEXTUS. (?)

See John M. Steadman, "Urania, Wisdom, and Scriptural Exegesis," Neophilologus, XLVII (1963), 61-73.

739. Heinsius, Daniel.

DE TRAGOEDIAE CONSTITUTIONE. (?)

See Paul R. Sellin, DANIEL HEINSIUS AND STU-ART ENGLAND (New York: Oxford University Press, 1968); Annette C. Flower, "The Critical Context of the Preface to Samson Agonistes," RES, X (1970), 409-23.

740. Heinsius, Daniel.

"First Pythian Ode of Pindar," in D. H. ORATIONES. (?)

```
          MAR        CM, XVIII, 289-90.
          See Pindar.
```

741. Helvicus, Christophorus.

THEATRUM HISTORICUM. (V)

```
          T          YP, II, 714.
```

742. Hemmingus ₍Hemmingsen₎, Nocolaus ₍Niels₎.

OPUSCULA THEOLOGICA. Geneva, 1568. (V)

```
          T          YP, II, 610, 712.
```

126

743. Henderson, Alexander.

A SERMON PREACHED BEFORE THE HONOURABLE HOUSE OF
LORDS, MAY 28, 1645. (?)

See G. W. Whiting, MILTON'S LITERARY MILIEU.

744. Henry of Huntington.

HISTORIARUM LIBRI VIII, in Sir Henry Savile's
RERUM ANGLICARUM SCRIPTORES POST BEDAM, q.v. (V)

CPB   YP, I, 390.
See W. R. Parker, MILTON, p. 841; H. Glicks-
man, "Sources of Milton's History of Britain,"
Wisconsin Studies in Language and Literature,
XI (1920), 105-44.

745. Henry VIII, King of England.

ASSERTIO SEPTEM SACRAMENTORUM ADVERSUS MARTINUM
LUTHERUM. (?)

K   YP, III, 337.

746. Heraclides of Pontus.

ALLEGORIAE IN HOMERI FABULAS DE DIJS. Basel, 1544.
(V)

Milton's autographed copy is now in the Uni-
versity of Illinois Library. See Harris F.
Fletcher, JEGP, XLVII (1948), 182-87; PQ,
XXVIII (1949), 72.

747. Heraclitus of Ephesus.

ON NATURE. (?)

CG   YP, I, 796.

748. Herberstein, Sigismund von, Baron.

COMMENTARIA RERUM MUSCOVITARUM. (?)

CPB   YP, I, 401, 409-10.
This questionable work was frequently bound
with Johannes Leunclavius's COMMENTARY ON THE
DEEDS OF THE MOSCOVITES, q.v., with which

127

        Milton was certainly familiar. See also
        Robert R. Cawley, MILTON AND THE LITERATURE
        OF TRAVEL.

749. Herennius, Caius.

        RHETORICA AD HERENNIUM. (?)

              E   YP, II, 401-03.

750. Hermas.

        THE PASTOR OF HERMAS. (*)

              CG   YP, I, 616, 780.

751. Hermogenes of Tarsus.

        ARS ORATORIA. (*)

              E   YP, II, 403.
        See D. L. Clark, "John Milton and 'the fitted
        stile of lofty, mean, or lowly'," Seventeenth-
        Century News, XI, iv (Winter, 1953), 5-9.

752. Herodian of Antioch.

        HISTORIAE ROMANAE SCRIPTORES LATINI MINORES. (V)

              1D   YP, IV, 448.

753. Herodianus.

        HISTORIAE. (V)

              R   YP, I, 554-57.

754. Herodotus.

        HISTORIARUM LIBRI. (V)

              R   YP, I, 588.
              E   YP, II, 400.
              1D   YP, IV, 382, 400, 434-37.
              SD   YP, IV, 744.

                          128

755. Hesiod.

      OPERA ET DIES. (*)

           PROL   YP, I, 239.
           E   YP, II, 394.
           NDX   CM, i, 888.

756. Hesiod.

      THEOGONIA. (*)

           PROL   YP, I, 221, 222, 223, 226, 228,
                           231, 237, 239, 250, 270, 279,
                           286, 289.
           E   YP, II, 394.
           NDX   CM, i, 888.

Hexam, Henry. Trans. of ATLAS by G. Mercator, q.v.,
and I. Hondius.

757. Heylyn, Peter.

      COSMOGRAPHY. (*)

           NDX   CM, i, 889.
           See Robert R. Cawley, MILTON AND THE LITERATURE
           OF TRAVEL; M. Y. Hughes, JOHN MILTON: COMPLETE
           POEMS AND MAJOR PROSE, pp. 280, 285.

758. Heylyn, Peter.

      THE HISTORY OF THAT MOST FAMOUS SAYNT AND SOULDIER
      OF CHRIST JESUS, ST. GEORGE OF CAPPADOCIA. (*)

           See M. Y. Hughes, JOHN MILTON: COMPLETE POEMS
           AND MAJOR PROSE, p. 687.

759. Heylyn, Peter.

      MICROCOSMUS. (*)

           NDX   CM, i, 889.
           See Sr. M. I. Corcoran, MILTON'S PARADISE.

760. Heylyn, Peter.

      THE REBELLS CATECHISME. (?)

See G. W. Whiting, MILTON'S LITERARY MILIEU.

761. Heywood, Thomas.

HIERARCHIE OF THE BLESSED ANGELS. (*)

NDX   CM, i, 889.
See J. M. Evans, PARADISE LOST AND THE GENESIS
TRADITION; M. Y. Hughes, JOHN MILTON: COMPLETE
POEMS AND MAJOR PROSE, pp. 237, 332, 344, 721.

762. Hierocles of Alexandria.

COMMENTARIUS IN AUREA PYTHAGOREORUM. (V)

MAR   CM, XVIII, 305, 307.
Milton refers to the Cambridge edition, but
there is nonesuch. Roger Daniel, the publisher
of the first edition, became the University
printer in 1632 but lost his privilege in 1650.
He continued his business in London where he
published this work in 1654.

763. Higden, Ranulf.

POLYCRONYCON. (V)

See H. Glicksman, "Sources of Milton's History
of Britain," Wisconsin Studies in Language and
Literature, XI (1920), 109.

764. Hilarius [Hilary].

"Enarratio," PSALM XXXIII, in OPERA. (?)

T   YP, II, 645.
CD   CM, XIV, 261.
Arnold Williams's notes to TETRACHORDON in the
Yale Prose indicate that Milton's reference to
Hilary was a mistake (he should have said
Jerome) and that at any rate his information
came from Erasmus; furthermore, Milton's
citation of Hilary in CHRISTIAN DOCTRINE seems
to indicate that his knowledge of the subject
came through Erasmus rather than original
study.

765. Hilarius.

130

TRACTATUS SUPER PSALMOS. (?)

See Sr. M. I. Corcoran, MILTON'S PARADISE.

766. Hill, Thomas.

THE SCHOOLE OF SKIL. (?)

See Grant McColley, PARADISE LOST.

767. Hippocrates.

DE AËRE, AQUIS, ET LOCIS. (?)

2D   YP, IV, 605.

768. Hippocrates.

THE ART. (V)

LO   CM, XI, 45.
Although modern scholars do not attribute THE
ART to Hippocrates, it is generally included
among the collections of the Hippocratic corpus.
Milton might have read it in any number of
editions.

769. HISTOIRE ENTIÈRE & VÉRITABLE DU PROCÈZ DE CHARLES STUART.
(V)

See W. R. Parker, MILTON, p. 960.

770. HISTORIAE AUGUSTAE SCRIPTORES. (V)

K   YP, III, 337.
1D   YP, IV, 341, 360, 448, 450.
A work by this name, ed. Isaac Casaubon (Paris,
1603), includes works of Spartianus, q.v., Gal-
licanus, Capitolinus, q.v., Pollio, q.v., Lampridius, q.v., and Vopiscus.

771. HISTORIAE ECCLESIASTICAE SCRIPTORES GRAECI. (V)

Ruth Mohl suggests that Milton used a Greek
text from editio princips of the first Robert
Estienne (Paris, 1544) or (Basel, 1562) with
a Latin translation. Bishop John Christerpher-
son and others published such a translation

131

(Geneva, 1612) which includes Esubius' HISTORIA
ECCLESIASTICA and DE VITA CONSTANTINI, Ruffinus'
HISTORIA ECCLESIASTICA, Socrates' HISTORIA,
Theodorit's HISTORIA, Sozomen's HISTORIA, Eva-
grius' HISTORIA, Theodorus's HISTORIA ECCLESIAS-
TICA, and Dorotheus' VITAE APOSTOLORUM AC PRO-
PHETARUM, qq.v.

772. HISTORIA MISCELLA. (V)

      CPB   YP, I, 430, 432.
This work is a collection of anonymous histories
in twenty-four books; it was first compiles "by
Paul, deacon of Aquileia, and later added to
and published by one Landulph, the wise author,
at the time of Leo IV, that is, in the year of
Chirst 806."

773. HISTORIAE PLURIMORUM SANCTORUM. (*)

      P   YP, I, 633.

774. Hobbes, Thomas.

    DE CIVE. (?)

      Intro.   YP, II, 35; YP, III, 72.

775. Hobbes, Thomas.

    DE CORPORE POLITICO: OR, THE ELEMENTS OF LAW, MORAL
AND POLITICK. (?)

      See Marjorie Hope Nicholson, "Milton and Hobbes,"
SP, XXIII (1926), 405-33; Don M. Wolfe, "Milton
and Hobbes: A Contrast in Social Temper," SP,
XLI (1944), 410-26.

776. Hobbes, Thomas.

    HUMANE NATURE. (?)

      See no. 775.

777. Hobbes, Thomas.

    LEVIATHAN. (?)

See M. Y. Hughes, JOHN MILTON: COMPLETE POEMS AND MAJOR PROSE, pp. 430, 818; see also no. 775.

778. Holinshed, Raphael.

CHRONICLES OF ENGLAND, SCOTLAND AND IRELAND. London, 1587. (V)

CPB   YP, I, 367, 372, 374, 387, 388, 395, 396, 403, 422, 423, 425, 426, 427, 428, 429, 433, 434, 435, 440, 441, 445, 446, 447, 448, 449, 453, 454, 455, 458, 461, 480, 481, 482, 483, 484, 485, 486, 487, 492, 493, 494, 496, 498, 499.

R   YP, I, 525, 526, 528, 529, 530, 531, 532, 533, 580, 581, 587, 594.

K   YP, III, 504.

O   YP, III, 306-07.

HB   CM, X, 5.

See W. R. Parker, MILTON, p. 842; H. Glicksman, "Sources of Milton's History of Britain," Wisconsin Studies in Language and Literature, XI (1920), 105-44.

779. Holland, Henry.

THE HISTORIE OF ADAM. (?)

See J. M. Evans, PARADISE LOST AND THE GENESIS TRADITION.

Holland, Philemon. See Ammianus Marcellinus' HISTORIAE.

Holstenius, Lucas. Ed. WORKS OF ST. ATHANASIUS OF ALEXANDRIA, q.v., (Rome, 1627).

2D   YP, IV, 617-18.

See Masson's LIFE, I, 798-805; J. M. French, THE LIFE RECORDS OF JOHN MILTON, I, 389-92.

780. Holy-Oke [Holyoke], Francis.

RIDERS DICTIONARIE. (?)

See John M. Steadman, "Urania, Wisdom, and Scriptural Exegesis," Neophilologus, XLVII (1963), 61-73.

133

781. Homer.

      BATRACHOMYOMACHIA. (?)

         PROL   YP, I, 273.

782. Homer.

      HOMERIC HYMNS. (?)

         NDX   CM, i, 901-03.

783. Homer.

      ILIAD. (V)

         1D   YP, IV, 358, 441.
         2D   YP, IV, 588.
         DDD   YP, II, 294.
         K   YP, III, 345-46.
         NDX   CM, i, 901-03.
         Jonathan Richardson said of Milton, "Homer
         he could Almost repeat without Book." See
         D. L. Clark, JOHN MILTON AT ST. PAUL'S SCHOOL.

784. Homer.

      ODYSSEY. (V)

         PROL   YP, I, 303.
         DDD   YP, II, 271, 294.
         E   YP, II, 415.
         AR   YP, III, 563.
         2D   YP, IV, 566.
         RJP   YP, IV, 898-99.
         NDX   CM, i, 901-03.
         See no. 783.

785. Hooker ⌜Vowell⌟, John.

      ORDER AND USAGE OF THE KEEPING OF PARLIAMENT IN
      ENGLAND. (?)

         1D   YP, IV, 485.
         Hooker incorporated MODUS TENENDI PARLIAMENTUM,
         ed. William Hakewill, into this work. Milton
         may have known Hooker's treatise, but the chances
         seem slim. See no. 704.

786. Hooker, Richard.

THE CAUSES OF THE CONTINUANCE OF THESE CONTENTIONS
CONCERNING CHURCH GOVERNMENT, in CERTAIN BRIEFE
TREATISES, q.v. (V)

Intro.   YP, I, 194.

787. Hooker, Richard.

OF THE LAWES OF ECCLESIASTICAL POLITIE. (V)

P   YP, I, 625.
A   YP, I, 688.
CG   YP, I, 759.
Intro.   YP, III, 116.

788. Horace.

OPERA. (V)

See John H. Finley, Jr., "Milton and Horace:
A Study of Milton's Sonnets," Harvard Studies
in Classical Philology, XLVIII (1937), 29-73;
John T. Shawcross, "Of Chronology and the Dates
of Milton's Translation from Horace and the NEW
FORCERS OF CONSCIENCE," SEL, III (1963), 77-
84. In JOHN MILTON AT ST. PAUL'S SCHOOL Donald
L. Clark suggests a toss-up between John Bond's
edition (London, 1606) and Lambin's (Paris, 1604)
until a definitive study has been made.

789. Horace.

ARS POETICA. (V)

E   YP, II, 404.
2D   YP, IV, 592.
RJP   YP, IV, 890.
NDX   CM, i, 911-12.

790. Horace.

EPISTLES. (V)

SD   YP, IV, 733.
T   YP, II, 639.
NDX   CM, i, 911-12.

135

791. Horace.

    ODES. (V)

        1D   YP, IV, 319, 358-59, 441.
        2D   YP, IV, 638, 685, 686.
        SD   YP, IV, 821.
        RJP   YP, IV, 918.
        NDX   CM, i, 911-12.

792. Horace.

    SATIRES. (V)

        1D   YP, IV, 527-28.
        SD   YP, IV, 748, 756.
        RJP   YP, IV, 900, 924, 936.

793. Horn, Andrew.

    LA SOMME APELLEE MIROIR DES JUSTICES VEL SPECULUM
    JUSTICIARIORUM. Trans. William Hughes as THE BOOKE
    CALLED THE MIRROUR OF JUSTICES. (V)

        K   YP, III, 398, 592.
        TKM   YP, III, 219.
        1D   YP, IV, 482, 490, 494.

794. Horsey, Sir Jerome.

    OBSERVATIONS IN HIS TRAVELS INTO RUSSIA, in
    Purchas or Hakluyt, qq.v. (V)

        HM   CM, X, 353, 382.

795. Hortensius, Quintus.

    MAXIMS. (?)

        2D   YP, IV, 643.
        PROL   CM, XII, 211, 243.

796. Hotamn, François.

    FRANCO-GALLIA. (V)

        CPB   YP, I, 459-60, 461, 501.
        1D   YP, IV, 420, 481.

```
        2D          YP, IV, 659.
        RJP         YP, IV, 948-49.
```

797. Hottinger, Johann Heinrich.

THESAURUS PHILOLOGICUS. (?)

See George N. Conklin, BIBLICAL CRITICISM AND
HERESY IN MILTON, pp, 62, 114-15.

798. Howell, James.

EPISTOLAE HO-ELIANAE, FAMILIAR LETTERS. (*)

MAR   CM, XVIII, 582.
On the verso of the title page is the signature
of Katherine Milton, believed authentic. When
she died the book more than likely passed into
Milton's own library.

Howell, James. Trans. Josephus' HISTORY OF THE LATTER
TIMES OF THE JEWS, q.v.

799. Hrabanus Magnentius.

COMMENTARIORUM IN GENESIM LIBRI QUATUOR. (?)

See Sr. M. I. Corcoran, MILTON'S PARADISE.

800. Hubertus, Conradus.

HISTORIA VERA: DE VITA, OBITU, SEPULTURA, ACCU-
SATIONE...CUMBUSTIONE...D. MARTINI BUCERI & PAULI
FAGII. (*)

MB   YP, II, 425.

801. Hunnius, Aegidius.

COMMENTARIUS IN EVANGELIUM DE JESU CHRISTO SECUN-
DUM MATTHAEUM, in OPERUM LATINORUM. (V)

T   YP, II, 612.

802. Hugh of St. Victore.

ADNOTATIONES ELUCIDATIORIAE IN PENTATEUCHON.

137

See Sr. M. I. Corcoran, MILTON'S PARADISE.

803. Hugh of St. Victore.

DE BESTIIS ET ALIIS REBUS. (?)

See Sr. M. I. Corcoran, MILTON'S PARADISE.

804. Hugh of St. Victore.

DE SACRAMENTIS. (?)

See Sr. M. I. Corcoran, MILTON'S PARADISE.

Hughes, William. See no. 793.

805. THE HUMBLE PETITION OF THE UNIVERSITY OF OXFORD, IN BEHALF OF EPISCOPACY AND CATHEDRALS. (V)

R   YP, I, 611.

806. Hus, John.

OPUSCULA. (*)

AR   CM, IV, 303, 340.
H   CM, VI, 75.
CG   YP, I, 788.

807. Hyginus, Gromaticus.

FABULAE. (?)

2D   YP, IV, 584.

Ibn Ezra ₍Abraham ben Meir Ibn Ezra₎. Scriptural com-mentator whose exegesis is found in Buxtorf's Bible, q.v.

808. Ignatius, St.

S. IGNATII ANTIOCHENI & MARTYRIS QUAE EXSTANT OMNIA. (V)

CPB   YP, I, 394.
R   YP, I, 541, 542, 546.
P   YP, I, 635, 636, 637.

138

Ignatius. See Polycarp.

809. Ingoldsby, William.

THE DOCTRINE OF THE CHURCH OF ENGLAND, ESTABLISHED
BY PARLIAMENT AGAINST DISOBEDIENCE AND WILFULL
REBELLION. (?)

See G. W. Whiting, MILTON'S LITERARY MILIEU.

810. Ingulf.

HISTORIA CROYLANDENSIS. Ed. Sir Henry Savile in
RERUM ANGLICARUM SCRIPTORES POST BEDAM. (V)

HB   CM, X, 194, 195, 208, 235, 236,
            243, 252, 253, 276, 289, 291,
            292, 295, 304.
See H. Glicksman, "Sources of Milton's History
of Britain," Wisconsin Studies in Language and
Literature, XI (1920), 105-44.

811. INSTRUMENT OF GOVERNMENT. (*)

Intro.   YP, IV, 229-34, passim; 261, 265-
            67.
This document was Cromwell's "constitution."

812. Irenaeus of Lyons, St.

ADVERSUS HAERESES. (V)

R   YP, I, 550, 567.
P   YP, I, 635, 639, 641, 642, 644.
AR   YP, II, 518.
1D   YP, IV, 391.

813. Irenaeus, St.

MARTYRDOM OF POLYCARP, in DIVI IRENAEI. (V)

P   YP, I, 642, 643.

814. Irenicus, Francis.

GERMANIAE EXEGESEOS. (V)

MAR   CM, XVIII, 572.

139

Isaiah Aharon ₍Isaiah ben Elijah₎.
Commentator on Book of Judges and Book of
Samuel; included in Buxtorf's Bible, q.v.

815. Isidore of Seville, St.

OPERA. (?)

ID   YP, IV, 395.
T   YP, II, 714.
Milton's knowledge of "isidorus Hispalensis"
in TETRACHORDON comes through Andraeus Alciatus, q.v.

816. Isidore of Seville, St.

DE ORTU ET OBITU PATRUM. (?)

See Sr. M. I. Corcoran, MILTON'S PARADISE.

817. Isidore of Seville, St.

DE VETERI ET NOVO TESTAMENTO QUAESTIONES. (?)

See Sr. M. I. Corcoran, MILTON'S PARADISE.

818. Isidore of Seville, St.

ETYMOLOGIAE. (?)

See Sr. M. I. Corcoran, MILTON'S PARADISE.

819. Isidore of Seville, St.

MYSTICORUM EXPOSITIONES SACRAMENTORUM SEU QUAES-
TIONES IN VETUS TESTAMENTUM. (?)

See Sr. M. I. Corcoran, MILTON'S PARADISE.

820. Isocrates.

AREOPAGITICUS. (?)

AR   YP, II, 486.
E   YP, II, 407.
NDX   CM, i, 980.
See Joseph Anthony Wettreich, Jr., "Milton's
AREOPAGITICA: Its Isocratic and Ironic Contexts,"

Milton Studies, IV (1972), 101-15.

821. Isocrates.

ISOCRATIS ORATIONES...ADJECIMUS QUOQUE H. WOLFII.
(?)

See D. L. Clark, JOHN MILTON AT ST. PAUL'S
SCHOOL.

822. Ivie, Thomas.

ALIMONY ARRAIGN'D, OR THE REMONSTRANCE AND HUMBLE
APPEAL OF THOMAS IVIE, ESQ. (?)

Intro.   YP, IV, 202-03.

823. James I, King of England.

BASILICON DORON. (?)

1D   YP, IV, 507.
2D   YP, IV, 551.

824. James I, King of England.

DAEMONOLOGIE. (?)

See Robert H. West, MILTON AND THE ANGELS.

825. James I, King of England.

A REMONSTRANCE...FOR THE RIGHT OF KINGS AND THE
INDEPENDENCIE OF THEIR CROWNES AGAINST AN ORATION
OF THE CARDINAL OF PERRON...TRANSLATED...BY R. B.
(*)

MAR   CM, XVIII, 575.

James V, King of Scotland. See Nicholas de Nicolay's
LA NAVIGATION DU ROY D'ECOSSE.

826. Jane, Joseph.

EIKON AKLASTOS. (V)

```
        RJP        YP, IV, 891-92.
        K          YP, III, 156, 161.
```

827. Jansonius, A.

    MUNDI FURIOSI. (?)

        HM   CM, X, 382.

828. Jansson ₍Jansonius₎, Jan ₍Johannes₎.

    ATLAS MARITIMUS. (*)

        See Amy Lee Turner, "Milton and Jansson's Sea
        Atlas," Milton_Q, IV (1970), 36-39.

829. Javelli ₍Javello₎, Chrysostom.

    EPITOME CHRYSOSTOMI IAVELLI CANAPITII, ORD. PRAE-
    DICATORUM, IN UNIVERSAM ARISTOTELIS PHILOSOPHIAM,
    TAM NATURALEM, QUAM TRANSNATURALEM. (*)

        PROL   YP, I, 260-61.
        See also no. 59.

830. Jenkinson, Anthony.

    VOYAGES, in Hakluyt, q.v. (?)

        HM   CM, X, 370, 372, 373, 383.
        Milton notes Jenkinson as one of the sources
        of HISTORY OF MUSCOVIA, but it seems likely
        that he knew him through Hakluyt or Purchas,
        qq.v.

831. Jermin, Michael.

    PARAPHRASTICALL MEDITATIONS, BY WAY OF COMMENTARIE,
    UPON THE WHOLE BOOKE OF THE PROVERBS OF SOLOMON. (?)

        See John M. Steadman, "Urania, Wisdom, and
        Scriptural Exegesis," Neophilologus, XLVII
        (1963), 61-73.

832. Jerome ₍Hieronymus₎, St.

    OPERA. Notes by Erasmus. Basel, 1524-26. (V)

```
            T         YP, II, 685.
            AR        YP, II, 518.
            CP        CM, VI, 17.
            1D        YP, IV, 349, 395.
            CD        CM, XV, 43.
            Milton's reference to "Epistle 82" in CHRISTIAN
            DOCTRINE matches the Basel edition.  See also
            W. R. Parker, MILTON, pp. 148, 285, 806.
```

833. Jerome, St.

        ADVERSUS PELAGIUS AD CTESIPHONTEM. (?)

            HB   CM, X, 88.

834. Jerome, St.

        AGAINST JOVINIAN. (*)

            DDD   YP, II, 236-37, 335.

835. Jerome, St.

        COMMENTARIA IN EVANGELIUM SECUNDUM MATTAEUM. (V)

            T   YP, II, 698.

836. Jerome, St.

        EPISTLE XVIII. (V)

            AR   YP, II, 510.

837. Jerome, St.

        EPISTLE LXXVII. (V)

            MB   YP, II, 448-49.

838. Jerome, St.

        EPISTLE TO EVANGELUS ⌜COMMENTARY ON TITUS⌝. (*)

            CG   YP, I, 776-77.
            K   YP, II, 515.

839. Jerome, St.

>   EPISTLE TO PAMMACHIUS. (?)

>   >   R   YP, I, 567.

840. Jerome, St.

>   LIBER HEBRAICARUM QUAESTIONUM IN GENESIM. (?)

>   >   See Sr. M. I. Corcoran, MILTON'S PARADISE.

841. Jerome, St.

>   LIVES OF ILLUSTRIOUS MEN. (*)

>   >   R   YP, I, 567.

842. John Malalas (the Orator) of Antioch.

>   CHRONOLOGY. (?)

>   >   P   YP, I, 634.
>   >   The CHRONOLOGY, according to J. Max Patrick in
>   >   the Yale Prose notes, "was not published until
>   >   the end of the seventeenth century. About 1640
>   >   it came to the attention of Ussher in the codex
>   >   of the MS. of Francis Barocci in the Bodleian
>   >   Library. Milton almost certainly had not read
>   >   it."

843. John of Salisbury.

>   POLICRATICUS. (?)

>   >   Intro.   YP, III, 111-12.
>   >   See Douglas Bush, THE RENAISSANCE AND ENGLISH
>   >   HUMANISM (Toronto, 1939), p. 103.

>   Johnson, Richard.
>   >   Milton notes in HISTORY OF MUSCOVIA his indebt-
>   >   edness to "Richard Johnson, Servant to Chancelor"
>   >   for information used therein; however, I can
>   >   find no evidence that Johnson's MS was ever pub-
>   >   lished independently. Milton's reference is
>   >   probably to Hakluyt, q.v.

Jonathan. One of "three most ancient Jewish commentators, Onkelos, Jonathan, and Hierosolymitanus." See
AP   YP, I, 902.

44. Jonson, Ben.

    EVERY MAN IN HIS HUMOUR. (?)

    C   YP, II, 743.

345. Jonson, Ben.

    PLEASURE RECONCILED TO VERTUE. (*)

        See C. H. Herford and Percy Simpson, BEN JONSON
        (Oxford, 1925), I, 307 ff.; Enid Welsford, THE
        COURT MASQUE (Cambridge, 1927), pp. 314-16.

846. Jonson, Ben.

    POETASTER. (*)

        See R. C. Fox, N&Q, n.s., IX (1962), 52-53.

847. Jonson, Ben.

    THE POET TO THE PAINTER. (?)

        See Michael Wilding, "Jonson, Sin, and Milton,"
        N&Q, n.s., XVII, xi (November 1970), 415.

848. Jonson, Ben.

    SEJANUS, HIS FALL. (?)

        COR   YP, I, 770.

849. Jonstonus ⌈Jonston⌉, Joannes, M.D., of Poland.

    A HISTORY OF THE CONSTANCY OF NATURE. Trans. J.
    Rowland. (?)

        See Kester Svendsen, MILTON AND SCIENCE.

850. Josephus, Flavius ⌈Joseph ben Matthias⌉.

    ANTIQUITATES JUDAICAE. (V)

145

```
K          YP, III, 582-83.
1D         YP, IV, 344, 355, 375, 409, 473.
CG         YP, I, 747.
DDD        YP, II, 327, 335.
T          YP, II, 644-47.
```

851. Josephus, Flavius.

DE BELLO JUDAICO. (*)

K   YP, III, 506, 552.

852. Josephus, Flavius.

CONTRA APIONEM, SEU DE ANTIQUITATE JUDAEORUM. (V)

1D   YP, IV, 370.

853. Josephus, Flavius.

HISTORY OF THE LATTER TIMES OF THE JEWS. Trans.
James Howell. (?)

Intro.   YP, IV, 182.

854. Jossipus ₍Yosippon; Joseph Ben Gorion; Abraham ben
David₎.

A COMPENDIOUS AND MOSTE MARUEYLOUS HISTORY OF THE
LATTER TIMES OF THE JEWES COMMUNE WEALE. (*)

1D   YP, IV, 410.

855. Joseph of Exeter.

DE BELLO TROJANO. (V)

HB   CM, X, 12.
See Harris Fletcher, "Milton's Homer, _JEGP_,
XXXVIII (April, 1939), 229-32.

Joses, Rabbi. See Jose Ben Halafta.

856. Joyner ₍_alias_ Lyde₎, William.

THE ROMAN EMPRESS. (?)

See W. R. Parker, MILTON, pp. 621, 1142-43.

857. Jovius, Paulus.

HISTORIA SUI TEMPORIS, in PAULI IOVII NOVOCOMENSIS
OPERA QUOTQUOT EXTANT OMNIA. (V)

CPB   YP, I, 368, 435, 492, 493, 506.

858. Jovius, Paulus.

MOSCHOVIA. (?)

See Robert R. Cawley, MILTON AND THE LITERATURE
OF TRAVEL.

859. Julian the Apostate [Flavius Claudius Iulianus Augustus].

IN CAESARIBUS. (?)

HB   CM, X, 38, 94, 95, 100.
R   YP, I, 557.
AR   YP, II, 508.
T   YP, II, 664.
1D   YP, IV, 415, 416.
SD   YP, IV, 823.

860. Julianus Salvius.

EDICTUM PERPETUUM. (V)

E   YP, II, 399.

861. Junius [Du Jon], Franciscus, the Elder.

TESTAMENTI VETERIS BIBLIA SACRA...IMMANUELE TREMEL-
LIO, & FRANCISCO JUNIO. (V)

T   YP, II, 615.
C   YP, II, 749.
CD   CM, XIV, 293; CM, XV, 127, 133, 165;
            CM, XVI, 359; CM, XVII, 309.

862. Justin Martyr.

OPERA. (V)

147

```
CPB          YP, I, 397, 437.
T            YP, II, 665-66, 693.
R            YP, I, 551.
P            YP, I, 632.
A            YP, I, 683.
C            YP, II, 736.
1D           YP, IV, 392.
```

863. Justinian I ⌈Flavius Anicius Justinian⌉.

   CODE, in CORPUS JURIS CIVILIS. (V)

```
      TKM          YP, III, 206.
      See no. 864.
```

864. Justinian I.

   CORPUS JURIS CIVILIS. (*)

```
      E            YP, II, 399.
      MB           YP, II, 442.
```
   In MILTON AND SCIENCE Kester Svendsen acknowled-
   ges that Milton's edition of Justinian is unknown; he suggests, however, that he probably
   used either Geneva, 1589, or Frankfurt, 1587.
   See W. R. Parker, MILTON, p. 882.

865. Justinian I.

   INSTITUTES, in CORPUS JURIS CIVILIS. (V)

```
      CPB          YP, I, 410, 411, 426, 438, 470,
                   471.
      1D           YP, IV, 457, 460.
      SD           YP, IV, 713.
      See no. 864.
```

Justiniani, Bernardo. See Justinianus Bernardus.

Justinus, M. Junians. See Trogus Pompeius.

866. Juvenal.

   SATYRAE. (V)

```
      PROL         YP, I, 249, 266, 280, 303.
      2D           YP, IV, 599.
      RJP          YP, IV, 893, 953.
```

```
HB          CM, X, 80.
W           CM, XVIII, 267.
LO          CM, XI, 49.
See D. L. Clark, JOHN MILTON AT ST. PAUL'S
SCHOOL.
```

Kallwitz, Seth. See Sethus Calvisius.

867. Keckermannus, Bartolomaeus.

> SYSTEMA LOGICAE. (?)
>
> > LO   CM, XI, 315, 431.
> > Milton quotes directly from Keckermann in THE
> > ART OF LOGIC, but I have been unable to locate
> > the source of the quotation, for Keckermann was
> > a prolific systemitizer, first at Heidelberg
> > and then at his native Danzig. This title and
> > no. 868 are the most likely candidates.

868. Keckermannus, Bartolomaeus.

> SYSTEMATIS LOGICI. (?)
>
> > LO   CM, XI, 315, 431.
> > See no. 867.

869. Kempe, William.

> THE EDUCATION OF CHILDREN IN LEARNING. (?)
>
> > E   YP, II, 386.

870. THE KEY OF SOLOMON THE KING. (?)

> This work is a manuscript; of the seven extant
> two antedate Milton. See Robert H. West, MIL-
> TON AND THE ANGELS, p. 206.

871. THE KINGS CABINET OPENED: OR CERTAIN PACKETS OF SECRET
LETTERS & PAPERS, WRITTEN WITH THE KINGS OWN HAND, AND
TAKEN IN HIS CABINET AT NASBY-FIELD, JUNE 14, 1645. (V)

> Intro.   YP, III, 148.
> K   YP, III, 397, 449, 484, 525, 526,
>   537, 538, 539, 541, 542, 544.
> RJP   YP, IV, 957.

149

872. Kieffer, Erhard, and Christopher Guntzer.

DISSERTATIONIS AD QUAEDAM LOCA MILTONI PARS PRIOR
ET POSTERIOR. (?)

See W. R. Parker, MILTON, pp. 507, 1063.

Kimchi, David. One of the commentators in Buxtorf's
Bible, q.v.

873. Kircher, Athanasius.

OEDIPUS AEGYPTIACUS. (?)

See Robert H. West, MILTON AND THE ANGELS.

874. Knolles, Richard.

THE GENERALL HISTORIE OF THE TURKES. (?)
See Robert R. Cawley, MILTON AND THE LITERATURE
OF TRAVEL; Elbert N. S. Thompson, "Milton's
Knowledge of Geography," SP, XVI (1919), 156.

875. Knox, John.

THE APPELLATION OF JOHN KNOXE FROM THE CRUELL AND
MOST UNJUST SENTENCE PRONOUNCED AGAINST HIM BY THE
FALSE BISHOPPES AND CLERGY OF SCOTLAND, WITH HIS
SUPPLICATION AND EXHORTATION TO THE NOBILITIE, AND
COMMUNALITIE OF THE SAME REALME. (V)

TKM   YP, III, 248.

876. Knox, John.

THE HISTORY OF THE REFORMATION OF THE CHURCH OF
SCOTLAND. (V)

TKM   YP, III, 224-25.
0   YP, III, 329.
2D   YP, IV, 661.

877. Labadie, Jean.

'AN ACCOUNT OF HIS SUFFERINGS.' (?)

"An account of ₍Labadie's₎ sufferings" was read

150

to Milton through the influence of Giles (?)
Dury, an elder of the French Church (Somerset
House Chapel) in London. Milton transmitted
a call from the London church to the minister
in Orange, but the Frenchman did not come to
England. See W. R. Parker, MILTON, pp. 525,
1068-69.

878. Lactantius, Lucius Caelicus Firmianus.

OPERA. (V)

CPB   YP, I, 363, 364, 369, 373, 422,
             490, 491.
R   YP, I, 561, 562.
Contrary to the editors of the Yale Prose,
Milton does give a page reference to Lactantius in MAR (CM, XVIII, 304); however, I have
been unable to match an edition with his
reference. The nearest is an Antwerp, 1532,
edition in which the reference given by Milton
appears on p. 16 rather than on p. 26. Could
this have been a slip of the pen of Milton's
part? See Kathleen Ellen Hartwell, LACTANTIUS
AND MILTON (Cambridge, Mass.: Harvard University
Press, 1929).

879. Lactantius, L. C. F.

DE IRA DEI. (V)

CPB   YP, I, 363.

880. Lactantius, L. C. F.

DIVINAE INSTITUTIONES. (V)

CPB   YP, I, 363, 364, 369, 422, 490,
             419.
R   YP, I, 561, 562.
T   YP, II, 695.
LO   CM, XI, 49.
MAR   CM, XVIII, 304.

881. Lactantius, L. C. F.

DE OPIFICIO DEI. (V)

CPB   YP, I, 373.

882. Laertius, Diogenes.

    LIVES AND OPINIONS OF EMINENT PHILOSOPHERS. (V)

        E   YP, II, 397.
        LO   CM, XI, 353-54.
        AR   YP, II, 495, 498, 523.

883. Lambard, William.

    ARCHEION OR A COMMENTARY UPON THE HIGH COURTS OF
    JUSTICE IN ENGLAND. (V)

        CPB   YP, I, 423-24, 449.
        Lambard's ARCHAIONOMIA was reprinted in Abraham
        Whelock's edition of Bede, q.v., in 1644. See
        W. R. Parker, MILTON, p. 842.

Lambinus ₍Lambin₎, Dionysius ₍Denys₎. Editor of Horace,
q.v.   COR   CM, XII, 307.

884. Lampridius, Aelius.

    HISTORIA, in HISTORIAE AUGUSTAE SCRIPTORES, q.v.
    (V)

        R   YP, I, 544-45.
        HB   CM, X, 84.
        1D   YP, IV, 448.

Landino, Cristoforo. Editor and annotator of LA COMEDIA
by Dante, q.v.

885. Langland, William.

    THE VISION OF PIERCE PLOWMAN. (V)

        R   YP, I, 579.
        AP   YP, I, 916.
        See W. R. Parker, MILTON, p. 222.

Langus ₍Lange₎, Johann. Trans. Justin Martyr's OPERA,
q.v.

886. La Place, Josué.

    DISPUTATIONES. (*)

See J. P. Pittion, "Milton, La Place and Socianism," RES, n.s. XXIII, 90 (May, 1972), 138-46.

887. Lapide, Cornelius a.

COMMENTARIA IN PENTATEUCHUM MOSIS. (?)

See Sr. M. I. Corcoran, MILTON'S PARADISE.

888. THE LATE CO ENANT ASSERTED. (?)

See G. W. Whiting, MILTON'S LITERARY MILIEU.

889. Latimer, Hugh.

FRUITFULL SERMONS. (V)

K   YP, III, 534.
R   YP, I, 532, 535.

890. Laud, William.

A RELATION OF THE CONFERENCE. (?)

R   YP, I, 522, 594, 603.
CG   YP, I, 826.
O   CM, VI, 252.

891. Laud, William.

A SPEECH DELIVERED IN THE STARR-CHAMBER. (?)

CG   YP, I, 785, 840.

892. Lavater, Ludwig.

IN LIBROS PARALIPOMENON SIVE CHRONICORUM. (V)

MS   CM, XVIII, 238.
LOR   CM, XI, 513.
See Audrey I. Carlisle, RES, n.s., V (1954), 249-55.

893. Lawes, Henry.

AYRES AND DIALOGUES. (V)

153

See W. R. Parker, MILTON, pp. 929, 1026.

894. Lawes, Henry.

CHOICE PSALMES. (V)

See no. 893.

895. Lawes, Henry.

SECOND BOOK OF AYRES. (*)

See no. 893.

896. Lawrence, Henry.

MILITIA SPIRITUALIS, OR A TREATISE OF ANGELS. (?)

See Robert H. West, MILTON AND THE ANGELS.

897. Lawrence, Henry.

OF OUR COMMUNION AND WARRE WITH ANGELS. (?)

See Robert H. West, MILTON AND THE ANGELS.

898. Leigh, Edward.

CRITICA SACRA; OBSERVATIONS ON ALL THE RADICES OR PRIMITIVE HEBREW OF THE OLD TESTAMENT. (*)

See George N. Conklin, BIBLICAL CRITICISM AND HERESY IN MILTON, pp. 14, 78.

899. Leigh, Edward.

CRITICA SACRA; OR, PHILOLOGICALL AND THEOLOGICALL OBSERVATIONS UPON ALL THE GREEK WORDS OF THE NEW TESTAMENT. (*)

See no. 898.

900. Leo III.

ECLOGUE, OR DELECTUS LEGUM COMPENDIARUS, FACTUS AB LEONE, ET CONSTANTINO, SAPIENTIBUS AUGUSTIS, EX IN-STITUTIONIBUS & DIGESTIS, & CODICE, & NOVELLIS MAGNI

154

ILLIUS JUSTINIANI CONSTITUTIONIBUS, in JURIS GRAECO-
ROMANI. (V)

TKM   YP, III, 218.

901. Leo VI, Emperor.

IMP. LEONIS AUGUSTI CONSTITUTIONES NOVELLAE. (V)

T   YP, II, 703.

902. Leo After, John.

AFRICAE DESCRIPTIO. (V)

CPB   YP, I, 382.
See W. R. Parker, MILTON, p. 842.

903. Leo Magnus, Pope.

LEONIS PAPE...EPISTOLAE CATHOLICAE. (V)

MB   YP, II, 452.

904. Lessabeus ₍Lessabé or de Leussauch₎, Jacques.

HANNONIAE URBIUM ET NOMINATIORUM LOCORUM. (*)

HB   CM, X, 16-17.

905. L'Estrange, Roger.

BE MERRY AND WISE; OR, A SEASONABLE WORD TO THE
NATION. (?)

See W. R. Parker, MILTON, pp. 548, 1073.

906. L'Estrange, Roger.

DOUBLE YOUR GUARDS. (?)

See W. R. Parker, MILTON, pp. 561, 1075.

907. L'Estrange, Roger.

EYE SALVE. (?)

155

See W. R. Parker, MILTON, pp. 561, 1075.

908. L'Estrange, Roger.

NO BLINDE GUIDES. (?)

See W. R. Parker, MILTON, pp. 561-62, 1073, 1075.

909. L'Estrange, Roger.

PHYSICIAN CURE THYSELF. (?)

See W. R. Parker, MILTON, pp. 561, 1075.

910. L'Estrange, Roger.

TREASON ARRAIGNED. (?)

See W. R. Parker, MILTON, pp. 561, 1075.

911. Leunclavius, Johannes.

COMMENTARY ON THE DEEDS OF THE MUSCOVITES IN THEIR WARS AGAINST THEIR NEIGHBORS, in Baron von Herberstein's COMMENTARIA RERUM MUSCOVITARUM, q.v. (?)

There is a good chance that Milton used Leunclavius as a source for BRIEF HISTORY OF MUSCOVIA, but he does not cite it.

912. Leunclavius, Johannes.

IURIS GRAECO-ROMANI TAM CANONICI QUAM CIVILIS TOMI DUO. Frankfort, 1596. (V)

CPB   YP, I, 401, 407, 408, 439.
T   YP, II, 685.
Intro.   YP, III, 218.

Leussauch, J. de. See Lessabeus.

913. Ley, John.

SUNDAY A SABBATH. OR A PREPARATIVE DISCOURSE FOR DISCUSSION OF SABBATARY DOUBTS. (V)

A   YP, I, 696.

156

914. Libanius.

    OPERA. (V)

        HB   CM, X, 93, 94.
        T   YP, II, 663-64.

915. THE LIFE AND REIGNE OF KING CHARLES, OR, THE PSEUDO-
MARTYR DISCOVERED. (*)

    See W. R. Parker, MILTON, p. 1001.

916. LIFE OF ADAM AND EVE. (?)

    This work is part of the Wheatley MS. See
Sr. M. I. Corcoran, MILTON'S PARADISE.

917. Lightfoot, John.

    HARMONY OF THE IV EVANGELISTS. (?)

    See George N. Conklin, BIBLICAL CRITICISM AND
HERESY IN MILTON.

918. Lightfoot, John.

    HORAE HEBRICAE ET TALMUDICAE. (?)

    See George N. Conklin, BIBLICAL CRITICISM AND
HERESY IN MILTON.

919. Lilburne, John.

    AS YOU WERE. (?)

    See W. R. Parker, MILTON, pp. 417, 1016.

920. Lilburne, John.

    ENGLAND'S NEW CHAINS DISCOVERED. (*)

    See W. R. Parker, MILTON, pp. 355, 960.

921. Lily, William.

    BREVISSIMA INSTITUTIO SEU RATIO GRAMMATICES COG-
NOSCENDAE, AD OMNIUM PUERORUM UTILITATEM PRAESCRIPTA.
(V)

E   YP, II, 380.

922. Lily, William.

   A SHORT INTRODUCTION OF GRAMMAR GENERALLY TO BE USED.
   (V)

      E   YP, II, 380.

923. Linacre, Thomas.

   DE EMENDATA STRUCTURA LATINI SERMONIS LIBRI SEX.   (V)

      G   CM, VI, 285.

924. Linschoten, Jan Huyghen van.

   HIS DISCOURS OF VOYAGES INTO THE EASTE AND WEST
   INDIES. (?)

      See Robert Cawley, MILTON AND THE LITERATURE
      OF TRAVEL.

925. Linschoten, Jan Huyghen van.

   VOYAGE TO GOA, AND OBSERVATIONS OF THE EAST INDIA.
   Ed. Samuel Purchas. (*)

      See S. Viswanathan, "Milton and Purchas' Lin-
      schoten: An Additional Source for Milton's
      Indian Figtree," MiltonN, II (1968), 43-45.

926. Lipsius, Justus.

   DE CONSTANTIA. (*)

      PROL   YP, I, 251.

927. Lipsius, Justus.

   SIXE BOOKES OF POLITICKES OR CIVIL DOCTRINE, WRITTEN
   IN LATINE...DONE INTO ENGLISH BY WILLIAM JONES. (?)

      TKM   YP, III, 119, 190, 338.

928. Littleton, Sir Thomas.

LES TENURES. (?)

        C   YP, II, 735.

929. Livy.

    HISTORIARUM AB URBE CONDITA. (V)

        K   YP, III, 565, 590.
        TKM   YP, IV, 208.
        1D   YP, IV, 442, 443.
        SD   YP, IV, 699.
        PROL   YP, I, 258, 267.
        A   YP, I, 669, 703.
        CG   YP, I, 791, 792.
        G   CM, VI, 331, 332, 337, 344, 347, 352.

    Lodge, Thomas. Trans. THE FAMOUS AND MEMORABLE WORKES
    OF JOSEPHUS, q.v.

930. Logan, Josias.

    VOYAGE TO PECHORA. (?)

        HM   CM, X, 382.
        Milton probably picked up Logan's account of
        his travels in Russia in Purchas, q.v.

931. Lombard, Peter.

    SENTENTIARUM LIBRI IV. (?)

        T   YP, II, 621.
        See Sr. M. I. Corcoran, MILTON'S PARADISE.

932. Longinus, Dionysius Cassius.

    DE SUBLIMITATE. (V)

        E   YP, II, 403.
        See E. M. W. Tillyard, "Milton and Longinus,"
        TIMES LITERARY SUPPLEMENT (28 August 1930), p.
        684.

933. Lovelace, Richard.

    LUCASTA. (?)

See W. R. Parker, MILTON, p. 369.

934. Loredano, Giovanni Francesco.

L'ADAMO. (?)

See "Introduction" to the edition by Roy C.
Flannagan and John Arthos (Gainesville, Fla.,
1967).

935. Lucan ₍Marcus Annaeus Lucanus₎.

BELLUM CIVILE. (*)

HB   CM, X, 48.
NDX   CM, ii, 1182-83.
See M. Y. Hughes, JOHN MILTON: COMPLETE POEMS
AND MAJOR PROSE, pp. 137, 255, 418.

936. Lucian.

OPERA. (*)

A   YP, I, 701.
RJP   YP, IV, 930.
COR   CM, XII, 103.
MAR   CM, XVIII, 277, 302.
In the allegedly Miltonic copy of Pindar, q.v.,
there is a reference to an edition of Lucian
by Johannes Benedictus.

937. Lucian.

MENIPPUS. (?)

C   YP, II, 722.
COLASTERION is a transliteration from the
Greek; Milton may have had Lucian's use of
it (MENIPPUS 14) in mind when he chose the
title of his tract.

Lucilius.
Only fragments of Lucilius' satires have come
down to posterity, and it is generally agreed
that Milton knew him through reputation and
through occasional quotations. His most famous allusion occurs in AREOPAGITICA (YP, II,
498-99).

160

938. Lucretius ₍Titus Lucretius Carus₎.

    DE RERUM NATURA. (V)

        E   YP, II, 395.
        RJP   YP, IV, 935.
        MAR   CM, XVIII, 326.
        G   CM, VI, 346.
        AR   YP, II, 498.

939. LUDUS COVENTRIAE, Parts I and II. (?)

        See Sr. M. I. Corcoran, MILTON'S PARADISE;
        Allan H. Gilbert, "Milton and the Mysteries,"
        SP, XVII (1920), 147-69.

940. Lullius ₍Lull₎, Ramón.

    OPERA. (?)

        AR   YP, II, 507.

    Luther, Martin.

        CPB   YP, I, 504-05.
        TKM   YP, III, 243 ff.
        T   YP, II, 688, 708, 712.
        A   YP, I, 734.
        AP   YP, I, 878, 901, 953.
        AR   YP, II, 553.
        1D   YP, IV, 337, 396.
        2D   YP, IV, 661.
        CD   CM, XVI, 375.
        TR   CM, VI, 169.
    Milton's COMMONPLACE BOOK quotation from Luther
    comes from Sleidan's COMMENTARIES, q.v., as do
    his references in THE TENURE OF KINGS AND MAGIS-
    TRATES. In TETRACHORDON Milton refers to Luther
    as "quoted by Gerard out of the Dutch"; see
    Johannes Gerhardus, LOCORUM THEOLOGICORUM.

941. Lycophron.

    ALEXANDRA. With commentary of Tzetzes. Geneva,
    1601. (V)

        MAR   CM, XVIII, 568.
    Milton's copy is now in the University of Il-
    linois Library. See W. R. Parker, MILTON, p.
    787.

Lycurgus.
In OF EDUCATION Milton recommends the "extoll'd remains" of several Greek law-givers, including Lycurgus. The legal code of Lycurgus was, according to Plutarch, never put into writing; Milton, therefore, knew him by reputation, probably through Xenophon, Plutarch, Herodotus, and Aristotle.

E YP, II, 398.
AR YP, II, 496.

942. Lydgate, John.

THE PURBES OF LYDGATE (UPON THE FALL OF PRYNCES). (?)

See Sr. M. I. Corcoran, MILTON'S PARADISE.

943. Lyranus, Nicholas.

TEXTUS BIBLIAE CUM GLOSSA ORDINARIA, NICOLAE DE LYRA POSTILLA. (?)

See John M. Steadman, "Urania, Wisdom, and Scriptural Exegesis," Neophilologus, XLVII (1963), 61-73.

944. Macrobius, Ambrosius Theodosius.

SATURNALIORUM. (V)

CPB CM, XVIII, 226.
A YP, I, 694.
2D YP, IV, 594.

Maecianus, Lucius Volusius.
Milton seems to have picked up a reference to ANNALES VOLUSII, a work known only by reputation, through Catullus.
2D YP, IV, 648.

945. Machiavelli, Niccolo.

TUTTE LE OPERE DI NICOLO MACHIAVELLI. (V)

CPB YP, I, 414-15, 421, 443-44, 456, 475, 477, 495, 496, 498, 499, 504, 506.

```
1D          YP, IV, 488-89.
AP          YP, I, 908.
DDD         YP, II, 321.
```
See W. R. Parker, MILTON, p. 883. Milton's
notes are from the DISCORSI and the DELL'ARTE
DELLA GUERRA rather than from IL PRINCIPE.

Magister Leo Hebraeus. See Ben Gerson.

Maistre Petit. See Kimchi.

946. Maimonides ₍Moses ben Maimon₎.

RABBI MOSIS MAIEMONIDIS LIBER DOCTOR PERPLEXORUM...
TRANSLATUS...A JOHANNE BUXTORFIUS. (V)

```
DDD         YP, II, 257.
1D          YP, IV, 354.
```

947. Malatesti, Antonio.

LA TRINA. (MS). (V)

```
2D          YP, IV, 617.
```

948. Maldonatus, Johannes.

COMMENTARIA IN IV EVANGELIA. (?)

```
T           YP, II, 640.
```
Evidence is slim indeed that Milton read this
work or no. 949; however, Maldonatus' commentary on the gospels was extremely popular
down to modern times and was widely reprinted,
and the treatise on angels and demons would
have been of great interest to Milton had he
seen it.

949. Maldonatus, Johannes.

TRAITÉ DES ANGES ET DEMONS. (?)

See no. 948.

950. Malory, Sir Thomas.

MORTE D'ARTHUR. (*)

See M. Y. Hughes, JOHN MILTON: COMPLETE POEMS
AND MAJOR PROSE, p. 480-81; W. R. Parker, MIL-
TON, p. 619.

951. Malvezzi, Virgilio Marquese.

DISCOURSES UPON CORNELIUS TACITUS. (V)

R   YP, I, 573.
MAR   CM, XVIII, 346, 493 ff., 575.

952. Manasses, Constantine.

BREVIARIUM HISTORICUM. (V)

See W. R. Parker, MILTON, p. 502.

953. Manilius, Marcus.

ASTRONOMICA. (V)

DDD   YP, II, 294.
E   YP, II, 396.
LO   CM, XI, 13.
MAR   CM, XVIII, 310.

954. Manso, Giovanni Bapttista, Marquis di Villa.

EROCALLIA OVVERO DELL' AMORE E DELLA BELLEZZA, DIA-
LOGHI XII...ET NEL FINE UN TRATTATO DEL DIALOGO.
(*)

See Michele De Filippis, "Milton and Manso:
Cups or Books?" PMLA, LI (1936), 745-56.

955. Mano, Giovanni Bapttista, Marquis di Villa.

I PARADOSSI. (?)

See no. 954.

956. Manso, Giovanni Bapttista, Marquis di Villa.

POESIE NOMICHE...DIVISE IN RIME AMOROSE, SACRE, E
MORALI. (*)

See no. 954.

957.   Manso, Giovanni Bapttista, Marquis di Villa.

VITA DI TORQUATO TASSO.   (?)

See no. 954.

958.   Mantova, Domenico.

POEMS.   (?)

See J. S. Smart, THE SONNETS OF MILTON, pp. 37, 71.

959.   Maplet, John.

A GREENE FOREST, OR A NATURALL HISTORIE.   (?)

See Kester Svendsen, MILTON AND SCIENCE.

Marinarius, Antonius.
Milton's reference to this "learned Carmelite" comes from Sarpi, q.v.   See also
T   YP, II, 638.

960.   Marianus Scotus.

CHRONICA.   (?)

HB   CM, X, 230.

961.   Marino, Giambattista.

L'ADONE.   (*)

See Gretchen Ludke Finney, "Comus, Drama Per Musica," SP, XXXVII (1940), 482-500; Anthony Mortimer, "The Italian Influence on COMUS," MiltonQ, VI (1972), 8-16.

962.   Marino, Giovanni Battista.

STRAGE DEGLI INNOCENTI.   Trans. Richard Crashaw as SOSPETTO D'HERODE.   (?)

See Grant McColley, PARADISE LOST; Ruth C. Wallerstein, RICHARD CRASHAW: A STUDY IN STYLE AND POETIC DEVELOPMENT (Madison: University of Wisconsin Press, 1959), p. 96.

963. Marlianus, Joannes Bartholomaeus.

    URBIS ROMAE TOPOGRAPHIA. (V)

        MAR   CM, XVIII, 576.
        See W. R. Parker, MILTON, p. 830.

964. Marlowe, Christopher, and George Chapman.

    HERO AND LEANDER. (*)

        NDX   CM, ii, 1217.
        See Herman Schaus, "Relationship of Comus to
        HERO AND LEANDER and VENUS AND ADONIS," UNI-
        VERSITY OF TEXAS STUDIES IN ENGLISH, XXV
        (1946), 129-41.

965. Marlowe, Christopher.

    TAMBURLAINE THE GREAT. (?)

        See William Leigh Godshalk, "Marlowe, Milton,
        and the Apples of Hell," MiltonQ, V (1971),
        34-35.

966. Marlowe, Christopher, and Thomas Nash.

    THE TRAGEDIE OF DIDO, QUEEN OF CARTHAGE. (?)

        NDX   CM, ii, 1217.

967. Marlowe, Christopher.

    THE TRAGICALL HISTORY OF THE LIFE AND DEATH OF
    DOCTOR FAUSTUS. (?)

        NDX   CM, ii, 1217.

968. Marshall, Stephen.

    A DIVINE PROJECT TO SAVE A KINGDOME. (?)

        See G. W. Whiting, MILTON'S LITERARY MILIEU.

969. Marshall, Stephen.

    REFORMATION AND DESORLATION: OR, A SERMON TENDING
    TO THE DISCOVERY OF THE SYMPTOMES OF A PEOPLE TO

WHOM GOD WILL BY NO MEANES BE RECONCILED. (?)

    See G. W. Whiting, MILTON'S LITERARY MILIEU.

970. Marshall, Stephen.

A SERMON PREACHED BEFORE THE HONOURABLE HOUSE OF COMMONS, NOW ASSEMBLED IN PARLIAMENT, AT THEIR PUBLIKE FAST, NOVEMBER 17, 1640. (?)

    See G. W. Whiting, MILTON'S LITERARY MILIEU.

971. Marston, John.

SCOURGE OF VILLANIE. THREE BOOKES OF SATYRES. (?)

    NDX   CM, ii, 1224.

972. Martial.

EPIGRAMMATA. (?)

PROL	YP, I, 225, 280.
AP	YP, I, 930.
1D	YP, IV, 319, 347, 475, 534.
2D	YP, IV, 564, 581, 608.
RJP	YP, IV, 899.
G	CM, VI, 341.
LO	CM, XI, 89, 129, 139, 143, 147, 163, 463.
HB	CM, X, 81.

See Donald L. Clark, JOHN MILTON AT ST. PAUL'S SCHOOL.

Martin of Tours, St.

Milton's knowledge of St. Martin was derived from Sulpicius Severus' OPERA, q.v. See also

R	YP, I, 538, 545, 558.
AP	YP, I, 944.
K	YP, III, 519.

973. Martini, Jacob.

ANNOTATIONES, in TRACTUM SPHAERAE IOANNIS DE SACRO-BOSCO, q.v. (?)

See Allen H. Gilbert, "Milton's Textbook of Astronomy," PMLA (1923), 297-307.

167

Martinius. Author of HEBREW GRAMMAR, adapted and translated by N. Udall, q.v.

Martyr, Justin. See Justin Martyr.

Martyr, Peter. See Vermilius.

974. Marvell, Andrew.

    REHERSAL TRANSPROSED. (*)

        See W. R. Parker, MILTON, pp. 629, 1145.

975. Marvell, Andrew.

    THE REHERSAL TRANSPROSED: THE SECOND PART. (*)

        See W. R. Parker, MILTON, pp. 630-31, 1146.

976. Mason, Francis.

    THE ADDITION OF FRANCIS MASON, in CERTAIN BRIEFE TREATISES, q.v. (V)

        Intro.   YP, I, 194.

977. Mason, Francis.

    THE VALIDITY OF THE ORDINATION OF THE MINISTERS OF THE REFORMED CHURCHES, in CERTAIN BRIEFE TREATISES, q.v. (V)

        Intro.   YP, I, 194.

Matthew Paris Monachus ⌈Matthew the Monk⌉.

    CPB   YP, I, 408, 449.
    T   YP, II, 685, 702-03.
    Milton got references to Matthew's CHRONICA MAIORA and HISTORIA ANGLORUM through Lambard and Leunclavius, qq.v. See also H. Glicksman, "Sources of Milton's History of Britain," <u>Wisconsin Studies in Language and Literature</u>, XI (1920), 105-44.

978. Matthew of Westminster ₍pseud.₎.

FLORES HISTORIARUM. (V)

See H. Glicksman, "Sources of Milton's History of Britain," <u>Wisconsin Studies in Language and Literature</u>, XI (1920), 105-44.

979. May, Thomas.

THE HISTORY OF THE PARLIAMENT OF ENGLAND: WHICH BEGAN NOVEMBER THE THIRD, M.DC.XL. London, 1647. (V)

See G. W. Whiting, "The Sources of EIKONOKLAS-TES: A Resurvey," <u>SP</u>, XXXII (1935), 74-102.

Mazzocchi, Domenico. See Ottavio Tronsarelli.

980. Mechovita, Maciej ₍also Maciej z Miechowa, Maciej Miechowita, Mathias von Michaw₎.

TRACTATUS DE DUABUS SARMATIIS ASIANA ET EUROPIANA ET DE CONTENTIS IN EIS. (?)

See Harris F. Fletcher, <u>PQ</u>, XX (1941), 501-11.

981. Mede, Joseph.

CLAVIS APOCALYPTICA. (?)

See Michael Fixler, MILTON AND THE KINGDOMS OF GOD, pp. 40-42.

982. Mede, Joseph.

THE WORKS OF THE PIOUS AND PROFOUNDLY-LEARNED JOSEPH MEDE. (?)

See George N. Conklin, BIBLICAL CRITICISM AND HERESY IN MILTON, pp. 43-44, 106-07.

983. A MEDICINE FOR MALIGNANCY. (?)

See G. W. Whiting, MILTON'S LITERARY MILIEU.

984. Mela, Pomponius.

DE SITU ORBIS. (V)

E   YP, II, 390-91.
HB   CM, X, 4, 49, 50.
See Robert R. Cawley, MILTON AND THE LITERATURE
OF TRAVEL.

985. Melancthon, Philip.

CHRONICI CARIONIS. (V)

MAR   CM, XVIII, 345.

986. Melancthon, Philip.

INITIA DOCTRINAE PHYSICAE. (?)

See Grant McColley, PARADISE LOST.

987. Melancthon, Philip.

LOCI COMMUNES THEOLOGICI. (V)

T   YP, II, 610, 708.
MB   YP, II, 422.
LOR   CM, XI, 507.

Memmius, Gaius.

1D   YP, IV, 350.
Milton quotes a line of Gaius Memmius preserved in Sallust's CATILINE, q.v.

988. Menander.

EX COMOEDIIS. (?)

AR   YP, II, 498.

989. Mercator, Gerard, and I. Hondius.

ATLAS: OR, A GEOGRAPHICKE DESCRIPTION OF THE WORLD.
(?)

See Sr. M. I. Corcoran, MILTON'S PARADISE;
Grant McColley, PARADISE LOST.

990. Mercator, Gerard.

   GALLIAE TABULAE GEOGRAPHICAE. (?)

   E   YP, II, 389.

991. Mercer, John.

   COMMENTARIUS IN GENESIN. (?)

   See Grant McColley, PARADISE LOST.

Mercurius Britannicus. See Joseph Hall's MUNDUS ALTER ET IDEM.

992. Mersenne, Marin.

   QUESTIONES CELEBERRIMAE IN GENESIM. (?)

   See Sr. M. I. Corcoran, MILTON'S PARADISE;
   Arnold Williams, "Commentaries on Genesis
   as a Basis for Hexaemeral Material in the
   Literature of the Late Renaissance," SP,
   XXIV (1937), 191-208.

Messalinus, Walo. Pseud for Claude de Saumaise, q.v.

993. MIDRASH KONEN. (?)

   See E. C. Baldwin, "Some Extra-Biblical Semitic
   Influences upon Milton's Story of the Fall of
   Man," JEGP, XXVIII (1929), 366-401.

994. MIDRASH RABBAH: BERESHITH RABBAH. (?)

   See Sr. M. I. Corcoran, MILTON'S PARADISE; no.
   993.

995. MIDRAH TEHILLIM. (?)

   See no. 993.

996. Minshew, John.

   DUCTOR IN LINGUAS: THE GUIDE INTO THE TONGUES. (*)

AP   YP, I, 880.

Modestinus, Herennius.

    T   YP, II, 611-12.
    Milton's knowledge of Modestinus apparently
    came through Dionysius Gothofredus's edition
    of Justinian's CORPUS JURIS CIVILIS, q.v.
    Modestinus, a Roman law expert, was included
    in the PANDECTS, that portion of the CORPUS
    composed of authoritative opinions on the law.

997. Modestus.

    DE RE MILITARI. (?)

        See W. R. Parker, MILTON, p. 853.

998. MODUS TENENDI PARLIAMENTUM. (MS). (V)

        See W. R. Parker, MILTON, pp. 501-02, 1061.

999. Montaigne, Michel Eyquem de.

    ESSAYS. (?)

        COR   YP, I, 329-30.
        See Anon. note in N&Q, 2nd series, V (6 Feb.
        1858), 115, which claims Milton's sometime
        possession of the Florio translation (London,
        1613); the copy in question allegedly had
        Milton's autograph.

1000. Montalván, Juan Pérez de.

    THE ILLUSTRIOUS SHEPHERDESS. (*)

        See W. R. Parker, MILTON, p. 989.

1001. Montalván, Juan Pérez de.

    THE IMPERIOUS BROTHER. (*)

        See W. R. Parker, MILTON, p. 989.

Montanus, Arias. See Pagnius' BIBLIA HEBRAICA.

1002. Montemayor, Jorge de.

DIANA. (*)

AR   YP, II, 525.
K   YP, III, 367.

Monteverdi, Claudio Zuan Antonio.
  See Edward Phillips' LIFE, and John Arthos,
  "Milton and Monteverdi," in MILTON AND THE
  ITALIAN CITIES, pp. 129-205.

1003. Moore, Andrew.

A COMPENDIUS HISTORY OF THE TURKS. (?)

  See Robert R. Cawley, MILTON AND THE LITERATURE
  OF TRAVEL, pp. 128-29.

1004. Moraes, Francesco de.

THE ₍FIRST &₎ SECONDE PART OF THE HISTORIE OF THE...
PRINCES PALMERIN OF ENGLAND. (*)

K   YP, III, 367.

1005. Moraes, Francesco de.

THE THIRD AND LAST PART OF PALMERIN OF ENGLAND. (*)

K   YP, III, 367.

1006. More, Alexander.

FIDES PUBLICA. (V)

Intro. YP, IV, 275, 276, 281.
SD   YP, IV, 687-825 passim.

1007. More, Alexander.

SUPPLEMENTUM. (V)

  See no. 1006.

1008. More, Henry.

AN EXPLANATION OF THE GRAND MYSTERY OF GODLINESS.
(?)

    See Robert H. West, MILTON AND THE ANGELS.

1009. More, Henry.

    ANTIDOTE AGAINST IDOLATRY. (?)

       See Robert H. West, MILTON AND THE ANGELS.

1010. More, Henry.

    CONJECTURA CABBALISTICA: OR A CONJECTURAL ESSAY
    OF INTERPRETING THE MINDE OF MOSES, ACCORDING TO
    A THREEFOLD CABBALA, VIZ., LITERAL, PHILOSOPHICAL,
    MYSTICAL OR DIVINELY MORAL. (?)

       See J. M. Evans, PARADISE LOST AND THE GENESIS
       TRADITION; Marjorie Hope Nicolson, "Milton
       and the CONJECTURA CABBALISTICA," PQ, VI (1927),
       1-18.

1011. More, Henry.

    ENTHUSIASMUS TRIUMPHATUS. (?)

       See Robert H. West, MILTON AND THE ANGELS.

1012. More, Hnery.

    IMMORTALITY OF THE SOUL. (?)

       NDX   CM, ii, 1311.
       See Robert H. West, MILTON AND THE ANGLELS.

1013. More, Henry.

    PLATONICAL SONG OF THE SOUL. (?)

       NDX   CM, ii, 1311.
       See Robert H. West, MILTON AND THE ANGLELS.

1014. More, Henry.

    PHILOSOPHICAL POEMS. (?)

See Robert H. West, MILTON AND THE ANGELS.

1015. More, Henry.

   THE SECOND LASH OF ALOZONOMASTIX. (?)

      See Robert H. West, MILTON AND THE ANGELS.

1016. More, Sir Thomas.

   UTOPIA. (V)

      AP   YP, I, 881.

1017. Morel, Guillaume.

   VERBORUM LATINORUM CUM GRAECIS ANGLICISQUE CONIUNCT-
   ORUM...COMMENTARIJ. (?)

      See John M. Steadman, "Urania, Wisdom, and
      Scriptural Exegesis," Neophilologus, XLVII
      (1963), 61-73.

   Morvyng, Peter. Trans. Josippus' DE BELLO JUDAICO, q.v.

1018. Moschus of Syracuse.

   IDYLS. (V)

      MAR   CM, XVIII, 279, 283.

   Moulin. See Du Moulin.

1019. Muffet, Peter.

   A COMMENTARIE UPON THE WHOLE BOOKE OF THE PROVERBS
   OF SALOMON. (?)

      See John M. Steadman, "Urania, Wisdom, and
      Scriptural Exegesis," Neophilologus, XLVII
      (1963), 61-73.

1020. Mulcaster, Richard.

   THE FIRST PART OF THE ELEMENTARIE. (?)

E   YP, II, 415.

1021. Mulcaster, Richard.

POSITIONS. (?)

E   YP, II, 415.

1022. Munster, Sebastian.

HEBRAICA BIBLIA. (?)

See John M. Steadman, "Urania, Wisdom, and Scriptural Exegesis," Neophilologus, XLVII (1963), 61-73.

1023. Muret, Marc Antoine.

VARIARUM LECTIONUM LIBRI XV. Paris, 1586. (V)

Milton's copy is now privately owned. See W. R. Parker, MILTON, p. 1122.

1024. Murtola, Gasparo.

DELLA CREAZIONE DEL MONDO. (?)

See Grant McColley, PARADISE LOST.

1025. Musculus [Mäuslin, Müslin, Moesel], Wolfgang.

IN EVANGELISTAM MATTHAEUM COMMENTARII. (V)

T   YP, II, 711.
CD   CM, XVII, 193.

1026. Musculus, Wolfgang.

IN GENESIM MOSIS. (?)

See Arnold Williams, "Milton and Commentaries on Genesis," MP, XXXVII (1940), 263-78.

1027. Nabbes, Thomas.

MICROCOSMUS, A MORALL MASKE. (?)

Nacmanides. Greek var. of Ben Nachman, q.v.

1028. Naevius, Anaeus.

      FRAGMENTA QUAE EXSTANT, in CORPUS OMNIUM VETERUM
      POETARUM LATINORUM. (?)

          AR   YP, II, 498.

1029. Nashe, Thomas.

      PIERCE PENNILESS'S SUPPLICATION TO THE DEVIL. (?)

        See Grant McColley, PARADISE LOST.

Naso. See Ovid.

1030. Needham, Marchamont.

      THE CASE OF THE COMMONWEALTH OF ENGLAND STATED. (*)

        See W. R. Parker, MILTON, p. 394.

1031. Needham, Marchamont [?].

      HUE AND CRY AFTER A WILFUL KING. (?)

          Intro.   YP, IV, 49-50.
          "On June 23, [1649] Milton was ordered by
          the Council of State to examine MERCURIUS
          PRAGMATICUS," of which Needham was the chief
          contributor and editor. One might reason-
          ably conjecture that Milton also read the
          anonymously issued HUE AND CRY, for which
          alleged authorship Needham had previously
          been confined to the Gatehouse.

1032. NEGOTIATION DE LA PAIX, ES MOIS D'AURIL & MAY 1575.
      CONTENANT LA REQUESTE & ARTICLES PRESENTEZ AU ROY
      PAR M. LE PRINCE DE CONDE, SEIGNEURS & GENTILSHOMMES
      DE LA RELIGION...AVEC LA RESPONSE DU ROY AUSDITS AR-
      TICLES. (?)

          MAR   CM, XVIII, 578-79.
          A Paris, 1576, edition has initials "J.M."

on the title-page.

1033. Nennius.

> HISTORIA BRITONUM. (MS). (V)
>
> | | |
> |---|---|
> | lD | YP, IV, 380, 490. |
> | HB | CM, X, 5, 30, 83, 90, 97, 116, 117, 120, 121, 122, 123, 127, 128, 129. |
>
> See H. Glicksman, "Sources of Milton's History of Britain," Wisconsin Studies in Language and Literature, XI (1920), 105-44. "It was largely to Usher, though in part also to Camden and Speed, that Milton seems to have owed his knowledge of the early British chronicler Nennius, whose HISTORIA, which did not appear in print until 1691, he used freely" (p. 106). Constance Nicholas, on the other hand, states that Glicksman is in error and cites persuasive evidence that Milton read Nennius in manuscript. See Nicholas's INTRODUCTION AND NOTES TO MILTON'S HISTORY OF BRITAIN, pp. 22-23.

Nepos. See Cornelius Nepos.

1034. Nicander.

> ALEXIPHARMACA. (V)
>
> E   YP, II, 395.

1035. Nicander.

> THERIACA. (V)
>
> E   YP, II, 395.

Nicanor, Lysimachus. Pseud. of John Corbet, q.v.

Nicephorus Gregoras. See Gregoras.

1036. Nicetas Acominate ɾor Choniateɿ.

> IMPERII GRAECI HISTORIA. (V)

```
CPB          YP, I, 508.
K            YP, III, 361.
```

1037. Nicolay, Nicholas de, sieur d'Arfeuille et Bel-Air.

NAVIGATION DU ROY D'ÉCOSSE JACQUES V, AUTOUR DE SON ROYAUME ET ISLES HÉBRIDES ET ORCHADES. (?)

MAR   CM, XVIII, 581-82.
A copy of this book, now lost, was said to contain the signature of Milton and some marginalia. See Jackson C. Boswell, "A Lost Book," MiltonQ, VII, ii (1973), 38-39, and "The Navigation of James V," The Bibliotheck, VI (1972) 118-20.

1038. Nieremberg, Juan Eusebio.

FLORES SOLITUDINIS. Trans. Henry Vaughan as MEDITATIONS. (?)

See J. M. French, THE LIFE RECORDS OF JOHN MILTON, III, 352; W. R. Parker, MILTON, p. 1122.

1039. NO FARTHER ADDRESSES. (V)

Intro.   YP, III, 149.
K   YP, III, 352, 471-484 passim.

1040. Nonius, Petrus Salaciensis.

ANNOTATIO IN EXTREMA VERBA CAPITIS DE CLIMATIBUS, ELIA VINETO INTERPRETE, in DE SPHAERA by Sacrobosco, q.v. (?)

See Allan H. Gilbert, "Milton's Textbook of Astronomy," PMLA, XXXVIII (1923), 297-307.

1041. Ochino, Bernardino.

DIALOGI XXX. (?)

See Louis A. Wood, THE FORM AND ORIGIN OF MILTON'S ANTI-TRINITARIAN CONCEPTION (London, 1911); J. H. Hanford, "Milton and Ochino," MLN, XXXVI (1921), 121-22.

1042. Ochino, Bernardino.

PREDICHE...NOMINATE LABERTINI DEL LIBRO. (?)

See no. 1041.

1043. Ochino, Bernardino.

TRAJEDY OR DIALOGUE OF THE UNJUST USURPED PRIMACY
OF THE BISHOP OF ROME. Trans. John Ponet. (?)

See no. 1041.

1044. Olaus Magnus.

HISTORIA DE GENTIBUS SEPTENTRIONALIBUS. Antwerp,
1558. (V)

MAR   CM, XVIII, 579.
NDX   CM, ii, 1389.
There is a copy of Olaus Magnus preserved at
the Milton Cottage at Chalfont St. Giles with
the initials "J.M." inscribed. Prior to the
Antwerp edition, there was one at Rome, 1555.
It was translated as A COMPENDIOUS HISTORY OF
THE GOTHS, SWEDES, & VANDALS, AND OTHER NORTH-
ERN NATIONS by J. S[treater (?), London, 1658.
See Harris Fletcher, PQ, XX (1941), 501-11.

Olympiodorus.
DDD   YP, II, 327-28.
HB   CM, X, 100.
Historian and skeptical philosopher, knowledge
of whom Milton seems to have picked up from
Photius, q.v.

1045. Oneklos.

TARGUM OF THE OLD TESTAMENT, in BIBLIA SACRA POLY-
GLOTTA. (?)

AP   YP, I, 902.
CD   CM, XV, 283.
See George N. Conklin, BIBLICAL CRITICISM AND
HERESY IN MILTON, pp. 58-59.

1046. Oppian.

CYNEGETICA. (V)

180

                   E   YP, II, 395.

1047. Oppian.

       HALIEUTICA. (V)

                   E   YP, II, 395.

1048. Origen.

       OPERA OMNIA. (*)

                   R   YP, I, 553, 567-68.
                   lD   YP, IV, 393.
                   H   CM, VI, 86.
                   See W. R. Parker, MILTON, pp. 147, 211, 285,
                   805, 809; Harry F. Robins, IF THIS BE HERESY:
                   A STUDY OF MILTON AND ORIGEN, (Urbana: Univer-
                   sity of Illinois Press, 1963).

1049. Origen.

       COMMENTARIA IN EVANGELIUM SECUNDUM MATTHAEUM.   (V)

                   MB   YP, II, 452.
                   T   YP, II, 695.

1050. Origen.

       IN CANTICUM CANTICORUM PROLOGUS.   (*)

                   CG   YP, I, 815.
                   Ralph A. Haug states, "It is likely Milton
                   found the reference in Paraeus. [q.v.]" W. R.
                   Parker (see references at no. 1048), on the
                   other hand, believes Origen was an integral
                   part of Milton's studies of the Horton period.

1051. Origen.

       PERIARCHON. (?)

                   See Sr. M. I. Corcoran, MILTON'S PARADISE.

1052. Ormonde, James Butler, Earl and Marquis of.

       ARTICLES OF PEACE. (V)

                               181

```
O          YP, III, 301, 303, 308.
K          YP, III, 473, 475, 487.
```

1053. Ormonde, James Butler, Earl and Marquis of.

DECLARATION TO MUNSTERMEN. (?)

```
O          YP, III, 309.
```

1054. Ormonde, James Butler, Earl and Marquis of.

PROCLAMATION CONCERNING THE PEACE. (V)

```
O          YP, III, 301.
```

1055. Orosius, Paulus.

HISTORIARUM ADVERSUM PAGANOS LIBRI VII. (V)

```
HB          CM, X, 39, 47, 48, 49, 80, 86,
            99, 221, 256, 257.
```
See H. Glicksman, "Sources of Milton's History
of Britain," <u>Wisconsin Studies in Language and
Literature</u>, XI (1920), 113; Constance Nicholas
INTRODUCTION AND NOTES TO MILTON'S HISTORY OF
BRITAIN, p. 38.

1056. Orpheus.

ARGONAUTICA. (*)

```
E          YP, II, 394.
```

1057. Orpheus.

DE LAPIDIBUS. (*)

```
E          YP, II, 394.
```

1058. Orpheus.

HYMNS. (V)

```
E          YP, II, 394.
1D         YP, IV, 382-83.
```
See Julia A. Humphreys-Edwards, "Milton's
'Il Penseroso,' 93-94," <u>N&Q</u>, XVI, iii (March
1969), 93.

1059. Ortelius, Abraham.

EPITOME DU THÉÂTRE DU MONDE. (?)

E   YP, II, 389-90.
A   YP, I, 697.
See Sr. M. I. Corcoran, MILTON'S PARADISE;
Robert R. Cawley, MILTON AND THE LITERATURE
OF TRAVEL; G. W. Whiting, MILTON'S LITERARY
MILIEU.

1060. Ortelius, Abraham.

THEATRUM ORBIS TERRARUM. (?)

See no. 1059.

Otanes ₍Persian historian (?)₎.
1D   YP, IV, 437.

1061. Otto, Bishop of Freising.

GESTA FRIDERICI IMPERATORIS. (?)

1D   YP, IV, 395.

1062. Ovid.

OPERA. (V)

See E. K. Rand, "Milton in Rustication," SP,
XIX (1922), 109-35; Donald L. Clark, MILTON
AT ST. PAUL'S SCHOOL; Davis P. Harding, MIL-
TON AND THE RENAISSANCE OVID.

1063. Ovid.

AMORES. (*)

See John M. Major, "Ovid's AMORES III.ix: A
Source for Lycidas," MiltonQ, VI, iii (October
1972), 1-3.

1064. Ovid.

ARS AMATORIA. (V)

```
              RJP          YP, IV, 916.


1065.  Ovid.

          DE TRISTIBUS.  (*)

               See no. 1062.


1066.  Ovid.

          EPISTOLAE EX PONTO.  (*)

               SD          YP, IV, 750.
               RJP         YP, IV, 899.
               See no. 1062.


1067.  Ovid.

          FASTI.  (*)

               K           YP, III, 584.
               See no. 1062.


1068.  Ovid.

          METAMORPHOSES.  (V)

               1D          YP, IV, 312, 380, 452, 518.
               2D          YP, IV, 556, 566, 569, 571.
               RJP         YP, IV, 941, 942.
               See no. 1062.


1069.  Paget, Thomas.

          A RELIGIOUS SCRUTINY CONCERNING UNEQUAL MARRIAGE.
          (?)

               See W. R. Parker, MILTON, p. 368.


1070.  Pagitt, Ephraim.

          HERESIOGRAPHY.  (?)

               See W. R. Parker, MILTON, pp. 582, 1093.


1071.  Pagninus, Xantis.


                         184
```

BIBLIA HEBRAICA. EORUNDEM LATINA INTERPRETATIO...
RECENTER BENEDICTI ARIAE MONTANI HISPAL. & QUORUNDAM
ALIORUM COLLATIO STUDIO, AD HEBRAICAM DICTIONEM DI-
LIGENTISSIME EXPENSA. (?)

See John M. Steadman, "Urania, Wisdom, and
Scriptural Exegesis," Neophilologus, XLVII
(1963), 61-73.

1072. Palladius, Rutilius Taurus AEmilianus.

DE RE RUSTICA. (V)

See W. R. Parker, MILTON, p. 852; Edward
Phillips, THEATRUM POETARUM (London, 1675),
pp. 211-12.

1073. Palmer, Herbert.

SCRIPTURE AND REASON: PLEADED FOR DEFENSIVE ARMES:
OR, THE WHOLE CONTROVERSIE ABOUT SUBJECTS TAKING
UP ARMES. WHEREIN BESIDES OTHER PAMPHLETS, AN AN-
SWER IS PUNCTUALLY DIRECTED TO DR. FERNES BOOKE,
ENTITLED, RESOLVING OF CONSCIENCE, ETC. (V)

TKM   YP, III, 252.

1074. Paraeus, David.

IN DIVINAM AD ROMANOS S. PAULI APOSTOLI EPISTOLAM
COMMENTARIUS. (V)

TKM   YP, III, 247-48.

1075. Paraeus, David.

IN GENESIN MOSIS COMMENTARIUS. (V)

DDD   YP, II, 246.
T   YP, II, 594, 596, 598, 599, 600,
               602, 607, 609.
See Sr. M. I. Corcoran, MILTON'S PARADISE.

1076. Paraeus, David.

IN PRIOREM AD CORINTHIOS EPISTOLAM S. PAULI...
COMMENTARIUS. (V)

```
DDD          YP, II, 289, 304.
C            YP, II, 749.
```

1077. Paraeus, David.

IN S. MATTHAEI EVANGELIUM COMMENTARIUS. (V)

```
DDD          YP, II, 285, 319.
T            YP, II, 641, 650, 652, 659, 673.
```

1078. Paraeus, David.

OPERUM THEOLOGICORUM. (V)

```
CG           YP, I, 815.
DDD          YP, II, 285, 289, 304, 319, 324,
             332, 352.
C            YP, II, 749.
```
See W. R. Parker, MILTON, pp. 211, 247, 374, 916-17.

1079. Parker, Samuel.

A REPROOF TO THE REHEARSAL TRANSPROSED. (*)

Andrew Marvell attributed THE TRANSPROSER REHEARSED to Parker. P. B. Anderson, SP, XLIV (1947), 504-18, suggests Samuel Butler, q.v., as the author. See W. R. Parker, MILTON, pp. 630, 1146.

1080. Parker, Samuel.

TENTAMINA DE DEO. (?)

See W. R. Parker, MILTON, p. 1088.

1081. Pascal, Blaise.

LES PROVINCIALLES, OR, THE MYSTERY OF JESUITISME. DISCOVERED IN CERTAIN LETTERS...THE SECOND EDITION CORRECTED, WITH LARGE ADDITIONALS. (V)

```
MAR          CM, XVIII, 581.
```

Paterculus. See Velleius Paterculus, G.

1082. Paulus Diaconus.

HISTORIA MISCELLA. Ingolstadt, 1603. (V)

CPB   YP, I, 430, 432.
HB   CM, X, 104, 106.
See W. R. Parker, MILTON, pp. 146, 150, 802-03,
806.

1083. Pausanias of Lydia.

GRAECIAE DESCRIPTIO. (*.)

PROL   YP, I, 246, 269.
HB   CM, X, 81.

1084. Peacham, Henry.

THE COMPLEAT GENTLEMAN. (?)

E   YP, II, 387, 409.

1085. Peacham, Henry.

THE VALLEY OF VARIETIE. (*)

See J. M. French, THE LIFE RECORDS OF JOHN
MILTON, I, 356; the London, 1638, edition has
the initials "J. M." on the title-page.

1086. Peele, George.

THE OLD WIVES TALE. (?)

See David Erskine Baker [and Isaac Reed],
BIOGRAPHIA DRAMATICA, II, 441.

1087. Pererius, Benedict.

COMMENTARIORUM ET DISPUTATIONUM IN GENESIM. (?)

See Sr. M. I. Corcoran, MILTON'S PARADISE;
Arnold Williams, "Commentaries on Genesis as
a Basis for Hexaemeral Material in the Literature of the Late Renaissance," SP, XXXIV
(1937), 191-208.

1088. Perkins, William.

    CHRISTIAN OECONOMIE. (V)

        DDD   YP, II, 341.

1089. Perkins, William.

    A DISCOURSE OF CONSCIENCE. (V)

        DDD   YP, II, 317.

1090. Perkins, William.

    DISCOURSE OF THE DAMNED ART OF WITCHCRAFT, in THE
    WORKES OF THAT FAMOUS AND WORTHY MINISTER OF CHRIST
    IN THE UNIVERSITIE OF CAMBRIDGE. (?)

    See Robert H. West, MILTON AND THE ANGELS.

1091. Perkins, William.

    A GODLY AND LEARNED EXPOSITION OF CHRISTS SERMON ON
    THE MOUNT. (V)

        DDD   YP, II, 320.

1092. Persius Flaccus, Aulus.

    SATIRES. (V)

        PROL   YP, I, 220, 239.
        Donald L. Clark notes in JOHN MILTON AT ST.
        PAUL'S SCHOOL the report by Gardiner that
        COMMENTAR ASCENTII ET AL. IN PERSIUM was bought
        for St. Paul's library and was, presumably,
        used by Milton.

    Petau, Denis. See Petavius, Dionysius.

1093. Petavius, Dionysius.

    DE THEOLOGICIS DOGMATIBUS. (?)

        1D   YP, IV, 391.

1094. Petavius, Dionysius.

OPUS DE DOCTRINA TEMPORUM. (?)

    1D   YP, IV, 391.

Peter Martyr. See P. M. Vermilius.

1095. Petrarca, Francesco.

OPERA. (*)

See J. S. Smart, THE SONNETS OF MILTON, pp. 93, 134, 138.

1096. Petrarca, Francesco.

APOLOGIA CONTRA GALLUM. (*)

    AP   YP, I, 895.

1097. Petrarca, Francesco.

LE RIME DEL PETRARCA BREVEMENTE SPOSTE PER LUDO-VICO CASTELVETRO. (?)

    COR   YP, II, 768.

1098. Petrarca, Francesco.

THE TRYUMPHES OF FRAUNCES PETRARCKE. Henrye Parker's translation of THE TRIUMPH OF LOVE. (?)

    COR   YP, II, 768.

1099. Petronius Arbiter, Titus.

SATYRICON. (?)

    AR   YP, II, 518.
    1D   YP, IV, 412, 468.
    RJP   YP, IV, 930.

Peyness, Thomas. Trans. J. L. Vives' THE OFFICE AND DUETIE OF AN HUSBAND, q.v.

1100. Peyton, Thomas.

    THE GLASSE OF TIME. (?)

        See Sr. M. I. Corcoran, MILTON'S PARADISE.

Phillip, William. Trans. Jan Juyghen van Linschoten's
DISCOURSE OF VOYAGES INTO THE EASTE AND WEST INDIES,
q.v.

1101. Phillips, Edward.

    THE MYSTERIES OF LOVE & ELEGANCE. (*)

        See W. R. Parker, MILTON, p. 989.

1102. Phillips, Edward.

    THE NEW WORLD OF ENLISH WORDS. (*)

        See Geoffrey M. Ridden, "Milton and Phillip's
        NEW WORLD OF WORDS," <u>MiltonQ</u>, VII, ii (1973),
        29-32; W. R. Parker, MILTON, p. 989.

1103. Phillips, John.

    MARONIDES OR VIRGIL TRAVESTIE: BEING A NEW PARA-
    PHRASE UPON THE FIFTH BOOK OF VIRGIL'S AENEIDS.
    (?)

        See W. R. Parker, MILTON, pp. 622, 1144.
        Phillips's paraphrase of Book V was publish-
        ed in London, 1672; Book VI in 1673.

1104. Phillips, John.

    MONTELIONS PREDICTIONS. (?)

        See W. R. Parker, MILTON, p. 1147.

1105. Phillips, John.

    SATYR AGAINST HYPOCRITES. (*)

        See W. R. Parker, MILTON, pp. 989-90.

1106. Phillips, John.

SPORTIVE WIT: THE MUSES' MERIMENT. A NEW SPRING
OF LUSTY DROLLERY, JOVIAL FANCIES, AND A LA MODE
LAMPOONS ON SOME HEROIC PERSONS OF THESE LATE
TIMES. (*)

See W. R. Parker, MILTON, pp. 477, 1047.

1107. Phillips, John, trans.

THE TEARS OF THE INDIANS: BEING AN HISTORICAL AND
TRUE ACCOUNT OF THE CRUEL MASSACRES AND SLAUGHTERS
...COMMITTED BY THE SPANIARDS...MADE ENGLISH BY
J. P. (*)

Phillips translated Bartolome de las Casas'
work in 1656. See W. R. Parker, MILTON, p.
1047.

1108. Philo Judaeus.

LEGUM ALLEGORIA. (V)

1D   YP, IV, 345.

1109. Philo Judaeus.

DE SPECIALIBUS LEGIBUS. (V)

1D   YP, IV, 344-45.
T   YP, II, 593, 646.

1110. Philo Judaeus.

MOSES. (?)

DDD   YP, II, 288.

1111. Philo Judaeus.

ON THE ACCOUNT OF THE WORLD'S CREATION GIVEN BY
MOSES. (?)

See Sr. M. I. Corcoran, MILTON'S PARADISE.

1112. Philodemus, Eutactus ⌈Antony Ascham⌉.

191

THE ORIGINAL & END OF CIVIL POWER. (?)

    See Michael Fixler, MILTON AND THE KINGDOMS OF
GOD.

1113. Philostratus, Flavius.

    APOLLONII TYANENSIS VITA. (?)

    A   YP, I, 729.

1114. Photius, Patriarch of Constantinople.

    BIBLIOTHECA. (V)

    P   YP, I, 633.
    DDD   YP, II, 327.

1115. Photius.

    NOMOCANON. (V)

    T   YP, II, 702.
    With the scholia of Theodore Balsamon, this
work goes by the above title; the text, however, is the same as Photius' SYNTAGMA CANONUM.

1116. Pico della Mirandola, Giovanni.

    ORATIO. (*)

    See Joseph A. Wittreich, Jr., "Pico and
Milton: A Gloss on Areopagitica," ELN, IX,
ii (December 1971), 108-10.

    PIERS PLOWMAN. See William Langland.

1117. Pietro Aretino.

    QUATTRO COMEDIE DEL DIVINO PIETRO ARETINO. (?)

    AR   YP, II, 518.

1118. Pigna.

    I ROMANZI, NÈ QUALI DELLA POESIA & DELLA VITA DELL'
ARIOSTO CON NUOVO MODE SI TRATA. (?)

CG   YP, I, 811.

1119. Pindar.

PINDARI OLYMPIA, PYTHIA, NEMEA, ISTHMIA. (V)

CG   YP, I, 815.
COR   YP, I, 324.
Maurice Kelley and S. D. Atkins argue quite
convincingly that the notations in a copy of
the Johannes Benedictus edition (Saumur, 1620),
long thought to be Milton's, are indeed not his
as is assumed in the Columbia Milton. See
"Milton and the Harvard Pindar," Studies in Bibliography, XVII (1964), 77-82. It is clear,
nevertheless, that Milton read Pindar in some
edition.

1120. PIRKÊ DE RABBI ELEAZER. (?)

See Sr. M. I. Corcoran, MILTON'S PARADISE;
Edward C. Baldwin, "Some Extra-Biblical Se-
mitic Influences upon Milton's Story of the
Fall of Man," JEGP, XXVIII (1929), 366-401.

1121. Piscator, Joannis.

COMMENTARIORUM IN OMNES LIBROS VETERIS TESTAMENTI.
(?)

See John M. Steadman, "Urania, Wisdom, and
Scriptural Exegesis," Neophilologus, XLVII
(1963), 61-73.

Piso.

Milton quotes Piso through Cicero's EPISTOLAE
AD FAMILARES, q.v.
SD   YP, IV, 744.
DDD   CM, III, 442.
1D   CM, VII, 315.

1122. Pitiscus ₍Petiscus₎, Bartholomaus.

TRIGONOMETRIA. (V)

E   YP, II, 392.

1123. Pits, John.

RELATIONUM HISTORICARUM DE REBUS. (?)

See W. R. Parker, MILTON, p. 1122.

1124. Plato.

OPERA. (V)

AP	YP, I, 891.
NDX	CM, ii, 1500-02.

See Herbert Agar, MILTON AND PLATO (Princeton:
Princeton University Press, 1928; Oxford: Oxford University Press, 1931); Irene Samuel,
PLATO AND MILTON (Ithaca, N. Y.: Cornell University Press, 1947).

1125. Plato.

APOLOGY. (*)

PROL	YP, I, 273, 302.
E	YP, II, 396.
T	YP, II, 583.
2D	YP, IV, 556, 591, 656.

1126. Plato.

CRITIAS. (?)

AR	YP, II, 526.

1127. Plato.

CRITO. (*)

E	YP, II, 396.

1128. Plato.

EPISTLES. (V)

1D	YP, IV, 383, 400, 438, 455.

1129. Plato.

EUTHYPHRO. (*)

```
               CG          YP, I, 841.

1130.  Plato.

          GORGIAS.  (?)
                    CG          YP, I, 846.
                    DDD         YP, II, 346.

1131.  Plato.

          LAWS.  (*)
                    COR         YP, I, 329.
                    CG          YP, I, 746, 753, 756, 819, 837,
                                840, 841, 849.
                    DDD         YP, II, 310.
                    E           YP, II, 377, 384, 385, 387, 408,
                                409, 414.
                    AR          YP, II, 496, 522, 523, 524, 526.
                    K           YP, III, 413, 498.
                    lD          YP, IV, 379, 383.

1132.  Plato.

          MENEXENUS.  (*)
                    E           YP, II, 396.

1133.  Plato.

          MENO.  (*)
                    DDD         YP, II, 294, 314.

1134.  Plato.

          PHAEDO.  (*)
                    PROL        YP, I, 291.
                    CG          YP, I, 801.
                    E           YP, II, 368, 396.
                    AR          YP, II, 530.

1135.  Plato.

          PHAEDRUS.  (*)
```

```
                PROL        YP, I, 295.
                CG          YP, I, 816, 821.
                AP          YP, I, 891.
                DDD         YP, II, 254.
                E           YP, II, 396.
                AR          YP, II, 523.
                2D          YP, IV, 589.
```

1136. Plato.

PHILEBUS. (?)

```
                E           YP, II, 396.
```

1137. Plato.

PROTAGORAS. (*)

```
                CG          YP, I, 769.
                DDD         YP, II, 314.
```

1138. Plato.

REPUBLIC. (*)

```
                PROL        YP, I, 236.
                CG          YP, I, 751, 819, 820-21, 840.
                AP          YP, I, 888, 891.
                E           YP, II, 377, 384, 387, 411.
                AR          YP, II, 522, 523, 526.
                K           YP, III, 408, 413.
```

1139. Plato.

SYMPOSIUM. (*)

```
                PROL        YP, I, 288.
                CG          YP, I, 801.
                AP          YP, I, 891-92.
                DDD         YP, II, 252.
                E           YP, II, 368, 396.
                AR          YP, II, 522, 523.
```
See Irene Samuel's PLATO AND MILTON, pp. 11-12,
23, 103-04, and chapt. 7 _passim_.

1140. Plato.

THEAETETUS. (V)

```
                    E           YP, II, 367.
                    See J. C. Maxwell, "Plato and Milton," MLR,
                    XLIII (1948), 409-10.


1141.  Plato.

           TIMAEUS.  (?)

                    DDD         YP, II, 314.
                    E           YP, II, 397.


1142.  Plautus.

           OPERA.  (V)

                    G           CM, VI, 333, 337, 338.
                    See D. L. Clark, JOHN MILTON AT ST. PAUL'S
                    SCHOOL.


1143.  Plautus.

           AMPHITRUO.  (*)

                    RJP         YP, IV, 951.


1144.  Plautus.

           AULULARIA.  (V)

                    1D          YP, IV, 428, 519.
                    RJP         YP, IV, 960.


1145.  Plautus.

           MILES GLORIOSUS.  (?)

                    RJP         YP, IV, 911.


1146.  Plautus.

           TRINUMMUS.  (V)

                    RJP         YP, IV, 913.


1147.  Pliny the Elder.
```

NATURALIS HISTORIA. (*)

```
PROL      YP, I, 280, 283.
E         YP, II, 390-91.
HB        CM, X, 48, 50.
```

1148. Pliny the Elder.

THE HISTORIE OF THE WORLD. Trans. Philemon Holland. (V)

```
MAR       CM, XVIII, 497.
NDX       CM, ii, 1504.
```
See G. W. Whiting, MILTON'S LITERARY MILIEU.

1149. Pliny the Younger.

EPISTOLAE. (?)

See Donald L. Clark, JOHN MILTON AT ST. PAUL'S SCHOOL.

1150. Pliny the Younger.

XII PANEGYRICI. (V)

```
1D        YP, IV, 445, 446, 447, 466.
```

1151. THE PLOT DISCOVERED AND COUNTERPLOTTED. (?)

```
MAR       CM, XVIII, 533, 580.
```
See TIMES LITERARY SUPPLEMENT, 28 Oct. 1936, p. 868.

1152. Plutarch.

LIVES. (V)

```
PROL      YP, I, 241, 267, 297, 298.
DDD       YP, II, 315, 348.
COR       YP, IV, 582-83.
1D        YP, IV, 536.
2D        YP, IV, 581, 585.
SD        YP, IV, 744.
RJP       YP, IV, 923.
HB        CM, X, 38.
LO        CM, XI, 45, 145, 239, 299.
CD        CM, XIV, 129.
MAR       CM, XVIII, 320.
```

                    NDX   CM, ii, 1506.
                    In his copy of Euripides, Milton made a note
                    to himself to consult the English translation
                    ⌈by North⌉ of Plutarch (London, 1610-12).

1153. Plutarch.

            MORALIA. (V)

                    PROL   YP, I, 237, 303.
                    E   YP, II, 384, 396, 397.
                    AR   YP, II, 496, 549.
                    2D   YP, IV, 577.

1154. Plutarch.

            ON THE EDUCATION OF CHILDREN. (V)

                    E   YP, II, 384.
                    Edward Phillips says he and his brother read
                    this work in Greek while studying with Mil-
                    ton.

            Polano, Pietro Soave. See Sarpi.

1155. Polanus, Amandus.

            THE SUBSTANCE OF CHRISTIAN RELIGION. (V)

                    CD   CM, XVI, 149, 151.

1156. Pollio, Trebellius.

            TYRANNI TRIGINTA, in HISTORIAE AUGUSTAE SCRIPTORES,
            q.v. (V)

                    1D   YP, IV, 341.
                    HB   CM, X, 34.

1157. Polyaenus.

            STRATEGEMATA. (V)

                    E   YP, II, 412.

1158. Polybius.

HISTORIA. (V)

    R   YP, I, 599.
    DDD   YP, II, 323.
    1D   YP, IV, 439.

1159. Polycarp.

POLYCARPI ET IGNATII EPISTOLAE. (V)

    MAR   CM, XVIII, 574.
    P   YP, I, 626-27, 634.
A copy of this work (Oxford, 1644) is preserved
in the Chapter Library of Ely Cathedral. T. O.
Mabbott believed the annotations Miltonic;
Maurice Kelley disagrees.

1160. Polycrates, Bishop of Ephesus.

ACTA TIMOTHEI, in HISTORIAE PLURIMORUM SANCTORUM.
(*)

    P   YP, I, 633-34.

Ponet, Jean.
    TKM   YP, III, 249.
See Sir Thomas Aston's A REMONSTRANCE, AGAINST
PRESBITERY.

1161. Pontanus, Johannes Isaacus.

RERUM DANICARUM HISTORIA. (V)

See C. H. Firth, "Milton as an Historian," PRO-
CEEDINGS OF THE BRITISH ACADEMY, III (1907-08),
227-57; H. Glicksman, "Sources of Milton's History of Britain," Wisconsin Studies in Language
and Literature, XI (1920), 109-10.

1162. Pontico Virunio, Ludovico.

BRITANNICAE HISTORIAE. (?)

See H. Glicksman, "Sources of Milton's History
of Britain," Wisconsin Studies in Language and
Literature, XI (1920), 110.

1163. Poole, Joshua.

> ENGLISH PARNASSUS, OR A HELP TO ENGLISH POESIE. (?)
>
>> See W. R. Parker, MILTON, pp. 507, 1062.

1164. Poole, Matthew.

> SYNOPSIS CRITICORUM ALIORUMQUE S. SCRIPTURAE IN-
> TERPRETUM. (?)
>
>> See George N. Conklin, BIBLICAL CRITICISM AND
>> HERESY IN MILTON, pp. 20, 58.

1165. Pordage, Samuel.

> MUNDORUM EXPLICATIO. (?)
>
>> See J. M. Evans, PARADISE LOST AND THE GENESIS
>> TRADITION.

1166. Powell, Thomas.

> THE ATTOURNEYS ACADEMY: OR, THE MANNER AND FORME OF
> PROCEEDING PRACTICALLY, UPON ANY SUITE, PLAINT OR
> ACTION WHATSOEVER, IN ANY COURT OF RECORD WHATSOEVER
> WITHIN THIS KINGDOME. (?)
>
>> C   YP, II, 741.

1167. POWERS TO BE RESISTED: OR A DIALOGUE ARGUING THE PARL-
> IAMENTS LAWFULL RESISTANCE OF THE POWERS NOW IN ARMES
> AGAINST THEM. (?)
>
>> See G. W. Whiting, MILTON'S LITERARY MILIEU.

1168. Primaudaye, Pierre de la.

> THE FRENCH ACADEMIE. (?)
>
>> See Kester Svendsen, MILTON AND SCIENCE.

1169. THE PRINCELY PELICAN. (*)

>> See W. R. Parker, MILTON, p. 369.

1170. Priscan of Athens.

GRAMMAR. (?)

PROL   YP, I, 284.

1171. Priscianus Caesariensis.

INSTITUTIONES GRAMMATICAE. (?)

2D   YP, IV, 664.

1172. Proclus.

DE ECLIPSIBUS EX PROCLO, in DE SPHAERA of Sacrobosco, q.v. (?)

See Allan H. Gilbert, "Milton's Textbook of
Astronomy," PMLA, XXXVIII (1923), 297-307.

1173. Procopius.

ANEKΔOTA ⌜Secret History⌝. (*)

T   YP, II, 701-02.
See H. Glicksman, "Sources of Milton's History
of Britain," Wisconsin Studies in Language and
Literature, XI (1920), 113.

1174. Procopius of Caesarea.

HISTORIARUM LIBRI VIII. Augsburg, 1607. (V)

CPB   YP, I, 416-17, 418, 488.
HB   CM, X, 101.
AP   YP, I, 873.

1175. Propertius, Sextus.

ELEGIES. (?)

PROL   YP, I, 289, 246.
DDD   YP, II, 346.
NDX   CM, ii, 1576-77.

1176. Prosper Tiro, Saint Aquitanus.

EPITOMA CHRONICON ⌜or CHRONICON CONSULARE⌝. (V)

       HB   CM, X, 97, 108, 109.

1177. Prudentius, Aurelius Clemens.

        PERISTEPHANON. (V)

           CPB   YP, I, 472.

1178. Prynne, William.

        A BREVIATE OF THE PRELATES INTOLERABLE USURPATIONS,
        BOTH UPON THE KINGS PREROGATIVE ROYALL, AND THE SUB-
        JECTS LIBERTIES. (?)

           A   YP, I, 730.

1179. Prynne, William.

        A BRIEFE MEMENTO TO THE PRESENT UNPARLIAMENTARY
        JUNTO TOUCHING THEIR PRESENT INTENTIONS AND PRO-
        CEEDINGS TO DEPOSE AND EXECUTE CHARLES STEWART,
        THEIR LAWFULL KING. (*)

           Intro.   YP, III, 44-45.
           TKM   YP, III, 195.

1180. Prynne, William.

        HIDDEN WORKS OF DARKNESS. (?)

           1D   YP, IV, 328.
           RJP   YP, IV, 913.

1181. Prynne, William.

        HISTORIOMASTIX: OR, THE PLAYERS SCOURGE AND ACT-
        ORS TRAGEDY. (?)

           See E. W. Kirby, WILLIAM PRYNNE: A STUDY IN
           PURITANISM (Cambridge, Mass., 1931), p. 27.

1182. Prynne, William.

        LAME GILES. (?)

           R   YP, I, 526.

1183. Prynne, William.

A LOOKING-GLASSE FOR ALL LORDLY PRELATES. (?)

R   YP, I, 520, 523, 590, 595, 598,
           610, 617.

1184. Prynne, William.

LORD BISHOPS NONE OF THE LORD'S BISHOPS. (?)

R   YP, I, 523, 576, 583, 590, 591,
           594, 603, 606, 609, 610, 612.

1185. Prynne, William.

THE POPISH ROYALL FAVOURITE. (*)

K   YP, III, 471, 515.
lD   YP, IV, 328.
RJP   YP, IV, 913.

1186. Prynne, William.

A QUENCH-COALE. (?)

R   YP, I, 526, 548.

1187. Prynne, William.

THE RE-PUBLICANS AND OTHERS SPURIOUS GOOD OLD
CAUSE. (?)

See W. R. Parker, MILTON, pp. 540, 1071.

1188. Prynne, William.

A TRUE AND PERFECT NARRATIVE. (?)

See W. R. Parker, MILTON, pp. 540, 1071.

1189. Prynne, William.

TWELVE CONSIDERABLE SERIOUS QUESTIONS TOUCHING
CHURCH GOVERNMENT. (V)

C   YP, II, 722-23.

1190. Psellus, Michael.

DE OPERATIONE DAEMONUM DIALOGUS. (V)

See Robert H. West, MILTON AND THE ANGELS, p. 205.

1191. Ptolemy.

GEOGRAPHIAE LIBRI OCTO GRAECO-LATINI...CUM TABULIS GEOGRAPHICIS AD MENTEM AUCTORIS RESTITUTIS PER GERARDUM MERCATOREM. (*)

See G. W. Whiting, MILTON'S LITERARY MILIEU.

1192. Pulci, Luigi.

IL MORGANTE MAGGIORE. (*)

AR   YP, II, 511.
NDX   CM, ii, 1599.

1193. Purbachius, Georgius.

NOVAE THEORICAE PLANETARUM, in Sacrobosco's DE SPHAERA, q.v. (?)

See Allen H. Gilbert, "Milton's Textbook of Astronomy," PMLA, XXXVIII (1923), 397-307.

1194. Purchas, Samuel.

HAKLUYTUS POSTHUMUS OR PURCHAS HIS PILGRIMES. London, 1625. (V)

CPB   YP, I, 368, 382-83.
HM   CM, X, 382.
See W. R. Parker, MILTON, p. 842; Leslie C. Tihany, PQ, XIII (1934), 305-6; Harris F. Fletcher, PQ, XX (1941), 501-11.

1195. Purchas, Samuel.

HIS PILGRIMAGE: OR RELATIONS OF THE WORLD AND THE RELIGIONS OBSERVED IN ALL AGES. (?)

See Robert R. Cawley, MILTON AND THE LITERATURE OF TRAVEL.

1196. Pursglove, William.

> VOIAGE TO PECHORA. (?)
>
>> HM   CM, X, 382.
>> Although Milton lists this work as one of his
>> sources for HISTORY OF MUSCOVIA, it seems more
>> likely that his true source was Purchas's
>> PILGRIMES; see no. 1194.

1197. Puteanus, Erycius.

> COMUS. (*)
>
>> See Ralph H. Singleton, "Milton's COMUS and the
>> COMUS of Erycius Puteanus," PMLA, LVIII (1943),
>> 949-57; Charles C. Mish, "COMUS and Bryce
>> Blair's VISION OF THEODORUS VERAX," MiltonN, I
>> (1967), 39-40.

1198. Quarles, Francis.

> EMBLEMS. (?)
>
>> NDX   CM, ii, 1607.

1199. Quarles, Francis.

> HISTORIE OF SAMSON, in DIVINE POEMS. (?)
>
>> See G. W. Whiting, MILTON'S LITERARY MILIEU.

1200. Quintilian ₍Marcus Fabius Quintilianus₎.

> INSTITUTIO ORATORIA. (V)
>
>> COR   YP, I, 331.
>> E   YP, II, 384.
>> LO   CM, XI, 21, 27, 113, 129, 205, 209,
>>   213, 223, 471.
>> See Donald L. Clark, JOHN MILTON AT ST. PAUL'S
>> SCHOOL.

1201. Quintus Smyrnaeus ₍Quintus Calaber₎.

> TROIA EXPUGNATA; SEU SUPPLEMENTUM HOMERI. ₍POST-
> HOMERICA₎. (V)

```
        E          YP, II, 401.
        2D         YP, IV, 595.


RACOVIAN CATECHISM.  See CATECHESIS ECCLESIARUM.


1202.  Rainolds, John.

        A DEFENCE OF THE JUDGMENT OF THE REFORMED CHURCHES.
        (?)

            Intro.      YP, I, 117.


1203.  Rainolds, John.

        JUDGEMENT OF DOCTOR REIGNOLDS CONCERNING EPISCOPACY,
        WHETHER IT BE GODS ORDINANCE.  EXPRESSED IN A LET-
        TER TO SIR FRANCIS KNOWLS...1588.  (V)

            Intro.      YP, I, 116.
            CG          YP, I, 763.


1204.  Rainolds, John.

        THE ORIGINALL OF BISHOPS AND METROPOLITANS: THE
        JUDGEMENT OF DOCTOR RAINOLDES, in CERTAIN BRIEFE
        TREATISES, q.v.  (V)

            Intro.      YP, I, 194.


1205.  Rainolds, John.

        THE OVERTHROW OF STAGE-PLAYES.  (?)

            Intro.      YP, I, 117.


1206.  Rainolds, John.

        SCRIPTA ANGLICANA.  (V)

            T           YP, II, 709-10.


1207.  Ralegh, Sir Walter.

        THE CABINET-COUNCIL: CONTAINING THE CHEIF ARTS OF
        EMPIRE, AND MUSTERIES OF STATE: DISCABINETED.  Lon-
        don, 1658.  (V)
```

Milton published Sir Walter's manuscript after
coming into possession of it upon the death of
"a Learned Man." CM, XVIII, 272-73.

1208. Ralegh, Sir Walter.

THE DISCOVERIE OF THE LARGE, RICH AND BEAUTIFUL EM-
PYRE OF GUIANA. (*)

See Robert R. Cawley, MILTON AND THE LITERATURE
OF TRAVEL.

1209. Ralegh, Sir Walter.

HISTORY OF THE WORLD. (V)

CPB   YP, I, 411.
See G. W. Whiting, MILTON'S LITERARY MILIEU,
pp. 39-63.

1210. Ramus, Peter.

CICERONIANUS. (?)

LOR   CM, XI, 507.

1211. Ramus, Peter.

DIALECTICAE...CUM COMMENTARIUS GEORGII DOWNAMI AN-
NEXIS. (*)

A   YP, I, 672.
LO   CM, XI, 5, 7, 19, 21, 57, 75, 83,
             105, 117, 127, 131, 147, 215, 217,
             231, 233, 255, 295, 297, 329, 355,
             395, 431, 487.
NDX   CM, ii, 1614-15.

1212. Ramus, Peter.

SCHOLAE DIALECTICAE OR ARISTOTELICAE ANIMADVERSI-
ONES. (?)

LO   CM, XI, 3, 487.
LOR   CM, XI, 501.

1213. Ramus, Peter.

SCHOLARUM PHYSICARUM. (?)

      LOR   CM, XI, 509.

1214. Ramus, Peter.

      VIA REGIA AD GEOMETRIAM. (*)

        E   YP, II, 386.

1215. Randolph, Thomas.

      ARISTIPPUS, OR THE JOVIAL PHILOSOPHER. (?)

        NDX   CM, ii, 1615.

1216. Randolph, Thomas.

      JOURNAL. (V)

            HM   CM, X, 382.
            CPB   YP, I, 465.
            An account of Randolph's adventures in Russia
            is in Hakluyt's THE PRINCIPALL NAVIGATIONS, q.
            v.

1217. Randolph, Thomas.

      POEMS. (?)

            COR   YP, I, 341.
            See J. S. Smart, THE SONNETS OF MILTON, p. 46.

1218. Rashi ₍Rabbi Solomon bar Isaac₎.

      PENTATEUCH WITH...COMMENTARY. (?)

            See Sr. M. I. Corcoran, MILTON'S PARADISE.
            Rashi's COMMENTARIES were included in Bux-
            torf's Bible, q.v.

1219. Ravenscroft, Thomas.

      DEUTEROMELIA: OR THE SECOND PART OF MUSICKS MELO-
      DIE. (?)

        C   YP, II, 741.

1220. Ravenscroft, Thomas.

>   WHOLE BOOK OF PSALMES. (?)

>> This work has music by John Milton, Sr., in it.
>> See W. R. Parker, MILTON, p. 800.

1221. Regio Monte, Ioannis de.

>   EXPOSITIO XXII EX LIBRO TERTIO EPITOMAE IOANNIS DE
>   REGIO MONTE IN ALMAGESTUM PTOLEMAEI, in DE SPHAERA
>   of Sacrobosco, q.v. (?)

>> See Allan H. Gilbert, "Milton's Textbook of
>> Astronomy," PMLA, XXXVIII (1923), 297-307.

1222. Ripa, Cesare.

>   DELLA PIU CHE NOVISSIMA ICONOLOGIA DI CESARE RIPA
>   PERUGINO...AMPLIATA DAL SIG. CAV. GIO. ZARATINO
>   CASTELLINI ROMANO. (?)

>> See John M. Steadman, "Urania, Wisdom, and
>> Scriptural Exegesis," Neophilologus, XLVII
>> (1963), 61-73.

1223. Rivet, André.

>   COMMENTARIUS IN LIBRUM SECUNDUM MOSIS, QUI EXODUS
>   APUD GRAECOS INSCRIBITUR, in OPERUM THEOLOGICORUM
>   QUAE LATINE EDIDIT. (V)

>> CPB   YP, I, 466-67.

1224. Rivet, André.

>   EXERCITATIONES IN GENESIN, in OPERA THEOLOGICA. (?)

>> See Arnold Williams, "Milton and Commentaries
>> on Genesis," MP, XXXVII (1940), 263-78.

1225. Rivet, André.

>   PRAELECTIONES IN CAPUT XX EXODI. (V)

>> CPB   YP, I, 419, 466.
>> See W. R. Parker, MILTON, p. 883.

1226. Rivet, André.

       THEOLOGICAE & SCHOLASTICAE EXERCITATIONES CXC IN
       GENESIN. (V)

          DDD   YP, II, 246, 297.

1227. Rivet, André.

       TRACTATUS TERTIUS, in OPERUM THEOLOGICORUM. (*)

          T   YP, II, 659.

1228. Robinson, Henry.

       AN ANSWER TO MR. WILLIAM PRYNN'S TWELVE QUESTIONS.
       (?)

          AR   YP, II, 569.
          Intro.   YP, II, 88.

1229. Robinson, Henry.

       THE FALSEHOOD OF MR. WILLIAM PRYN'S TRUTH TRIUMPH-
       ING. (?)

          Intro.   YP, II, 121.

1230. Robinson, Henry.

       JOHN THE BAPTIST, FORERUNNER OF CHRIST JESUS. (?)

          Intro.   YP, II, 87-88.
          AR   YP, II, 542, 546.

1231. Robinson, Henry.

       LIBERTY OF CONSCIENCE. (*)

          Intro.   YP, II, 83-84.
          AR   YP, II, 569.
          Intro.   YP, III, 67.
          Although I, personally, find little evidence
          to certify Milton's acquaintance with Robin-
          son's LIBERTY OF CONSCIENCE, Ernest Sirluck
          seems convinced, and I bow to his superior
          knowledge.

1232. Roger of Hoveden.

> CHRONICA. Ed. Sir Roger Savile, in RERUM ANGLICARUM SCRIPTORES POST BEDAM, q.v. (V)
>
>> HB   CM, X, 180, 181, 195, 201, 223, 240, 242, 252, 307.
>> See H. Glicksman, "Sources of Milton's History of Britain," <u>Wisconsin Studies in Language and Literature</u>, XI (1920), 105-44; Constance Nicholas, INTRODUCTION AND NOTES TO MILTON'S HISTORY OF BRITAIN, p. 105.

1233. Rogers, Daniel.

> MATRIMONIALL HONOUR. (?)
>
>> See William Haller, "Hail Wedded Love," <u>ELH</u>, XIII (1946), 79-97.

Romanus, St. Clement. See Clement.

1234. Rosse, Alexander.

> COMMENTUM DE TERRAE MOTU CIRCULARI. (?)
>
>> See Grant McColley, PARADISE LOST.

1235. Rosse, Alexander.

> THE FIRST BOOKE OF QUESTIONS AND ANSWERS UPON GENESIS. (?)
>
>> See J. M. Evans, PARADISE LOST AND THE GENESIS TRADITION.

1236. Rosse, Alexander.

> MEL HELICONIUM: OR, POETICAL HONEY, GATHERED OUT OF THE WEEDS OF PARNASSUS. (?)
>
>> MAR   CM, XVIII, 376, 589.
>> Milton's alleged autograph is in the New York Public Library copy. See footnote nine in Grant McColley's "Milton's Dialogue on Astronomy: the Principal Immediate Sources," <u>PMLA</u>, LII (1937), 729.

1237.   Rosse, Alexander.

> THE NEW PLANET NO PLANET; OR, THE EARTH NO WANDER-
> ING STAR. (V)
>
> > See J. M. Evans, PARADISE LOST AND THE GENESIS
> > TRADITION.

1238.   Rosse, Alexander.

> PANSEBEIA; OR, A VIEW OF ALL RELIGIONS IN THE WORLD.
> (V)
>
> > See Grant McColley, "The Epic Catalogue of
> > PARADISE LOST," ELH, IV (1937), 180-91.

1239.   Rota, Bernardino.

> SONNETTI ET CANZONI. (?)
>
> > NDX   CM, ii, 1699.
> > See J. S. Smart, THE SONNETS OF MILTON, pp. 37,
> > 111.

1240.   Rovai, Francesco.

> POEMS. (?)
>
> > COR   YP, II, 767.
> > Other than a remark by Dati, there is no evi-
> > dence that Milton knew Rovai's poetry; more-
> > over, Dati's letter is dated 1647, and Rovai's
> > POEMS were not published until 1652 (in Florece,
> > edited by Niccolo Rovai, perhaps a brother of
> > the poet).

1241.   Rowland, John.

> POLEMICA, SIVE SUPPLEMENTUM AD APOLOGIAM ANONYMAN.
> (V)
>
> > See W. R. Parker, MILTON, p. 433.

1242.   Rowland, John.

> PRO REGE & POPULO ANGLICANO APOLOGIA CONTRA JOHAN-
> NIS POLYPRAGMATICI...DEFENSIONEM. (V)

```
          SD          YP, IV, 698, 767.
          RJP         YP, IV, 875 ff.
```

1243. Rupertus.

DE OPERIBUS SANCTAE TRINITATIS. (?)

See Sr. M. I. Corcoran, MILTON'S PARADISE.

1244. Rutherford, Samuel.

LEX, REX: THE LAW AND THE PRINCE. (?)

Intro.   YP, III, 77 ff.

1245. Rutilius Namatianus, Claudius.

DE REDITU SUO ITINERARIUM. (?)

HB   CM, X, 98.

1246. Ryff, Petrus.

QUAESTIONES GEOMETRICAE, IN EUCLIDIS ET P. RAMI
ΣΤΟΙΧΕΙΩΣΙΝ. (?)

E   YP, II, 387.

Saadiah ₍Gaon₎. Commentator on Book of Daniel in Buxtorf's Bible, q.v.

1247. Sabellicus, Cocceius ₍Marco Antonio Coccio Sabellico₎.

RAPSODIAE HISTORICAE ENNEADUM. (V)

HB   CM, X, 106.

Sabi, Dom.
          MAR   CM, XVIII, 304.
          Possibly Angelus Sabinus or Georgius Sabinus,
          both of whom were editors of numerous classical
          works. Of the two, Angelus Sabinus is the more
          probable, for he emended a piece by Lactantius,
          q.v., in the WORKS (Rome, 1474).

1248. Sacro Bosco, Johannes de ₍John Halifax of Holywood₎.

DE SPHAERA. (V)

E   YP, II, 387, 389, 392.
See Allen H. Gilbert, "Milton's Textbook of
Astronomy," PMLA, XXXVIII (1923), 297-307.

1249. Sadlar, John.

RIGHTS OF THE KINGDOM. (V)

K   YP, III, 399.

1250. Sallust ₍Sallustinus Crispus, Gaius₎.

BELLUM CATILINAE. (V)

CG   YP, I, 812.
AP   YP, I, 903.
K   YP, III, 441.
1D   YP, IV, 350, 442.
SD   YP, IV, 744.

1251. Sallust.

BELLUM IUGURTHINUM. (V)

1D   YP, IV, 349, 442, 512.

1252. Sallust.

HISTORIAE. (*)

E   YP, II, 400.
COR   CM, XII, 90-94.
See Donald L. Clark, JOHN MILTON AT ST. PAUL'S
SCHOOL.

Salmasius. See Claude de Saumaise.

Salzilli, Giovanni. Roman literary friend of Milton;
See Milton's Latin verses, "Ad Salsillum."

Sancta Clara. See Christopher Davenport.

1253. Sandys, Sir Edwin.

EUROPAE SPECULUM, OR A VIEW OR SURVEY OF THE STATE
OF RELIGION IN THE WESTERN PARTS OF THE WORLD. (V)

R   YP, I, 553.

1254. Sandys, George.

CHRIST'S PASSION: A TRAGEDY. (?)

A verse translation of Grotius's Latin, q.v.

1255. Sandys, George.

OVID'S METAMORPHOSIS ENGLISHED. (?)

See M. Y. Hughes, JOHN MILTON: COMPLETE POEMS
AND MAJOR PROSE, pp. 25, 420.

1256. Sandys, George.

PARAPHRASE UPON THE DIVINE POEMS. (?)

See M. Y. Hughes, JOHN MILTON: COMPLETE POEMS
AND MAJOR PROSE, p. 473.

1257. Sandys, George.

A RELATION OF A JOURNEY BEGUN ANNO DOM. 1610. (*)

NDX   CM, ii, 1724.
See M. Y. Hughes, JOHN MILTON: COMPLETE POEMS
AND MAJOR PROSE, pp. 550, 590; Robert R. Caw-
ley, MILTON AND THE LITERATURE OF TRAVEL.

1258. Sannazaro, Jacopo.

DE PARTU VIRGINIS. LAMENTATIO DE MORTE CHRISTI,
PISCATORIA. (*)

NDX   CM, ii, 1725.
See M. Y. Hughes, MILTON'S MINOR POEMS, pp.
xix-xx.

Sappho.
NDX   CM, ii, 1725.
Milton apparently read a fragment of Sappho's

216

preserved by a scholiast on Sophocles, ELECTRA, V, 148.

1259. Sarpi, Paolo.

HISTORIA DEL CONCILIO TRIDENTINO. (V)

CPB	YP, I, 396, 397, 398, 402, 406-07, 424, 451, 467, 500, 501, 502.
R	YP, I, 581, 595.
K	YP, III, 511, 589.

1260. Sarpi, Pietro.

HISTORY OF THE INQUISITION. (*)

A   YP, II, 492, 503.

1261. Saumaise, Claude de.

AD IOANNEM MILTONUM RESPONSIO. (*)

See J. M. French, THE LIFE RECORDS OF JOHN MILTON, V, 461.

1262. Saumaise, Claude de.

DE EPISCOPIS AC PRESBYTERIS, CONTRA D. PETAVIUM LOIOLITAM DISSERTATIO PRIMA. (V)

CG	YP, I, 781.
1D	YP, IV, 391, 397, 429, 449.
2D	YP, IV, 563.

1263. Saumaise, Claude de.

DEFENSIO REGIA PRO CAROLO I. (V)

2D	YP, IV, 559 ff.
RJP	YP, IV, 889 ff.

1264. Saumaise, Claude de.

LIBRORUM DE PRIMATU PAPAE, PARS PRIMA, CUM APPARATU ACCEDERE DE OEDEM PRIMATU, NILI & BARLAAMI TRACTATUS. (V)

```
        1D          YP, IV, 314 ff.
        2D          YP, IV, 563, 601.
        RJP         YP, IV, 919.
```

1265. Saumaise, Claude de.

PLINIANAE EXERCITATIONES IN CAII JULII SOLINI POLY-
HISTORIA. (?)

```
        1D          YP, IV, 461.
        2D          YP, IV, 569.
```

1266. Saumaise, Claude de.

SIMPLICII COMMENTARIUS IN ENCHIRIDION EPICTETI. (?)

```
        1D          YP, IV, 430.
```

1267. Savile, Sir Henry, ed.

RERUM ANGLICARUM SCRIPTORES POST BEDAM PRAECIPUI,
EX VETUSTISSIMIS CODICIBUS MANUSCRIPTIS NUNC PRI-
MUM IN LUCEM EDITI. (V)

```
        CPB         YP, I, 369-70, 386, 388, 390, 450,
                      452.
```
Savile's anthology includes works by:
William of Malmsbury, Henry of Huntingdon, q.
v., Roger of Hovedon, q.v., Ingulf, q.v.

1268. Savonarola, Girolamo.

ORACOLO DELLA RENOVATIONE DELLA CHIESA. Venice,
1560. (V)

```
        CPB         YP, I, 423.
        A           YP, I, 683.
```

Scaliger, Joseph Juste. Ed. Lycophron's ALEXANDRA,
q.v., and Marcus Manilius's ASTRONOMICON, q.v.

1269. Scaliger, Julius Caesar.

POETICES. (V)

```
        AP          YP, I, 879.
```

1270. Schickhard, William.

      JUS REGIUM HEBRAEORUM E TENEBRIS RABBINICIS ERUTUM
      & LUCI DONATUM. (V)

          CPB   YP, I, 460.
          1D   YP, IV, 350, 355.
          See W. R. Parker, MILTON, p. 883.

1271. Schindler, Valentinus.

      LEXICON PENTAGLOTTON. (?)

          See George N. Conklin, BIBLICAL CRITICISM AND
          HERESY IN MILTON, pp. 13-14, 57-58, 63.

1272. Schneidewein ₍Oinotomus₎, Johann.

      IN QUATTUOR INSTITUTIONUM IMPERIALIUM JUSTINIANI
      IMP. LIBROS COMMENTARII. (V)

          C   YP, II, 754.

1273. Schotti ₍Schott₎, Andraeus.

      OBSERVATIONUM HUMANARUM. (V)

          MAR   CM, XVIII, 320.

1274. Scot, Reginald.

      THE DISCOVERIE OF WITCHCRAFT...A TREATISE UPON THE
      NATURE AND SUBSTANCE OF SPIRITS AND DIVELS. (?)

          See Grant McColley, PARADISE LOST; Robert H.
          West, MILTON AND THE ANGELS.

1275. Scot, Thomas.

      PHILOMYTHIE, OR PHILOMYTHOLOGIE. (?)

          See Sr. M. I. Corcoran, MILTON'S PARADISE.

      Scribonius. See Daniel Widdowes.

1276. Scudamore, James, trans.

THE SIXTY-SIX ADMONITORY CHAPTERS OF BASILIUS TO HIS
SON LEO. (?)

 T   YP, II, 703.
 See W. R. Parker, MILTON, p. 817.

1277. Sedgwick, William.

 A SECOND VIEW OF THE ARMY REMONSTRANCE. (?)

  See G. W. Whiting, MILTON'S LITERARY MILIEU.

1278. Seissel, Claude de.

 LA GRAND MONARCHIE DE FRANCE. Trans. Johannes Sleidan, DE MONARCHIA FRANCIAE SIVE DE REPUBLICA GALLIAE
 ET REGUM OFFICIIS. (V)

  CPB   YP, I, 549, 494, 495.
  TKM   YP, III, 200.
  RJP   YP, IV, 948.

1279. Selden, John.

 DE DIIS SYRIIS. (?)

  NDX   CM, ii, 1765.

1280. Selden, John.

 DE IURE NATURALI & GENTIUM, IUXTA DISCIPLINAM
 EBRAEORUM. London, 1640. (V)

  CPB   YP, I, 403.
  DDD   YP, II, 350.
  AR   YP, II, 513.
  1D   YP, IV, 422.
  See Eivion Owen, "Milton and Selden on Divorce,"
  SP, XLII (1946), 233-57; Arthur Barker, MILTON
  AND THE PURITAN DILEMMA, pp. 114 ff.; W. R. Par-
  ker, MILTON, p. 883.

1281. Selden, John.

 ILLUSTRATIONS, in Drayton's POLY-OLBION, q.v. (?)

  A   YP, II, 529.

1282. Selden, John.

UXOR HEBRAICA, SEU DE NUPTIIS & DIVORTIS EX IURE
CIVILI, ID EST, DIVINO & TALMUDICO, VETERUM EBRAE-
ORUM, LIBRI TRES. London, 1646. (V)

CPB	YP, I, 402.
2D	YP, IV, 625.
CD	CM, XV, 171.
H	CM, VI, 72.

Selden, John, ed. Sir John Fortescue's DE LAUDIBUS
LEGUM ANGLIAE, q.v.

1283. Seneca, Lucius Annaeus.

OPERA. (?)

See Donald L. Clark, JOHN MILTON AT ST. PAUL'S
SCHOOL.

1284. Seneca, Lucius Annaeus.

THE WORKES OF LUCIUS ANNAEUS SENECA. Trans. Thomas
Lodge. (?)

MAR	CM, XVIII, 579-80.
NDX	CM, ii, 1768.

1285. Seneca, Lucius Annaeus.

AD LUCILIUM, in EPISTOLAE MORALES. (*)

1D	YP, IV, 456.
SD	YP, IV, 699.
RJP	YP, IV, 953.

1286. Seneca, Lucius Annaeus.

DE BENEFICIIS. (V)

C	YP, II, 745.
1D	YP, IV, 456.

1287. Seneca, Lucius Annaeus.

HERCULES FURENS. (V)

221

```
        TKM          YP, III, 213.
        1D           YP, IV, 446.
        2D           YP, IV, 590-91.
```

1288. Seneca, Lucius Annaeus.

   HERCULES OETAEUS. (?)

```
        COR          YP, II, 769, 772.
```

1289. Seneca, Lucius Annaeus.

   QUESTIONES NATURALES. (V)

```
        E            YP, II, 390, 392.
```

1290. Seneca, Lucius Annaeus.

   THE TROJAN WOMEN. (?)

   See Gerald Stacy, "The Senecan Messenger in
   SAMSON AGONISTES," Forum, XIV, iv (1973), 32-
   35.

1291. Servius, Marius [or Maurus Servius Honoratus].

   COMMENTARY ON VERGIL. (*)

```
        MS           CM, XVIII, 234.
        NDX          CM, ii, 1779.
```

1292. Severus, Sulpitius.

   SACRAE HISTORIAE LIBRI DUO. (V)

```
        CPB          YP, I, 415-16, 440.
        R            YP, I, 538, 543, 545, 553, 557, 558,
                     568, 574.
        P            YP, I, 647.
        A            YP, I, 944.
        K            YP, III, 519.
        1D           YP, IV, 349, 432.
        H            CM, VI, 89.
```

   Seyssel, Claude. See Seissel.

1293. Shakespeare, William.

WORKS. ₍First folio.₎ (?)

NDX   CM, ii, 1782-83.
See Alwin Thaler, "The Shakespearian Element
in Milton," PMLA, XL (1925), 645-91; George
Coffin Taylor, "Shakespeare and Milton Again,"
SP, XXIII (1926), 189-99.

1294. Shakespeare, William.

WORKS. ₍Second folio.₎ (*)

See W. R. Parker, MILTON, p. 120; Ethel Seaton,
"COMUS and Shakespeare," ESEA, XXXI (1945), 68-
80.

1295. Shakespeare, William.

AS YOU LIKE IT. (?)

C   YP, II, 756.
Perhaps a Shakespearean allusion, but the comparison of the life of a man to "a Scene" was
almost proverbial.

1296. Shakespeare, William.

RICHARD THE THIRD. (V)

K   YP, III, 361.

1297. Shakespeare, William.

VENUS AND ADONIS. (*)

See Herman Schaus, "Relationship of COMUS to
HERO AND LEANDER and VENUS AND ADONIS," University of Texas Studies in English, XXV (1946),
129-41.

1298. Shakespeare, William.

THE WINTER'S TALE. (?)

See James H. Sims, "Perdita's 'Flowers O' th'
Spring' and 'Vernal Flowers' in LYCIDAS," SQ,
XXII, i, 87-90.

1299. Sidney, Sir Philip.

ARCADIA. (V)

```
CPB          YP, I, 371, 372, 463, 464.
AR           YP, II, 525.
K            YP, III, 362, 363, 366.
NDX          CM, ii, 1791.
```

1300. Sidney, Sir Philip.

THE DEFENSE OF POESIE. (V)

```
AP           YP, I, 811, 813, 816, 817, 818.
```

1301. Sigebert of Gembloux.

CHRONICA SIGEBERTI GEMBLACENSIS. (?)

```
HB           CM, X, 128, 161, 162, 163, 165,
             167, 169, 181, 182, 183, 185.
```

1302. Sigonius, Carolus.

COMMENTARY ON THE SACRED HISTORY OF BLESSED SUL-
PICIUS SEVERUS. (V)

```
CPB          YP, I, 575.
```

1303. Sigonius, Carolus.

DE REGNO ITALIAE. (V)

```
CPB          YP, I, 444, 478, 489.
1D           YP, IV, 420.
R            YP, I, 478-79.
See W. R. Parker, MILTON, p. 150.
```

1304. Sigonius, Carolus.

DE REPUBLICA HEBRAEORUM. (V)

```
CPB          YP, I, 575.
```

1305. Sigonius, Carolus.

HISTORIARUM DE OCCIDENTALI IMPERIO. (V)

```
CPB        YP, I, 375, 431, 437.
HB         CM, X, 92, 93, 97, 101, 112, 205.
```
See H. Glicksman, "Sources of Milton's History
of Britian," Wisconsin Studies in Language and
Literature, XI (1920), 105-44. Constance
Nicholas believes Milton used the 1593 edition
of Sigonius; see INTRODUCTION AND NOTES TO MIL-
TON'S HISTORY OF BRITAIN, p. 61. Ruth Mohl,
on the other hand, prefers Wechel's edition
(Frankfurt, 1618); see her notes in the Yale
Prose.

1306. Sikes, George.

THE LIFE AND DEATH OF SIR HENRY VANE. (*)

```
NDX        CM, ii, 1794.
```
See also a note on page 656 of vol.XVIII
of the Columbia Milton.

1307. Silius Italicus.

PUNICA. (?)

```
NDX        CM, ii, 1795.
```
See Donald L. Clark, JOHN MILTON AT ST. PAUL'S
SCHOOL.

1308. Simeon of Durham.

DE OBSESSIONE DUNELMI, in Twysden's HISTORIAE ANGLI-
CANAE SCRIPTORES X, q.v. (V)

```
HB         CM, X, 180-315 passim.
NDX        CM, ii, 1796.
```

1309. Simeon of Durham.

HISTORIA DE DUNELMENSI ECCLESIA, in Twysden's
HISTORIAE ANGLICANAE SCRIPTORES X, q.v. (V)

```
HB         CM, X, 180-315 passim.
NDX        CM, ii, 1796.
```

1310. Simeon of Durham.

HISTORIA DE GESTIS REGUM ANGLORUM, in Twysden's
HISTORIAE ANGLICANAE SCRIPTORES X, q.v. (V)

```
HB          CM, X, 180-315 passim.
NDX         CM, ii, 1796.
```

1311. Simeon Metaphrastes.

ACTS OF PETER AND PAUL, or COMMENTARY ON SAINTS
PETER AND PAUL. (?)

P   YP, I, 647.
Although Milton spoke knowingly of "fabulous
Metaphrastes," I have yet to make his acquaint-
ance.

Simplicius. Commentator on EPICTITUS, q.v.

1312. Sinibaldus, Johann Benedict.

GENEANTHROPEIA ₍TEN BOOKS ON THE GENERATION OF
MAN₎. Rome, 1642. (V)

CPB   YP, I, 414.

Sinnamus, Johannes. See Cinnamus.

1313. Skelton, John.

MAGNYFYCENCE, A GOODLY INTERLUDE. (?)

See Robert L. Ramsay, "Morality Themes in Milton's Poetry," SP, XV (1918), 150.

1314. Sleidan, Johannes ₍Johann Philippson₎.

COMMENTARII DE STATU RELIGIONIS ET REIPUBLICAE,
CAROLO QUINTO, CAESARE. Strassburg, 1555. (V)

CPB   YP, I, 373, 381, 390, 436, 456,
             497, 499, 504, 505.
AP   YP, I, 901.
MB   YP, II, 428.
TKM   YP, III, 223, 243.
K   YP, III, 443-44, 468, 533.
H   CM, VI, 82.
See W. R. Parker, MILTON, p. 882. The editors
of the Yale Prose call attention to two trans-
lations: A FAMOUSE CRONICLE OF OURE TIME, CAL-
LED SLEIDANES COMMENTARIES...TRANSLATED...BY
IHON DAUS (London, 1560), and a translation

by Edmund Bohun (London, 1589); see YP, III, 443, 533.

1315. Smalcius, Valentin.

REFUTATIO THESIUM...FRANTZII. (?)

See George N. Conklin, BIBLICAL CRITICISM AND HERESY IN MILTON, pp. 82-83.

1316. Smectymnuus.

AN ANSWER TO A BOOKE ENTITULED, AN HUMBLE REMON-STRANCE. (V)

Intro.   YP, I, 78, 84.

1317. Smectymnuus.

A VINDICATION OF THE ANSWER TO THE HUMBLE REMON-STRANCE, FROM THE UNJUST IMPUTATIONS OF FRIVOLOUS-NESSE AND FALSEHOOD. (V)

Intro.   YP, I, 78, 84.

1318. Smith, George.

ENGLANDS PRESSURES: OR, THE PEOPLES COMPLAINT. (?)

See G. W. Whiting, MILTON'S LITERARY MILIEU.

1319. Smith, Henry.

PREPARATIVE TO MARRIAGE. (?)

See William Haller, "Hail Wedded Love," ELH, XIII (1946), 79-97.

1320. Smith, James, and Sir John Mennes.

WIT RESTOR'D IN SEVERALL SELECT POEMS NOT FORMERLY PUBLISH'T. (?)

See W. R. Parker, MILTON, p. 499.

1321. Smith, Richard.

VILLATIONIS SUAE DE MEDIO ANIMARUM STATU RATIO
EPISCOPO CHALCEDONENSI. Trans. Thomas White as
THE MIDDLE STATE OF SOULS. (?)

See J. M. French, THE LIFE RECORDS OF JOHN
MILTON, IV, 274; CM, XVIII, 656 notes an
alleged Milton autograph.

1322. Smith, Sir Thomas.

COMMONWEALTH OF ENGLAND. (V)

CPB	YP, I, 420, 440, 442, 443, 453, 454.
TKM	YP, III, 221.
1D	YP, IV, 476.
R	YP, I, 539.

See W. R. Parker, MILTON, p. 842.

1323. Smith, Sir Thomas.

DE RECTA ET EMENDATA LINGUAE GRAECAE PRONUNTIATIONE.
(?)

To which is appended a tract advocating reform
of the English alphabet. Proper pronunciation
was long of prime interest to Milton; perhaps
he knew this work as well as others of Sir
Thomas.

1324. Smith, Sir Thomas.

SIR THOMAS SMITHES VOIAGE AND ENTERTAINMENT IN RUS-
SIA. (?)

HM   CM, X, 378, 379, 382.
Milton's knowledge of Sir Thomas's embassy to
Russia probably came from Purchas, q.v. See
also Robert R. Cawley, MILTON AND THE LITERATURE
OF TRAVEL.

1325. Socinus, Faustus, the Elder.

PRAELECTIONES THEOLOGICAE. ₍Vol. I of the BIBLIO-
THECA FRATRUM POLONORUM.₎ (?)

See George N. Conklin, BIBLICAL CRITICISM AND
HERESY IN MILTON, pp. 43-44.

1326.   Socrates Scholasticus.

       CHURCH HISTORY, in ECCLESIASTICAE HISTORIAE AUTORES.
       (V)

CPB	YP, I, 376-77, 380, 383, 393-94, 400, 406, 417-18, 433.
R	YP, I, 577.
AP	YP, I, 944.
AR	YP, II, 509.
HB	CM, X, 97.
P	YP, I, 634.
R	YP, I, 556, 562.

       See W. R. Parker, MILTON, pp. 146, 149, 802-
       03.

1327.   Solinus, Gaius Julius.

       POLYHISTORIA.   Ed. Salmasius, in PLINIANAE EXERCIT-
       ATIONES IN CAII JULII SOLINI POLYHISTORIA.   (*)

1D	YP, IV, 461.
2D	YP, IV, 569-70.
HB	CM, X, 50.
E	YP, II, 391.

      Solon.
       In OF EDUCATION Milton recommends the "extol'd
       remains" of several Greek law-givers, includ-
       ing Solon. None of Solon's writings were avail-
       able to Milton, however; he knew him by rep-
       utation only, probably through Plutarch and
       Aristotle.   See YP, II, 398-99; NDX, CM, ii,
       1825.

1328.   Sophocles.

       TRAGEDIES OF SOPHOCLES.   (*)

E	YP, II, 398.
NDX	CM, ii, 1836.

1329.   Sophocles.

       AJAX.   (*)

C	YP, II, 729.

1330. Sophocles.

  ANTIGONE. (V)

    1D   YP, IV, 441.
    2D   YP, IV, 585.

1331. Sophocles.

  ELECTRA. (V)

    CG   YP, I, 905.

1332. Sophocles.

  OEDIPUS TYRANNUS. (V)

    CG   YP, I, 803.
    1D   YP, IV, 440-41.

1333. Sophocles.

  TRACHINIAE. (V)

    E   YP, II, 398.

  Sophron Mimus.
    Fragments of Sophron's works remain; he is
    known, however, mainly through quotations of
    grammarians who use his famous mimes to il-
    lustrate the Doric dialect and by reputation,
    for he was highly regarded in antiquity.
    Milton twice cites Plato's fondness for Soph-
    ron's works, gets the fact from Diogenes
    Laertius, q.v. See
    AP   YP, I, 879.
    AR   YP, II, 523.

1334. Southam, Thomas.

  VOYAGES OF SOUTHAM. (?)

    HM   CM, X, 382.
    Milton's reference is probably the account
    found in Hakluyt's PRINCIPALL NAVIGATIONS,
    q.v.

1335. Sozomen, Hermius Salamanes.

>HISTORIA, in ECCLESIASTICAE HISTORIAE AUTORES.
>(V)
>
>| | |
>|---|---|
>| CPB | YP, I, 376-77, 398. |
>| R | YP, I, 555, 556, 562. |
>| K | YP, III, 513, 517. |
>| 1D | YP, IV, 416, 418. |
>| H | CM, VI, 64. |
>| HB | CM, X, 99, 100, 149. |

1336. Spanheim, Friedrich.

>DUBIORUM EVANGELICORUM. (V)
>
>| | |
>|---|---|
>| T | YP, II, 675. |
>| 2D | YP, IV, 567, 630. |
>| SD | YP, IV, 727-28, 787. |

1337. Sparke, John.

>VOYAGES OF SPARKS. (?)
>
>| | |
>|---|---|
>| HM | CM, X, 382. |
>
>Milton's reference is probably to Hakluyt's
>PRINCIPALL NAVIGATIONS, q.v.

1338. Spartianus, Aelius.

>HADRIANI, CARACALLI, DIDIUS JULIANUS, etc., in
>SCRIPTORES HISTORIAE AUGUSTAE, q.v. (V)
>
>| | |
>|---|---|
>| K | YP, III, 337. |
>| HB | CM, X, 81, 84, 86, 87. |
>| 1D | YP, IV, 341, 360, 448, 450. |

1339. Speed, John.

>HISTORIE OF GREAT BRITAINE. London, 1623. (V)
>
>| | |
>|---|---|
>| CPB | YP, I, 378, 387, 389, 396, 400-01, 419, 426, 427, 428, 445, 447, 448, 449, 454, 458, 463, 479, 480, 485, 486, 487, 493, 494, 502. |
>| R | YP, I, 525, 528, 529, 530, 531, 532, 533, 554, 580, 581, 586, 587. |
>| K | YP, III, 343. |
>
>See Constance Nicholas, INTRODUCTION AND NOTES

231

TO MILTON'S HISTORY OF BRITAIN, p. 17. Professor Nicholas is convinced Milton used the 1627 edition of Speed. See W. R. Parker, MILTON, p. 842.

Speiss-Hammer, Johannes. See Cuspianus.

1340. Spelman, Sir Henry.

CONCILIA, DECRETA...IN RE ECCLESIASTICA ORBIS BRITANNIAE. (V)

CFB   YP, I, 449.
HB   CM, X, 148.
H   CM, VI, 71
See H. Glicksman, "Sources of Milton's History of Britain," Wisconsin Studies in Language and Literature, XI (1920), 105-44.

1341. Spencer, John.

DE LEGIBUS HEBRAEORUM RITUALIBUS ET EARUM RATIONIBUS LIBRI TRES. (?)

Harris F. Fletcher says of DE LEGIBUS, "It would, of course, have been completely unknown to ⌐Milton¬ as a book, although he may have known the author and have been familiar with the whole project of the book" (MILTON'S RABBINICAL READINGS, p. 294). As usual, Professor Fletcher covers himself with maybe's and might-have-been's, but the space and attention given to the book leads one to believe that he considers it a major influence on the intellectual development of John Milton.

1342. Spenser, Edmund.

THE FAERIE QUEEN: THE SHEPHEARDS CALENDER, TOGETHER WITH THE OTHER WORKS OF ENGLAND'S ARCH-POET. (V)

CG   YP, I, 857.
AR   YP, II, 516.
K   YP, III, 390.
HB   CM, X, 17.
A   YP, I, 722-23.
NDX   CM, ii, 1849-50.
See Edwin Greenlaw, "A Better Teacher than Aquinas," SP, XIV (1917), 196-217; "Spenser's

Influence on PARADISE LOST," SP, XVII (1920), 320-59.

Spenser, Edmund.
A VIEW OF THE PRESENT STATE OF IRELAND, in Campion's HISTORY OF IRELAND (Dublin, 1633), q.v. (*)

1343. Spondanus ₍De Sponde₎, Jean.

HOMER QUAE EXTANT OMNIA...COMMENTARIIS. PINDARI QUINETIAM THEBANI EPITOME ILIADOS. (?)

MAR   CM, XVIII, 276, 277, 299.

1344. Stafford, Anthony.

NIOBE, OR HIS AGE OF TEARES. (?)

See Grant McColley, PARADISE LOST.

1345. Starkey, George.

THE DIGNITY OF KINGSHIP ASSERTED IN ANSWER TO MR. MILTON. (?)

See W. R. Parker, MILTON, pp. 560, 1074.

1346. Statius, Publius Papinus.

SILVAE: THEBIAS. (?)

PROL   YP, I, 249.
NDX   CM, ii, 1869.

1347. Stephanus, Carolus.

DICTIONARIUM HISTORICUM GEOGRAPHICUM, POETICUM. (?)

See John M. Steadman, "Urania, Wisdom, and Scriptural Exegesis," Neophilologus, XLVII (1963), 61-73.

Stephanus, Henri. See Estienne.

233

1348. Stephanus, Robertus.

       THESARUS LINGUAE LATINAE. (?)

           See John M. Steadman, "Urania, Wisdom, and
           Scriptural Exegesis," _Neophilologus_, XLVII
           (1963), 61-73.

1349. Steuart, Adam.

       ZERUBBABEL TO SANBALLAT AND TOBIAH: OR, THE FIRST
       PART OF THE DUPLY TO M. S. ALIAS TWO BRETHREN...
       WHEREUNTO IS ADDED THE JUDGEMENT OF THE REFORMED
       CHURCHES OF FRANCE, SWITZERLAND, GENEVA &C. CON-
       CERNING INDEPENDENTS, WHO DONDEMNE THEM WITH AN
       UNANIMOUS CONSENT. (V)

           K   YP, III, 563, 583-84.
           Steuart is also the "A. S." of Milton's
           sonnet "On the New Forcer of Conscience,"
           line 8.

1350. Stobaeus, Johannes.

       OPERA. (*)

           1D   YP, IV, 438.

1351. Stobaeus, Johannes.

       SENTENTIAE. (?)

           E   YP, II, 399.

1352. Stow, John.

       ANNALES, OR GENERAL CHRONICLE OF ENGLAND. (V)

           CPB   YP, I, 370-71, 372, 378, 382, 386,
                     387, 390, 395, 424, 430, 431, 432,
                     435, 440, 450, 452, 453, 479, 480,
                     481, 484, 491, 494.
           R   YP, I, 533.
           See W. R. Parker, MILTON, pp. 841-42.

1353. Strabo.

       GEOGRAPHICA. (?)

```
AP          YP, I, 890.
HB          CM, X, 49, 50, 51, 52.
See Robert R. Cawley, MILTON AND THE LITERA-
TURE OF TRAVEL.
```

1354. Stubbe, Henry.

CLAMOR, RIXA, JOCI, MENDACIA, FURTA, CACHINI, OR,
A SEVERE ENQUIRY. (?)

See W. R. Parker, MILTON, pp. 507, 1062.

1355. Stubbe, Henry ₍?₎.

A LIGHT SHINING OUT OF DARKNESS. (?)

See W. R. Parker, MILTON, pp. 540, 1071.

```
Sturmius, John.
          Milton translated a comendatory statement
          by Sturmius in his foreword to THE JUDGE-
          MENT OF MARTIN BUCER; the statement, however,
          was taken from Bucer's SCRIPTA ANGLICANA,
          ed., Conradus Hubertus, q.v., (Basel, 1577),
          rather than directly from a work by Sturmius.
          MB          YP, II, 423, 433.
          T           YP, II, 710.
          LOR         CM, XI, 511.
```

1356. Suetonius Tranquilus, Gaius.

DE VIRIS ILLUSTRIBUS. (?)

```
          2D          YP, IV, 594.
```

1357. Suetonius Tranquilus, Gaius.

DE VITA CAESARUM XII. (V)

```
          CG          YP, I, 770.
          T           YP, II, 672.
          K           YP, III, 342, 439, 467-68, 546, 590.
          1D          YP, IV, 388, 404, 451.
          SD          YP, IV, 744, 822.
          RJP         YP, IV, 944.
          HB          CM, X, 34, 53, 56, 63, 80.
          NDX         CM, ii, 1891.
```

See H. Glicksman, "Sources of Milton's History of Britain," <u>Wisconsin Studies in Language and Literature</u>, XI (1920), 105-44.

1358. **SUIDAS.** (?)

        LO   CM, XI, 21.
        MAR   CM, XVIII, 317.
        The title of a lexicon, not an author, although this distinction is not clearly shown in Milton's writings.

1359. Swan, John.

        SPECULUM MUNDI. (?)

           See Grant McColley, PARADISE LOST.

Sylvester, Joshua. Translator of Guillaume Du Bartas, q.v. See also Hilda M. Hulme, "On the Language of PARADISE LOST: Its Elizabethan and Early Seventeenth-Century Background," LANGUAGE AND STYLE IN MILTON (1968), pp. 65-101.
        NDX   CM, ii, 1906-07.

1360. Symmons, Edward.

        A MILITARIE SERMON, WHEREIN BY THE WORD OF GOD, THE NATURE AND DISPOSITION OF A REBELL IS DIS-COVERED, AND THE KINGS **TRUE** SOULDIER DESCRIBED AND CHARACTERIZED. (?)

           See G. W. Whiting, MILTON'S LITERARY MILIEU.

1361. Syncellus, Georgius.

        CHRONOGRAPHIA, in CORPUS **BYZANTINAE** HISTORIAE. (*)

           See Denis Saurat, LA PENSÉE DE MILTON, pp. 255 ff.; Harris F. Fletcher, MILTON'S RABBINICAL READINGS, pp. 282-83.

1362. Tacitus.

        ANNALES. (V)

           AR   YP, II, 499, 518.
           T   YP, II, 672.

```
              1D              YP, IV, 343, 389, 407, 442, 443.
              2D              YP, IV, 586.
```

1363. Tacitus.

    DE VITA IULII AGRICOLAE. (V)

```
              AR              YP, II, 552.
              1D              YP, IV, 479.
              HB              CM, X, 48, 59, 64, 80.
```

1364. Tacitus.

    DIALOGUS DE ORATORIBUS. (V)

```
              1D              YP, IV, 448-49.
```

1365. Tacitus.

    HISTORIAE. (V)

> HB   CM, X, 50, 53, 56, 57, 63, 70, 71.
> See H. Glicksman, "Sources of Milton's History
> of Britain," _Wisconsin Studies in Language and_
> _Literature_, XI (1920), 105-44. See Milton's
> letter to Henry de Brass (CM, XII, 90-94) for
> his judgement of Tacitus as an historian. See
> also Edwin B. Benjamin, "Milton and Tacitus,"
> _Milton Studies_, IV (1972), 117-40.

1366. Talon ₍Talaeus₎, Omer ₍Audomari₎.

    INSTITUTIONES ORATORIAE. (?)

```
              LOR             CM, XI, 499.
```

1367. Talon, Omer.

    OEUVRES. (?)

```
              LOR             CM, XI, 499.
```

1368. Talon, Omer.

    PRÉFACES ET DISCOURS. (?)

```
              LOR             CM, XI, 499.
```

1369. Talon, Omer.

    RHETORICA. (?)

        See Donald L. Clark, JOHN MILTON AT ST. PAUL'S
        SCHOOL.

1370. Tasso, Torquato.

    AMINTA. (*)

        See Mario Praz, "Milton and Poussin," SEVENTEEN-
        TH CENTURY STUDIES PRESENTED TO SIR HERBERT
        GRIERSON (Oxford, 1938), p. 202.

1371. Tasso, Torquato.

    DISCORSI DELL'ARTE POETICA: ED IN PARTICOLARE SOPRA
    IL POEMA EROICA. (V)

        E   YP, II, 404-05.
        See F. T. Prince, THE ITALIAN ELEMENT IN MILTON'S
        VERSE.

1372. Tasso, Torquato.

    DISCORSI DEL POEMA HEROICO. (*)

        CG   YP, I, 815-18.
        E   YP, II, 405.
        See John Buxton, "A Note on PARADISE LOST, X.
        71-79," RES, XV (1964), 52-53; J. S. Smart, THE
        SONNETS OF MILTON, p. 35.

1373. Tasso, Torquato.

    IL GOFFREDO [GERUSALEME LIBERATA]. (V)

        CPB   YP, I, 385.
        NDX   CM, ii, 1914-15.
        The editors of the Columbia Milton use Fairfax's
        translation, GODFREY OF BULLOIGNE: THE RECOVERIE
        OF JERUSALEM (Lonodn, 1600), as their touchstone
        rather than considering Milton's use of the
        original.

1374. Tasso, Torquato.

    IL MONDO CREATO. (*)

See Albert R. Cirillo, "Tasso's IL MONDO
CREATO: Providence and the Created Universe,"
Milton Studies, III (1971), 83-102.

1375. Tasso, Torquato.

LE SETTE GIORNATE DEL MONDO CREATO. (?)

See Grant McColley, PARADISE LOST.

1376. Tassoni, Alessandro.

DIECI LIBRI DI PENSIERI DIVERSI. (V)

CPB   YP, I, 469, 470.

1377. Tatian.

ORATIO AD GRAECOS, in ORTHODOXOGRAPHA THEOLOGIA
SACROSANCTAE. (?)

See Sr. M. I. Corcoran, MILTON'S PARADISE.

1378. Taubman, Friderich.

BELLUM ANGLICUM, in MELODAESIA. (?)

See Grant McColley, PARADISE LOST.

1379. Taylor, Jeremy.

LIBERTY OF PROPHESYING. (?)

NDX   CM, ii, 1917.

1380. Taylor, John.

THE NOBLE CAVILIER CARACTERISED, AND A REBELLIOUS
CAVILLER CAUTERISED. (?)

See G. W. Whiting, MILTON'S LITERARY MILIEU.

1381. Temple, Thomas.

CHRIST'S GOVERNMENT IN AND OVER HIS PEOPLE. (?)

See G. W. Whiting, MILTON'S LITERARY MILIEU.

1382. Teresa of Avila, St.

> LIBROS DE LA B. MADRE TERESA [THE INTERIOR CASTLE].
> (?)
>
> > See Sr. M. I. Corcoran, MILTON'S PARADISE.

1383. Terence.

> COMOEDIAE SEX EX RECENSIONE HEINSIANA. Leyden,
> 1635. (V)
>
> | | |
> |---|---|
> | LO | CM, XI, 177, 197, 217, 291, 353, 423. |
> | G | CM, VI, 329, 331, 336, 341, 342, 343, 344, 346, 353. |
> | NDX | CM, ii, 1927. |
>
> See J. M. French, THE LIFE RECORDS OF JOHN
> MILTON, I, 291-92. Milton's copy is in the
> Harvard College Library.

1384. Terence.

> ANDRIA. (V)
>
> | | |
> |---|---|
> | C | YP, II, 748. |
> | RJP | YP, IV, 952. |
> | LO | CM, XI, 353. |

1385. Terence.

> EUNUCHUS. (V)
>
> | | |
> |---|---|
> | 1D | YP, IV, 309, 313. |
> | SD | YP, IV, 726. |
> | RJP | YP, IV, 901. |

1386. Terence.

> PHORMIO. (*)
>
> | | |
> |---|---|
> | RJP | YP, IV, 911. |

1387. Tertullian.

> OPERA. Ed. Nicolaus Rigaltius. Paris, 1634. (V)
>
> | | |
> |---|---|
> | CPB | YP, I, 362. |

```
              P           YP, I, 644, 645.
              C           YP, II, 736.

1388.  Tertullian.

           ADVERSUS MARCIONEM.  (V)

              R           YP, I, 552.
              T           YP, II, 644.

1389.  Tertullian.

           ADVERSUS PRAXEAM.  (?)

              See Sr. M. I. Corcoran, MILTON'S PARADISE.

1390.  Tertullian.

           APOLOGETICUS.  (V)

              CPB         YP, I, 433.
              1D          YP, IV, 392-93, 414.

1391.  Tertullian.

           DE ANIMA.  (?)

              See Sr. M. I. Corcoran, MILTON'S PARADISE.

1392.  Tertullian.

           DE JEJUNIIS.  (V)

              CPB         YP, I, 367.

1393.  Tertullian.

           DE RESURRECTIONE CARNIS.  (?)

              See Sr. M. I. Corcoran, MILTON'S PARADISE.

1394.  Tertullian.

           DE SPECTACULIS.  (V)

              CPB         YP, I, 362, 489-90.
```

1395.   Tertullian.

      EXHORTATION TO CHASTITY. (?)

          DDD   YP, II, 236.

1396.   Tertullian.

      ON THE CROWN. (V)

          TKM   YP, III, 202.

1397.   Theocritus.

      IDYLLS. (V)

PROL	YP, I, 289.
AP	YP, I, 887.
E	YP, II, 394-95.
RJP	YP, IV, 895.
MAR	CM, XVIII, 314, 345.
NDX	CM, ii, 1935.

1398.   Theodoret.

      HISTORIA ECCLESIASTICA, in ECCLESIASTICAE HISTORIAE
      AUTORES. (V)

CPB	YP, I, 377, 498.
AR	YP, II, 508.
1D	YP, IV, 393-94.
H	CM, VI, 64.
R	YP, I, 533, 543, 545, 555, 556, 557, 607.
P	YP, I, 634.

1399.   Theodoret, Bishop of Cyrus.

      HAERETICARUM FABULARUM COMPENDIUM. (?)

          See Sr. M. I. Corcoran, MILTON'S PARADISE.

1400.   Theodoret, Bishop of Cyrus.

      IN LOCA DIFFICILIA SCRIPTURAE SACRAE QUAESTIONES
      SELECTAE. IN GENESIN. (?)

          See Sr. M. I. Corcoran, MILTON'S PARADISE.

1401. Theodoret, Bishop of Cyrus.

> ON GOD'S PROVIDENCE ₍THE MORROR OF DIVINE PROVIDENCE.₎ (?)

>> See Sr. M. I. Corcoran, MILTON'S PARADISE.

1402. Theodorus Belvederensis.

> HISTORIA ECCLESIASTICA, in ECCLESIASTICAE HISTORIAE AUTORES. (*)

>> K   YP, III, 514.
>> See W. R. Parker, MILTON, p. 803; YP, I, 377.

1403. Theognis.

> ELEGIES. (V)

>> 1D   YP, IV, 441-42.

1404. Theon, Aelius, of Alexandria.

> THEONI SCHOLIA ₍on Aratus₎, q.v. (*)

>> See Maurice Kelley and Samuel D. Atkins, "Milton's Annotations of Aratus," PMLA, LXX (1955), 1090-1106.

1405. Theophanes, St.

> CHRONOGRAPHIA. (V)

>> See W. R. Parker, MILTON, p. 502.

1406. Theophilus of Antioch, St.

> APOLOGY TO AUTOLYCUS, in ORTHODOXOGRAPHA. (?)

>> See Sr. M. I. Corcoran, MILTON'S PARADISE.

1407. Theophrastus.

> AETIOLOGY. (V)

>> E   YP, II, 390.

1408. Theophrastus.

ENQUIRY. (V)

E   YP, II, 390.

1409. Thomas, Thomas.

THOMAE THOMASII DICTIONARIUM. (?)

See John M. Steadman, "Urania, Wisdom, and
Scriptural Exegesis," Neophilologus, XLVII
(1963), 61-73.

Thomasinus of Padua. See Tomasini.

1410. Thuanus [de Thou], Jacobus Augustus.

HISTORIARUM SUI TEMPORIS. (V)

CPB   YP, I, 370, 372, 380, 404, 408,
             409, 410, 412, 413, 414, 421, 441,
             445, 446, 455, 457, 459, 461, 462,
             465, 466, 500, 501.
MB   YP, II, 428-29.
TKM   YP, III, 226-27.
O   YP, III, 306, 313.
2D   YP, IV, 659-60.

1411. Thucydides.

DE BELLO PELOPENNESIACO. (V)

E   YP, II, 400.
CD   CM, XV, 191.
NDX   CM, ii, 1945.
See W. R. Parker, MILTON, p. 1122. CM, XVIII,
572 notes a copy purportedly autographed by
Milton.

1412. Tibulus, Albius.

ELEGIA. (?)

COR   YP, II, 768, 771.
1D   YP, IV, 313.
NDX   CM, ii, 1947.

244

1413. Timaeus of Locri.

ON THE SOUL OF THE WORLD AND NATURE. (V)

E   YP, II, 396-97.

1414. Tomasini, Jacob Philipp.

PETRARCHA REDIVIVUS...ACCESSIT NOBILISSIMAE POEM-
INAE LAURAE BREVIS HISTORIA. Padua, 1635. (V)

CPB   YP, I, 468.

1415. THE TRANSPROSER REHEARSED, OR THE FIFTH ACT OF MR.
BAYES'S PLAY. (V)

Author unknown; attrib. to Samuel Butler and
Samuel Parker. See W. R. Parker, MILTON, pp.
629, 1145.

Trebellius Pollio. Author of TYRANII TRIGINTA, in
HISTORIAE AUGUSTAE SCRIPTORES, q.v.

Tremellius, Immanuele. See Franciscus Junius, Sr.

1416. Trissino, Giovanni Giorgio.

L'ITALIA LIBERATA DAI GOTI. (?)

NDX   CM, ii, 1978.

1417. Trissino, Giovanni Giorgio.

SOFONISBA. (?)

See M. Y. Hughes, JOHN MILTON: COMPLETE POEMS
AND MAJOR PROSE, p. 538; F. T. Prince, THE
ITALIAN ELEMENT IN MILTON'S VERSE, pp. 145-68.

1418. Trogus Pompeius.

JUSTINA EPITOMA HISTORIARUM PHILIPPICARUM TROGI
POMPEII. (V)

1D   YP, IV, 472.

1419.　Tronsarelli, Ottavio, and Domenico Mazzocchi.

LA CATENA D'ADONE. (*)

See Gretchen Ludke Finney, "Comus, Dramma Per Musica," <u>SP</u>, XXXVII (1940), 482-500.

1420.　Trostius, Martinus.

NOVUM DOMINI NOSTRI JESU CHRISTI TESTAMENTUM SYRIACÈ, CUM VERSIONE LATINA. (V)

T　　　　YP, II, 647.

1421.　Tuningus, Gerardus.

IN QUATUOR LIBROS INSTITUTIONUM JURIS CIVILIS DIVI JUSTINIANI COMMENTARIUS. (*)

T　　　　YP, II, 611.

1422.　Turberville, George.

ECLOGS. (?)

See Grant McColley, PARADISE LOST.

1423.　Turberville, George.

EPITAPHS, EPIGRAMS, SONGS AND SONNETS. (?)

See William E. Sheidley, "'Lycidas': An Early Elizabethan Analogue by George Turbervile," <u>MP</u>, LXIX, iii (1972), 228-30.

Twyne, Thomas. Trans. THE WONDERFUL WOORKMANSHIP OF THE WORLD by Lambert Daneau, q.v.

1424.　Twysden, Sir Roger, ed.

HISTORIAE ANGLICANAE SCRIPTORES X. (V)

Twysden's anthology includes works by: Simeon of Durham, q.v., John Brompton, q.v., Ailredi (or AElred), q.v., John Prior Hagustaldensis, Richard Prior Hagustaldensis, Radulphi de Diceto, Gervase of Canterbury (Gervasius

Dorobornensis), William Thorn, Henry Knight-
on, Thomae Stubbs. That Milton knew and used
Twysden's work there is no doubt (see W. R.
Parker, MILTON, p. 466), but he refers to only
three of the historians included, and those
are the only ones I have cross-referenced.

Tymme, Thomas. See Adrichomius's URBIS, HIEROSOLIMAE
DESCRIPTIO.

Tzetzes. See Lycophron's ALEXANDRA.

1425. Udall, John.

> KEY OF THE HOLY TONGUE. Adapted and translated
> from P. Martinius's HEBREW GRAMMAR. (?)
>
> > See Donald L. Clark, JOHN MILTON AT ST. PAUL'S
> > SCHOOL.

1426. Urfé, Honoré d'.

> ASTRÉE. (?)
>
> > K -   YP, III, 366.

1427. Urstissius, Christianus.

> ELEMENTA ARITHMETICAE, LOGICIS LEGIBUS DEDUCTA.   (V)
>
> > E   YP, II, 387.
> > See W. R. Parker, MILTON, p. 852.

1428. Ussher, James.

> BRITANNICARUM ECCLESIARUM ANTIQUITATES.   (V)
>
> > HB   CM, X, 109, 125.
> > See H. Glicksman, "Sources of Milton's History
> > of Britain," Wisconsin Studies in Language and
> > Literature, XI (1920), 105-44.

1429. Ussher, James.

> A GEOGRAPHICALL AND HISTORICALL DISQUISITION, TOUCH-
> ING...ASIA, in CERTAIN BRIEFE TREATISES, q.v.   (V)

Intro.   YP, I, 194.

1430. Ussher, James.

THE ORIGINALL OF BISHOPS AND METROPOLITANS, SET
DOWN BY JAMES ARCH-BISHOP OF ARMAGH, in CERTAIN
BRIEFE TREATISES, q.v. (V)

Intro.   YP, I, 194.

1431. Uziel, Jonathan.

TARGUM. Portions printed in BIBLIA POLYGLOTTA
WALTONI, q.v. (*)

See Harris F. Fletcher, MILTON'S RABBINICAL
READINGS, pp. 239-42.

1432. Valerianus, Pierius Bellunensis.

COMPENDIUM IN SPHAERAM, in DE SPHAERA by Sacrobosco,
q.v. (?)

See Allan H. Gilbert, "Milton's Textbook of
Astronomy," PMLA, XXXVIII (1923), 297-307.

1433. Valerius Flaccus.

ARGONAUTICA. (?)

COR   YP, II, 769, 770.

1434. Valerius Maximus.

FACTA ET DICTA MEMORABILIA. (V)

HB   CM, X, 38.
G   CM, VI, 329, 346.
See H. Glicksman, "Sources of Milton's History
of Britain," Wisconsin Studies in Language and
Literature, XI (1920), 111.

Valesius, Henricus ₍Henry de Valois₎. See Ammianus
Marcellinus.

Valla, Laurentius. Trans. Thucydides, q.v.

1435. Valvasone, Erasmo di.

　　　　L'ANGELEIDA. (?)

　　　　　　See Grant McColley, PARADISE LOST.

1436. Varchi, Benedetto.

　　　　I SONETTI DI M. BENEDETTO VARCHI. Venice, 1555.
　　　　(V)

　　　　　　Milton's copy is in the New York Public Li-
　　　　　　brary. See Maurice Kelley, BNYPL, LXVI (1962),
　　　　　　499-504.

1437. Varro, Marcus Terentius.

　　　　DE RE RUSTICA. (V)

　　　　E　　　　　YP, II, 388.
　　　　RJP　　　　YP, IV, 958.
　　　　G　　　　　CM, VI, 335, 339, 352.
　　　　LO　　　　CM, XI, 299.
　　　　See W. R. Parker, MILTON, p. 852.

1438. Vatablus ₍Vatable or Vatablé₎, Franciscus.

　　　　NOTES TO THE OLD TESTAMENT, in Robert Étienne's
　　　　BIBLIA, q.v. (?)

　　　　T　　　　　YP, II, 614.

1439. Veer, Gerrit de.

　　　　THE TRUE AND PERFECT DESCRIPTION OF THREE VOYAGES.
　　　　Trans. from the Dutch by W. Phillip. (?)

　　　　　　See Robert R. Cawley, MILTON AND THE LITERATURE
　　　　　　OF TRAVEL.

1440. Vegetius ₍F. Vegetius Renatus₎.

　　　　ARTIS VETERINARIAE SIVI MULO-MEDICINAE. (?)

　　　　SD　　　　YP, IV, 750.

1441. Vegetius ₍F. Vegetius Renatus₎.

DE RE MILITARI. (?)

    RJP   YP, IV, 891.
    See W. R. Parker, MILTON, p. 853.

1442. Velleius Paterculus, Gaius.

    HISTORIAE ROMANAE. (V)

        G   CM, VI, 337.

Vellutello, Alesandro. Editor and commentator on
Dante's LA COMEDIA, q.v.

Verax, Theodorus. See Clement Walker.

1443. Vergilius, Polydorus.

    ANGLICAE HISTORIAE LIBRI XXVI. (V)

        MAR   CM, XVIII, 328, 329.
        HB   CM, X, 3.
        CPB   YP, I, 456.

1444. Verheiden, Jacobus.

    PRAESTANTIUS ALIQUOT THEOLOGORUM QUI ROM. ANTI-
    CHRISTUM PRAECIPUE OPPUGNARUNT EFFIGIES. (V)

        MB   YP, II, 427, 429.

1445. Vermilius ₁Vermigli, Pietro Martire₁, P. M.

    COMMENTARY ON THE TWO BOOKS OF SAMUEL. (?)

        Bound with no. 1446 in the third, enlarged
        edition of that work. See R. Mohl's note
        YP, I, 455-56.

1446. Vermilius, P. M.

    IN LIBRUM IUDICUM D. PETRI MARTYRIS VERMILIJ...
    COMMENTARIJ DOCTISSIMI. (V)

        CPB   YP, I, 455-56.
        TKM   YP, III, 221, 247.

```
MB        YP, II, 427, 478.
1D        YP, IV, 396.
2D        YP, IV, 661.
SD        YP, IV, 725.
CD        CM, XVII, 193.
See W. R. Parker, MILTON, pp. 883, 922.
```

1447. Vermilius, P. M.

IN PRIMUM LIBRUM MOSIS. (?)

See Arnold Williams, "Milton and Commentaries on Genesis," MP, XXXVII (1940), 263-78.

1448. Vermilius, P. M.

IN SELECTISSIMAM D. PAULI PRIOREM AD CORINTHIOS... COMMENTARII DOCTISSIMI. (V)

T   YP, II, 681, 711, 716.

1449. Vermilius, P. M.

LOCI COMMUNES D. PETRI MARTYRIS VERMILII. Trans. Anthonie Marten, THE COMMON PLACES...DOCTOR PETER MARTYR. (V)

C   YP, II, 711, 752.

1450. Vicars, John.

THE LOOKING-GLASSE FOR MALIGNANTS. (?)

See G. W. Whiting, MILTON'S LITERARY MILIEU.

1451. Vida, Marco Girolamo.

CHRISTIADOS. (*)

See Olin H. Moore, "The Infernal Council," MP, XVI (1918), 186-93; R. C. Fox, "Vida and 'Samson Agonistes'," N&Q,(1959), 370-72.

1452. Vida, Marco Girolamo.

DE ARTE POETICA. (?)

NDX   CM, ii, 2034.
See M. Y. Hughes, MILTON'S MINOR POEMS, pp.
xix-xx.

1453. Viger, François.

DE PRAECIPIUS GRAECAE DICTIONIS IDIOTISMIS. (V)

MAR   CM, XVIII, 306.

1454. Villani, Giovanni.

CRONICHE. (V)

CPB   YP, I, 366, 367.
See W. R. Parker, MILTON, p. 883.

1455. A VINDICATION OF THE LATE VOW AND COVENANT. (?)

See G. W. Whiting, MILTON'S LITERARY MILIEU.

1456. Vinetus, Eliae, ed.

SCHOLIA, Ioannis de Sacrobosco's DE SPHAERA, q.v.
(V)

See Allan H. Gilbert, "Milton's Textbook of
Astronomy," PMLA, XXXVII (1923), 297-307.

Virgidemiae. See Joseph Hall.

1457. Virgil.

OPERA OMNIA. (V)

NDX   CM, ii, 2026-29.
Which edition of Virgil Milton used is unclear;
however, many think it probable that he used
one with a commentary by T. Donati and Servius
(Basel, 1613). Donald L. Clark suggests COM-
MENTAR. VALENTIS ET SCALIGERI IN VIRGIL (Antwerp, 1575) in JOHN MILTON AT ST. PAUL'S SCHOOL.

1458. Virgil.

AENEID. (V)

```
     1D          YP, IV, 312, 445, 503.
     2D          YP, IV, 580-81, 609, 639, 653.
     SD          YP, IV, 726.
     RJP         YP, IV, 898, 947.
     See E. K. Rand, "Milton in Rustication," SP,
     XIX (1922), 109-35.
```

1459. Virgil.

     CATALEPTON. (*)

          PROL   YP, I, 225.

1460. Virgil.

     ECLOGUES. (V)

```
          PROL      YP, I, 239.
          E         YP, II, 396.
          C         YP, II, 757.
          RJP       YP, IV, 894, 910, 911.
```

1461. Virgil.

     GEORGICS. (V)

```
          PROL      YP, I, 239.
          E         YP, II, 396.
          1D        YP, IV, 347, 348, 509.
          2D        YP, IV, 654.
```

Virunnius. See Pontico Virunio, Ludovico.

1462. VITA ADAE ET EVAE. (?)

          See E. C. Baldwin, "Some Extra-Biblical Sem-
          itic Influences upon Milton's Story of the
          Fall of Man," JEGP, XXVIII (1929), 366-401.

1463. Vitruvius Pollio, Marcus.

     DE ARCHITECTURA. (V)

          E   YP, II, 390.

1464. Vives, Juan Luis.

      DE TRADENDIS DISCIPLINIS. (?)

          E   YP, II, 358, 366, 368, 386, 394,
                      401, 413.

1465. Vives, Juan Luis.

      THE OFFICE AND DUETIE OF AN HUSBAND. Trans. Thomas
      Peynell. (?)

          See Sr. M. I. Corcoran, MILTON'S PARADISE.

1466. Völkel, Johannes.

      DE VERA RELIGIONE. (?)

          See George N. Conklin, BIBLICAL CRITICISM AND
          HERESY IN MILTON, p. 73.

      Volusius. See Maecianus, Lucius Volusinus.

1467. Vondel, Joost van den.

      ADAM IN BALLINGSCHAP. (?)

          See George Edmundson, MILTON AND VONDEL.

1468. Vondel, Joost van den.

      LUCIFER, in DICHTERLIJKE WERKEN. (?)

          See George Edmundson, MILTON AND VONDEL; J. J.
          Moolhuizen, VONDELS LUCIFER EN MILTONS VER-
          LOREN PARADIJS.

1469. Vondel, Joost van den.

      SAMSON, OF HEILIGE WRAECK. (?)

          See George Edmundson, MILTON AND VONDEL.

      Voragine, Jacobus de. See Caxton.

1470. Vossius, Isaac.

VERSES ON ROVAI. (?)

| COR | CM, XII, 297. |
| P | YP, I, 635. |

Vowell, John. See Hooker, John.

Vulcanius, Bonaventura. Ed. Callimachus's OPERA, q.v.

1471. Walker, Clement.

ANARCHIA ANGLICANA: OR, THE HISTORY OF INDEPENDENCY. THE SECOND PART. (*)

See W. R. Parker, MILTON, p. 968.

1472. Walker, Clement.

AN ANSWER TO COL: NATHANIEL FIENNES. (?)

AR   YP, II, 505.

1473. Waller, Edmund.

"Summer-Islands" and "Night Piece" in POEMS. (?)

NDX   CM, ii, 2055.

1474. Walton, Brian, ed.

BIBLIA SACRA POLYGLOTTA. (*)

See W. R. Parker, MILTON, p. 499.

1475. Walwyn, William.

THE COMPASSIONATE SAMARITANE. (V)

Intro.   YP, II, 87.

1476. Ward, Robert.

ANIMADVERSIONS OF WARRE, OR A MILITARIE MAGAZINE OF THE TRUEST RULES, AND ABLEST INSTRUCTIONS, FOR

THE MANAGING OF WARRE.   London, 1639.   (V)

CPB   YP, I, 374.

1477.   Waring, Thomas.

A BRIEF NARRATIVE OF THE...REBELLION AND BUTCHERIE
IN IRELAND.   (V)

See W. R. Parker, MILTON, p. 959.

1478.   Watson, Richard.

THE PANEGYRIKE AND THE STORME...BY ED. WALLER...
ANSWERED.   (?)

See W. R. Parker, MILTON, pp. 541, 1071.

1479.   Weemse, John.

THE CHRISTIAN SYNAGOGUE.   (?)

See George N. Conklin, BIBLICAL CRITICISM AND
HERESY IN MILTON, p. 21.

1480.   Weemse, John.

PORTRAITURE OF THE IMAGE OF GOD IN MAN.   (*)

See Sr. M. I. Corcoran, MILTON'S PARADISE.

1481.   Wesenbechius ₍Wesenbeck₎, Mattaeus.

IN PANDECTAS JURIS CIVILIS & CODICIS JUSTINANEI,
LIB. IIX COMENTARII.   (V)

T   YP, II, 693, 715.

Weyer, Jean.   See Wierus, Johannes.

1482.   Whately, William.

A BRIDE-BUSH.   (?)

See William Haller, "Hail Wedded Love," ELH,
XIII (1946), 79-97.

1483. Whately, William.

　　　　A CARE-CLOTH. (?)

　　　　　　　See William Haller, "Hail Wedded Love," <u>ELH</u>,
　　　　　　　XIII (1946), 79-97.

1484. Wheloc, Abraham, ed.

　　　　ANGLO-SAXON CHRONICLE. (V)

　　　　　　　NDX　　　　CM, i, 65.
　　　　　　　See H. Glicksman, "Sources of Milton's History
　　　　　　　of Britain," <u>Wisconsin Studies in Language and
　　　　　　　Literature</u>, XI (1920), 105-44.

　　　　White, Thomas. See Smith, Richard.

1485. Whitney, Geffrey.

　　　　CHOICE OF EMBLEMES. (?)

　　　　　　　See Gayle Edward Wilson, "Emblems in PARADISE
　　　　　　　REGAINED," <u>MiltonQ</u>, VI, iv (December 1972), 77-
　　　　　　　81; Mario Praz, STUDIES IN SEVENTEENTH-CENTURY
　　　　　　　IMAGERY (Rome, 1964).

1486. Whittingham, William.

　　　　A BRIEF DISCOURSE OF THE TROUBLES BEGUN AT FRANKEFORD
　　　　IN...1554 ABOUT THE BOOKE OF COMMON PRAYER AND CERE-
　　　　MONIES. (V)

　　　　　　　TKM　　　　　　YP, III, 251.

　　　　Whittingham, William. Wrote "Preface" to Christopher
　　　　Goodman's OF OBEDIENCE, q.v.

1487. Wickins, William.

　　　　ARGUMENTS AGAINST BOWING AT THE NAME OF JESUS. (?)

　　　　　　　R　　　　　　YP, I, 526.

1488. Widdowes, Daniel.

　　　　NATURAL PHILOSOPHY. Trans. and abridged from

G. A. Scribonius's RERUM NATURALIUM DOCTRINA METHOD-
ICA. (?)

> See Kester Svendsen, MILTON AND SCIENCE.

1489. Wierus ₍Weyer or Wier₎, Johannes.

> HISTOIRES DISPUTES ET DISCOURS DES ILLUSIONS ET IM-
POSTURES DES DIABLES. (?)

>> See Robert H. West, MILTON AND THE ANGELS.

1490. Wierus ₍Weyer or Wier₎, Johannes.

> PSEUDO-MONARCHIA DAEMONUM. (?)

>> NDX   CM, ii, 2076.

Wigandus, Johann.
A learned Lutheran divine cited by Arnisaeus,
q.v., from whom Milton probably took the reference. See
> T   YP, II, 712.

1491. Wilkins, John.

> DISCOURSE THAT THE EARTH MAY BE A PLANET, OR, A
DISCOURSE CONCERNING A NEW PLANET. (V)

>> See Grant McColley, "Milton's Dialogue on
Astronomy: The Principal Immediate Sources,"
PMLA, LII (1937), 728-62.

1492. Wilkins, John.

> THE DISCOVERY OF A WOLRD IN THE MOONE. (V)

>> See Grant McColley, "Milton's Dialogue on
Astronomy: The Principal Immediate Sources,"
PMLA, LII (1937), 728-62.

Willes, Richard, See Eden, Sir Richard.

1493. Willet, Andrew.

> HEXAPLA IN GENESIN. (?)

See Sr. M. I. Corcoran, MILTON'S PARADISE.

1494. William of Malmesbury.

DE GESTIS REGUM ANGLORUM, in Savile's RERUM ANGLI-
CARUM, q.v. (V)

CPB   YP, I, 370, 378, 386, 388, 390,
         450, 452.
NDX   CM, ii, 1203-04.
See H. Glicksman, "Sources of Milton's History
of Britain," Wisconsin Studies in Language and
Literature, XI (1920), 105-44; W. R. Parker,
MILTON, p. 841.

1495. Willoughby, Sir Hugh.

JOURNAL. (?)

HM   CM, X, 382.
Milton's reference is probably to Hakluty or
Purchas, qq.v.

1496. Wither, George.

COLLECTION OF EMBLEMES. (?)

See Evert M. Clark, "Milton and Wither," SP,
LVI (1959), 626-46; Lyle H. Kendall, Jr.,
"Sonnet XIX and Wither's Emblem III.xlvii,"
MiltonN, III (1969), 57.

1497. Witichind [Witichindus, Wittekind, Widukind].

RES GESTAE SAXONICAE. (*)

HB   CM, X, 114, 115.
Milton might well have taken his reference to
Witichind from Camden or Ussher. See Constance
Nicholas, INTRODUCTION AND NOTES TO MILTON'S
HISTORY OF BRITAIN, pp. 73-74.

1498. Wollebius, Johannes.

ABRIDGMENT OF CHRISTIAN DIVINITIE. (?)

See Grant McColley, PARADISE LOST.

1499.   Wollebius, Johannes.

        CHRISTINAE THEOLOGIAE COMPENDIUM. (V)

                See Maurice Kelley, PMLA, L (1935), 156-65, and
                N&Q, (1966), 259-60; J. M. Steadman, Harvard
                Theological Review, LIII (1960), 155-56.

1500.   Wolseley, Sir Charles.

        CASE OF DIVORSE AND RE-MARRIAGE. (?)

                See W. R. Parker, MILTON, pp. 634, 1147.

        Wycliffe, John.
                DIALOGUS or SPECULUM ECCLESIAE MILITANTIS is
                cited third-hand by Milton from Arnisaeus of
                Halberstad, q.v., who cites him from Corasius
                of Tolouse. Milton bitterly complains that
                the poverty of English libraries forced him
                to such straits, and one wonders if he ever
                had the opportunity to overcome what he clear-
                ly considered a hardship and handicap. See
                T   YP, II, 707-08.
                DDD   YP, II, 231-32.

1501.   Xenophon.

        OPERA. (V)

                AP   YP, I, 891.
                LO   CM, XI, 151, 167.
                E   YP, II, 396.

1502.   Xenophon.

        ANABASIS. (V)

                E   YP, II, 396.

1503.   Xenophon.

        APOLOGY FOR SOCRATES. (*)

                E   YP, II, 396.

1504.   Xenophon.

BANQUET ⌈Symposium⌉. (*)

    E   YP, II, 396.

1505. Xenophon.

    CYROPAEDIA. (V)

        CG   YP, I, 751.
        E   YP, II, 396.

1506. Xenophon.

    HIERO. (V)

        1D   YP, IV, 438-39.

1507. Xenophon.

    MEMORABILIA. (*)

        A   YP, I, 719.
        E   YP, II, 396.

1508. Xiphilinus, Johannes.

    EPITOME OF DIO CASSIUS. (V)

        1D   YP, IV, 360, 399.

1509. YORK PLAYS: IV, V, VI. (?)

    See Allan H. Gilbert, "Milton and the Mysteries,"
    SP, XVII (1920), 147-69.

1510. Young, Thomas.

    CERTAIN CONSIDERATIONS TO DISSUADE MEN FROM FURTHER
    GATHERING OF CHURCHES. (?)

    See Arthur Barker, "Milton's Schoolmasters,"
    MLR, XXXII (1937), 517-37.

1511. Young, Thomas.

    DIES DOMINICA. Trans. as THE LORD'S DAY. (?)

See Arthur Barker, "Milton's Schoolmasters,"
MLR, XXXII (1937), 517-37.

1512.   Young, Thomas.

HOPE'S ENCOURAGEMENT.   (?)

See Arthur Barker, "Milton's Schoolmasters,"
MLR, XXXII (1937), 517-37.

1513.   Zabrella.

ON THE DECRETALS.   (?)

P   YP, I, 628.

Zaleucus.
In OF EDUCATION Milton recommends the "extoll'd
remains" of several Greek law-givers, including
Zaleucus. Two paragraphs attributed to Zaleucus are included in Johannes Stobaeus" SENTEN-
TIAE, q.v., p. 279; there is a slight possibility that Milton knew Zaleucus through that
source. See YP, II, 398-99.

1514.   Zanchius, Jerome.

DE FINE SAECULI.   (V)

2D   YP, IV, 586.
CD   CM, XVI, 341.

1515.   Zanchius, Jerome.

DE OPERIBUS DEI INTRA SPATIUM SEX DIERUM CREATIS
OPUS.   (V)

CD   CM, XV, 267.
NDX   CM, ii, 2137.
See Arnold Williams, "The Motivation of Satan's
Rebellion in PARADISE LOST," SP, XLII (1945),
253-68; J. M. Evans, PARADISE LOST AND THE GENE-
SIS TRADITION.

1516.   Zanchius, Jerome.

DE UNO VERO DEO.   (V)

262

2D   YP, IV, 586.

1517.   Zanchius, Jerome.

OPERUM THEOLOGICORUM.   (?)

See Robert H. West, MILTON AND THE ANGELS.

Zell, Mattäus.
          Milton praised Zellius's leadership in the
          Reformation at Strassburg and as a pedagogue;
          whether he read his books is open to question.
          See
          MB   YP, II, 433.
          T   YP, II, 710.

1518.   Zesen, Filip von.

DIE VERSCHMÄHETE DOCH WIEDER ERHÖHETE MAJESTÄHT.
(?)

See W. R. Parker, MILTON, pp. 582, 1093.

1519.   Zosimus.

HISTORIAE.   (V)

          R   YP, I, 554-57.
          HB   CM, X, 88, 89, 94, 96, 97, 99, 101,
                        104.
          See H. Glicksman, "Sources of Milton's History
          of Britain," Wisconsin Studies in Language and
          Literature, XI (1920), 105-44.

1520.   Zwingli, Huldrich.

OPERA.   (V)

          TKM   YP, III, 245-46.
          CPB   YP, I, 497.
          AR   YP, I, 550.
          1D   YP, IV, 338, 396, 453.
          2D   YP, IV, 661.

263

Un grand nombre d'ouvrages qui sont plein de pillage et qui ont éte bien pillés.